10.00 AD

THE SKILL FACTOR IN POLITICS

Eugene Bardach

.

The Skill Factor In Politics

REPEALING THE
MENTAL COMMITMENT LAWS
IN CALIFORNIA

.

UNIVERSITY OF CALIFORNIA PRESS
BERKELEY, LOS ANGELES, LONDON 1972

University of California Press
Berkeley and Los Angeles, California

University of California Press, Ltd.
London, England

Copyright © 1972 by
The Regents of the University of California
ISBN: 0-520-02042-1
Library of Congress Catalog Card Number: 79-157820

Printed in the United States of America

To Nancy and Elizabeth

Contents

Acknowledgments

This book grows out of a doctoral dissertation and hence, out of the advice and encouragement given by its faculty sponsors, Herbert Mc-Closky, Aaron Wildavsky, and Andie Knutsen at the University of California, Berkeley. I wish to acknowledge also my more general debt to Professor McClosky for his intellectual and moral tutelage since my earliest years in graduate school.

Friends, colleagues, and students have generously read portions of the manuscript over the past several years and have offered many valuable criticisms. May they continue to be so generous even after observing how little I may seem to have profited by their suggestions. My colleagues in the Political Science Department at Brandeis University, especially Bob Art, Martin Levin, and Ken Waltz, bore the earliest and therefore the heaviest burdens. More recently the burdens have fallen to my colleagues, especially Bob Biller and Arnold Meltsner, in the Graduate School of Public Policy, University of California, Berkeley. At various times, I also received advice and encouragement from Joan Bamberger, Jack Citrin, David Elkins, Darius W. Gaskins, Jr., Gary Hershdorfer, Robert Jervis, Andrew McFarland, Nelson Polsby, and Paul Sniderman. My old friends, David Blicker, Frank Furstenberg, Jr., Laurel Weinstein Eisner, and Marcel Teitler, kibitzed merrily from the sidelines. They graciously accept responsibility for all the defects in this volume.

My wife Nancy edited the dissertation manuscript with abundant good will and intelligence. My daughter Elizabeth, still too young to read (much less edit), collected and decorated the many pages of unproductive statistical output. And these were the smallest of their contributions.

Financial assistance came from numerous sources and assumed many forms. During the academic year 1966–1967 I held a National Science Foundation Dissertation Year Fellowship. From the NSF Division of

Social Sciences I received a generous grant to support my field work. This grant was authorized under the foundation's valuable program, Improving Doctoral Dissertation Research in the Social Sciences. I received additional financial aid from the Graduate Division of the University of California, Berkeley, and from the Office of the Dean of Faculty at Brandeis University. I am much indebted to the Brandeis Politics Department and to the Department of Political Science at the University of California, Berkeley, for significant clerical assistance. During 1970–1971 a grant from the National Institute of Mental Health supported much of the statistical analysis in the present work which I was unable to complete before submitting my dissertation.

Patsy Fosler, Charles Goldman, and Irene Herman assisted me in most of the computer analysis. Monique Williamson and Lois Robertson ably typed and retyped the final manuscript.

Finally, I wish to express my thanks to the hundreds of individuals and organizations that, in one way or another, facilitated my research. They were patient with me well beyond the requirements of duty. I hope they will take no offense at whatever misinformed or uninspired renderings of their attitudes or conduct have crept into the following pages. All errors of fact and interpretation are my own responsibility.

Introduction: Political Skill and the Problems of Politics

From the early fall of 1966 through the late summer of 1967, I charted the course of mental health politics in California. During that period I was surprised by not a few events. Some surprises measured my own personal failings, no doubt, but others I took as a measure of the low estate of scientific knowledge about politics. Failures of the first sort I hope to be excused from describing. One outstanding failure of the second kind, though, is worth recounting, for it provoked the search for remedies described in this book.

In most jurisdictions in the United States the procedures whereby the state detains and commits persons alleged to be mentally ill are of extremely doubtful legal, moral, and practical worth. In California a small group of state legislators and legislative staff concluded that the entire complex of legal and treatment institutions that rested on this dubious base and in turn helped to support it were so hopeless that only very fundamental changes could produce visible improvements. The group worked for some two years, from 1965 to 1967, identifying components of the problem, designing solutions, gathering public support, and winning the approval of the legislature and the governor. Experienced observers of California mental health politics, including some within the group of reformers itself, initially gave the attempt low odds on succeeding. Custom, ideology, and vested interests all appeared to stand squarely in the doorway to change. My own brief reconnaissance of the situation in May 1966, that is, some eight to ten months after the reform effort had been launched, suggested that, although the odds had improved substantially, no prudent man would have risked more than a few dollars to back the reformers. Over the next twelve months, how-

1

ever, prospects brightened continually. In early May 1967, according to the same experienced observers, the odds had improved to about even money. Over the next two months, though, they declined rapidly. In early July the reform effort had virtually been killed, and a careful bettor would have asked at least 100-to-1 odds before wagering on its success in the current legislative session.

Yet, one month later, the reform had been accomplished. What accounts for the failure of experienced observers (and our fictional bettor) to predict the actual outcome? Aided by some acquaintance with the literature of political science, I myself turned in a *somewhat* better record than most of my experienced informants, because I tended always to give more weight than they to factors that I intuitively associated with political skill. The reform group, I sensed, enjoyed a huge superiority in this respect over their various opponents. Yet my own judgments were grounded more in intuition than in theory. I was hard put to explain the substantive basis for my intuition. At the same time, I felt that it ought to be possible to give such an explanation.

In the pages that follow, I shall examine the varieties of political skill as they appear in only one political context, namely, California mental health politics in the mid-1960s. But because this policy-making system shares features with many others, certain conclusions can probably be generalized to levels of government other than the state, to states other than California, and to policy areas other than mental health.

I should emphasize at this point what this examination is not about. It is not about skill in running for office, sustaining successful insurgency movements, conducting palace coups, building an ideal political community, taming foreign enemies, developing the economies of the Third World, or about saving our souls (individually or collectively). Nor is it about the relative importance of skill as opposed to other factors. I do not dwell on questions of how people come to be skillful or of what praiseworthy or pernicious deeds they are likely to do with their skill. All these are questions for future scientific research and for philosophical analysis.

Before attempting to develop a formal theory of political skill, I had already accumulated a fairly complete record of the events from the mental commitments issue, as well as from four other issues in the California mental health field. This record of events was my principal point of departure and return. A brief account of how this record was completed may be in order.

Initially, I had set out to study the process of how issues arise. After many months of designing a procedure for creating data I hoped would bear on the question, the results of implementing its first steps persuaded me that many of my initial assumptions about the process were incorrect and that the study ought to be abandoned. By that time, however, the mental commitments issue was well underway and generating quantities of fascinating data. Some of these data were especially striking in view of one of my initial assumptions, namely, that an actor's attention being drawn to political events outside his usual perceptual field was highly problematic. I found this to be true to an extent I had scarcely imagined. Far more remarkable, though, was that when actors did expand their perceptual field in this way, they rarely initiated the process or spent much energy in carrying it on. The energy source was almost always in the actor's milieu, not in himself. Indeed the fundamental energy source appeared even more remote than the actor's personal milieu, which appeared to be transmitting energy from the larger process of political competition itself. A very complicated process having relatively little to do with individual disposition or choice and relatively much to do with the political system itself was almost certainly at work.

Moreover, whatever might have been the processes linking the system to milieus and milieus to individuals, they seemed to be working relatively well. Most actors, I discovered, were ignorant of most political goings-on most of the time—but very often there was a remarkable convergence of actors, information, and timely opportunities for action. These convergencies did not meet any absolute standard of frequency or of excellence, but I discovered relatively few instances of frustration or anger about cases of nonconvergence. In addition, almost all expressions of frustration or anger were directed at what were believed to have been calculated efforts at inhibiting information from circulating to particular individuals or groups. Not infrequently, these expressions were warranted by the facts, although in no case was the information flow inhibited by an especially opaque screen of secrecy. Frustrating as these facts may have been to the actors, they provided the academic researcher, myself, with additional evidence that the attention-flagging processes embedded in the political system were significant, highly versatile, and probably quite complex.

As I continued to observe the mental commitments controversy, I came to realize that the leaders of the reform effort had had a lot to do with the way these processes were operating in that contest. To me it

3

seemed that their operations were very successful and that these reflected some special political talent. It thus became clear that, by following the commitment contest carefully and by noting all the tactical decisions of the reform coalition's leadership—particularly decisions about whose attention they tried to attract or distract, with what means, and at what times—one could accumulate a rich source of data about both the political system and the nature of political skill.

About halfway through my projected year of fieldwork, that is, some time in February 1967, I also decided to develop a set of comparative data. I began to canvass the recent history of California mental health politics for controversies whose development might provide a useful comparative framework. After gathering preliminary material on nine such controversies, I decided to investigate fully three of these. One, the transfer of the Bureau of Social Work in July 1966 from the Department of Mental Hygiene to the Department of Social Welfare, was chosen because it had been a highly divisive contest and because some of the leaders from the commitment reform effort had also been involved. The Mendocino Plan controversy I selected because it had taken place entirely within the Department of Mental Hygiene and had involved no elected officials. The struggle by the California State Psychological Association to reverse the attorney general's stricture against the practice of psychotherapy by nonmedical personnel was chosen because it was clearly relevant to some of the activists in the generally attentive mental health public but of only marginal relevance to most. It would, therefore, provide a useful perspective on the phenomenon of selective inattention. The struggle was also in progress at the time I was doing my fieldwork. Finally, I added a fifth contest to my list, the controversy over the fiscal 1968 budget for the state hospitals for the mentally ill, because it exploded during March 1967 when I was in an excellent position to track it from its very beginnings. It was also the only contest in which the mass public became significantly involved.

In effect, then, I hit upon the topic of political skill largely fortuitously but accumulated data on the subject both designedly and haphazardly. Unfortunately, it was not possible to devise rigorous hypothesis-testing procedures or to develop accurate and reliable measures of attitudes or activity. The only attempt to supplement methods of field observation, interviewing, and documentary analysis with more refined tools was a mail questionnaire administered to some 1,300 persons in a supposedly attentive public at the end of August 1967. A total of 583 usable questionnaires were returned. The questionnaire and the sampling procedure are described in Appendixes A and B, respectively.

POLITICAL SKILL AS A QUALITY OF ACTION

It is certainly true that some politicians are more skillful than others, and that a few are a great deal more skillful. Yet, the usual connotations of the adjective "skillful" mistakenly suggest that the quality is a personal capacity, trait, or talent. True, there may be personal characteristics that facilitate the learning of political skills, but these are logically distinct from skill itself. In this book, I shall describe skill as a quality of political action. The action is political problem solving, and the qualities of skill are efficiency, inventiveness, and creativity, the relevant criteria of quality depending, of course, on the type of problem. To make this distinction between the qualities of the actor and the qualities of his actions more clear, let us employ an analogy.

With regard to driving an automobile we would be describing the skill of driving, the action, if we spoke of slowing down at dangerous intersections, accelerating slightly in a turn, downshifting when descending steep grades, and moving to the left-hand lane when passing. We would be describing the skill of the driver, the person, were we to speak of his familiarity with local traffic patterns, his knowledge of shortcuts, his quick braking reflexes, and his capacity to anticipate the behavior of other drivers.

Notice that it would be impossible to understand the skill of the driver had we not already understood some of the requirements and problems of driving. How else could we have known that knowledge of shortcuts and braking reflexes were relevant skills of a driver? Similarly, we can talk meaningfully of the skills of the political actor only after we have clarified the nature of political problems. It would be pointless to say, for instance, that timing was an important skill if we were not clear what goals, constraints, and options were being predicated for which timing was relevant. In short, before we can talk about political skill, we must state our conception of the nature of political problems.

The insufficiency of describing skill as a personal trait is suggested by the following passage written by Aaron Wildavsky, a well-known political scientist and a sensitive observer of the political process at many levels of government. One of the several reasons that the planning coalition in Oberlin, Ohio, scored so many victories in the late 1950s and early

1960s, suggests Wildavsky, was the unusual skill with which they carried on their activities. What were these skills? Wildavsky writes:

> For the most part, in Oberlin, it consists of rather simple kinds of actions. First, the collection of information so that one is better informed than others. Second, the development of a rationale for approaching those who make the decision. Third, the use of citizens committees and Council Commissions to test community sentiment, to gather support, and to ward-off opposition. Fourth, open meetings to give opponents a chance to vent grievances, to convince the doubtful, and to comply with feelings of procedural due process so that no one can accurately say that he was not given a chance to present his views. Fifth, ceaseless persuasion through personal contact, the newspaper, and official bodies. Finally, and this is perhaps most subtle, an appreciation of group dynamics and a *general sense of strategy* which includes pinpointing the crucial individuals and persuading opinion leaders of important groups such as Negroes. A good example is the choice of a slate in the 1959 election which was designed by the planners to blunt criticism of their alleged radicalism.[1]

Wildavsky's list nicely illustrates some skillful actions carried on in a very concrete political context. Yet, he does little to suggest why these actions were skillful. To answer this question, he would have had to propose a set of rather more abstract propositions about political problems, political actions, and the qualities (or attributes) of those actions that could intuitively be recognized as being skillful. Moreover, we may note on Wildavsky's list a large residual category called "a general sense of strategy," for which only one illustration is provided!

THE PROBLEMS OF POLITICS: SOME EXISTING THEORIES

Nowhere in the literature of political science, unfortunately, is there a coherent and systematic statement of the problems an actor encounters when he ventures into the policy-making process. Fragments are everywhere, but we find a coherent theory nowhere. Consider, for example, Richard Neustadt's often cited essay *Presidential Power*.[2] Neustadt writes that the president's power is "the product of

[1] Emphasis added. Aaron Wildavsky, *Leadership in a Small Town* (Totowa, New Jersey: Bedminster Press, 1964), pp. 267–277.
[2] New York: John Wiley, 1960.

his vantage points in government, together with his reputation in the Washington community and his prestige outside" (p. 179). He himself can enhance or dissipate his power "by the things he says and does. Accordingly, his choice of what he should say and do, and how and when, are his means to conserve and tap the sources of his power. Alternatively, choices are the means by which he dissipates his power" (p. 179). But what are the better and the worse choices? How can we tell a good choice from a bad one? Neustadt's implied answer is that the quality of his choices "will often turn on whether he perceives his risk in power terms and takes account of what he sees before he makes his choice" (p. 179). But exactly how should the president "take account of" what he sees? Should the president *never* jeopardize his public prestige or his image of professional competence? Obviously, Neustadt could not intend such a prescription, yet he says nothing else about how to take account of what the president sees. Neustadt's contribution has been to remind us that wanting to look good is a useful and laudable motive for a president (or any other political actor, for that matter); but he tells us little about how the president can in fact make, as well as seem to make, the right choices.

Another problem with Neustadt's argument is that it does not deal with the question of how to use power creatively. What, after all, is the president to do with all the power he has managed to conserve? In *Who Governs?* Robert Dahl delineates a less conservative ideal-typical political actor, Mayor Richard Lee of New Haven, a virtuoso "political entrepreneur":[3]

> Although the kinds and amounts of resources available to political man are always limited and at any given moment fixed, they are not . . . permanently fixed as to either kind or amount. Political man can use his resources to gain influence and he can then use his influence to gain more resources. Political resources can be pyramided in much the same way that a man who starts out in business sometimes pyramids a small investment into a large corporate empire. To the political entrepreneur who has skill and drive, the political system offers unusual opportunities for pyramiding a small amount of initial resources into a sizable political holding [p. 227].

The question now becomes, What can be done with all the political resources the mayor has managed to accumulate? Influence policy, of

[3] New Haven: Yale University Press, 1961.

course, by which Dahl means "successfully initiate or veto proposals for policies" (p. 163). But what does it mean to successfully initiate or veto? Vetoing seems clear enough, but successful initiation is more ambiguous. The crucial problem is that the success of the initiative can be determined only *post hoc*. Can we not develop a standard, though, for determining whether or not an actor's resources are, at any point in a policy controversy, being employed so as to lead to success? While Dahl's descriptions of the controversies in three issue areas are extremely suggestive, he provides only the rudiments of a significant theoretical criterion: build and control large and diverse coalitions of supporters. This can be accomplished by making promises and commitments and offering certain kinds of patronage and opportunities for conviviality and social intercourse (pp. 95–100). Still, we may ask, what is it about these coalitions that leads to success?

The answer to this question must depend partly on the institutional context in which the controversy is being waged. Since many significant controversies engage the attention of a legislative body, let us consider the question of success in legislative politics. A superficially appealing answer is that success depends on winning a majority. Recognizing the existence of legislative committees and subcommittees, and at the state and national level of bicameralism, we might elaborate this answer to read, "Success depends on building successive majorities in each arena in which a bill is considered."[4] Such an answer, however, does not take us very far. It does not account for success that comes from defeating bills. Are we to say, for instance, that Howard Smith, as chairman of the House Rules Committee, never enjoyed success when he refused to grant a rule to a bill? It is certainly a one-sided view of the process that refuses to credit conservative forces with success but accords to them only the dubious honor of blocking, thwarting, and frustrating. This answer also does not admit of different degrees of success. Does it not seem fair to say, for instance, that a large majority is a sign of greater success than a narrow majority? Or that a majority built arduously against strong opposition is a greater success than a majority based on routine work by the majority party whips on an issue of legislative organization?

Outside legislative arenas the utility of the successive-majorities criterion diminishes even further. Suppose that an administrator in the

[4] A good example of this line of analysis may be found in Louis A. Froman, Jr., *The Congressional Process* (Boston: Little Brown, 1967), pp. 16–19.

public service is prepared to decide an issue strictly on the basis of how various coalitions of interest groups and his administrative subordinates line up. The meaning of a numerical majority in such a context is vague at best, and we might be tempted to say that the decision would favor the side with the most influence. But what could this mean precisely? The capacity to reward or sanction the decision maker, one might suppose. But would it also include the influence that comes from persuading him that their views are, in some sense, meritorious? If so, what does merit have to do with what Dahl calls the coalition's "political resources"? On the basis of what can be found in or inferred from Dahl's writings, or from the work of others who have used the notion of resources, it is difficult to answer this question. The picture of the political process that moves from resources to influence to success seems to be missing something. Persuading authorities to endorse a proposal on its merits—however they may define them—is not an analytically or empirically trivial link in the process.

THE PROBLEMS OF POLITICS:
OVERVIEW OF ANOTHER MODEL

In my own analytic model, the success of a policy proposal ultimately means receiving authorization from officials ("the authorities") with the prerogative to give or withhold it. This in turn depends on the proposal's winning a certain amount of support from interests both inside and outside the circle of officials. In this scheme, "support" is a hypothetical construct, a bookkeeping figure that rises and falls throughout the course of the contest. Every interest can choose, at any time, to give or withhold its own quantum of support. Interests differ in how much support they can contribute, because the authorities weigh their endorsements differently for a variety of reasons, including considerations of merit. If by the time the contest is concluded the proposal has reached some finite (but unspecifiable) level of support called "enough," it is authorized; otherwise it is not.

If we postulate a rational entrepreneur trying to accumulate enough support for a proposal, we can easily see that one of his political problems will be to identify and select from among the several plausible combinations of interests those that will produce this level of support. This entails, at a minimum, designing a proposal and some acceptable, if unrevealed, alternatives; ascertaining the disposition of the various

9

interests who might support them; and assessing how weighty their views are among the relevant authorities.

A second major problem is to persuade these weighty and well-disposed interests to register their support. This entails recruiting a coalition of interests that will not merely register their own support but that will also work actively to solicit the support of others. Whatever means the entrepreneur and his coalition employ to do this work, we may call "political resources." Thus, the second major problem the entrepreneur faces is analogous to the first: to activate a coalition of allies whose combination of resources might plausibly win for the proposal "enough" support.

A third major problem is to defend one's own side from counterattack by opposition groups or alliances. This involves elements of gamesmanship, particularly sabotage of the opposition's support and resources, and maneuvers based on timing considerations.

Finally, there is the problem of developing and sustaining, for the duration of the contest, the capacity to play the role of entrepreneur effectively. To a large extent, this capacity is organizational and managerial, but there are also points of strategic doctrine to be mastered and cognitive skills to be learned.[5]

---

[5] This model of the policy process is probably closer to Dahl's than to any other model described in political science literature. It differs from Dahl's, however, in several respects. First, it utilizes the construct of political support, principally as a bookkeeping term. In Dahl's model, resources are used either to obtain additional resources by pyramiding or to control certain decisions. There is no way to describe the skill of an entrepreneur who consistently achieves near successes but loses for merely fortuitous reasons. In the present model, such an entrepreneur is credited with achieving "much" support, say, even though this quantity is short of "enough." Secondly, my own classification of political resources (in chapters 9 and 10) is based on an inventory of the entrepreneur's strategic political requirements rather than on social and psychological resources like money or status. In general, the present model differs from other models of political exchange by virtue of its focusing on production rather than distribution processes. See, for instance, R. L. Curry, Jr., and L. L. Wade, *A Theory of Political Exchange* (Englewood Cliffs: Prentice-Hall, 1968), especially chapter 1. There are many difficulties with the existing models on political exchange, but it suffices to point only to their inability to explain political support freely and joyfully subscribed—"on the merits," say—or political opposition never adequately recompensed. Production, as one economist defines it, is "all the processes of combining and coordinating materials and forces in the creation of some valuable good or service." Sune Carlson, *A Study on the Pure Theory of Production* (New York: Kelley and Millman, 1956), p. 1. Hence we can treat support as the valued good produced, political resources as the materials and forces used in production, and entrepreneurial skill as pertaining to the combining and coordinating tasks.

These four major problems are those of the entrepreneur already engaged in action. They are the most difficult of his problems, and the skills used to solve them are, therefore, the most intriguing as well as the most important. Our full discussion of them does not occur until the last four chapters of this book, chapters 9 to 12, since such a discussion requires illustrative specimens of both political problems and political skills, which are implicitly recorded in the five case studies narrated in chapters 4 to 8.

No sensible entrepreneur would leap directly into action—if he could help it—without prior mapping of the programmatic and the political contours of the area into which he was moving. The first three chapters describe the nature of these mapping problems and some procedures for solving them. The problem specimens are drawn from the domain of California mental health politics. Unfortunately, the problems never troubled any of the actors I observed at work, since none of them was entering the domain as a novice. They all carried maps in their heads. Hence, I could not observe their methods for drawing them. I myself, however, entered the domain of California mental health politics as a neophyte, and I experienced some difficulty mapping its contours. In effect, the procedures suggested in the next three chapters emerged by way of retrospection on how my own experience as a novice could have been made less onerous and inefficient.

At the conclusion of this book I shall argue that the institutions and processes of representative government need an infusion of political skills such as this book describes. The larger and more diverse the sources of this diffusion, the better. Policy analysts in training, like our students at the Graduate School of Public Policy, are an especially rich source of fresh entrepreneurial skills. Part-time citizen activists, freshly elected or appointed public officials, and veteran politicos—all can and should contribute. It is to my students and to this wider audience that the arguments in this book are addressed.

Part I

MAPPING THE CONTOURS
OF THE ATTENTIVE PUBLIC

1
Mapping Existing Policies and Their Audiences

MAPPING EXISTING POLICIES

The first problem a political entrepreneur must solve in trying to change policy in a given area is to understand the existing set of programs and practices in the area. He ought, in effect, to know what the policies are— conceiving policies quite broadly and including those that are public and private, official and unofficial, costly and nearly costless, planned and unplanned, explicit and implicit. If the entrepreneur is a veteran observer of the policy area, this problem is solved almost unconsciously. It is more difficult for the novice—for instance, the new recruit to a legislator's staff or the policy analyst just imported by one agency from another agency with very dissimilar policy concerns.

The novice is fortunate who can find an old-timer to show him the ropes and describe the policy area. Yet even if such informants can be found, their reliability must be checked by independent means. The principal danger is not that they will be biased—consulting a large variety of informants reduces this risk—but that their coverage will be incomplete. They are especially likely to omit some of the most important policies, those that are private, unofficial, low cost, unplanned, and implicit. Unfortunately, there is no easy way for the novice to understand all the existing programs and practices in the policy area, for that is a product of insight as well as knowledge. However, it is not too difficult to discover the institutions, groups, and individuals who operate in this area. Once this is accomplished it is easier to analyze how well they operate, to what purpose, and to what possibilities for change they are subject.

The relevant operators may be found by the use of tracer elements, that is, certain critical resources that circulate through the system of programs and practices. By tracking the movement of these resources from one operating site to another, it is possible to identify most of the important institutions, groups, and individuals in the policy area. In locating the operators of the mental health treatment system in California, I have worked with three such tracers: money, manpower, and clients (that is, those who are treated by the system).[1] Tracking the flow of just these three from one site to another will probably produce a serviceable first approximation of the important programmatic contours of any policy area in which government provides services, treatment, or regulation to the general public. Of course, special technology in a particular policy area may make it desirable to use additional tracer resources, although using more than six or seven such tracers would probably only complicate the task without creating much additional information of real value.

It is important to stress that this procedure answers no questions about the moral value or the effectiveness of existing policy. It helps only with the question, What is worth considering? Therefore, when one tracer element has already identified an institution, program, practice, or process, it is probably useless to identify it once more via its connection with other such features. After all, the object of this exercise is not to model the workings of the system but only to identify its relevant components.

Figure 1 shows the results of applying the recommended procedure to the California mental health system. Beginning with the state Department of Mental Hygiene (DMH), I asked myself, What are the sources of each of the three tracer resources as they come into the DMH, and where does the DMH send such resources? (The DMH was chosen as a starting point because it was the most prominent public agency officially charged with administering programs in this policy system.) Since the department was scarcely involved at all in the flow of manpower and clients, sketching any flow lines other than the budgetary would merely have cluttered the diagram. Nevertheless, thinking about all three resource flows is a necessary part of the method. The result of being so systematic may perhaps be suggested by the fact that we have identified the communities where state hospitals are located as somehow involved in the

---

[1] By "treatment" I do not necessarily mean to imply a benevolent or even appropriate relationship. The system treated some clients well, others poorly.

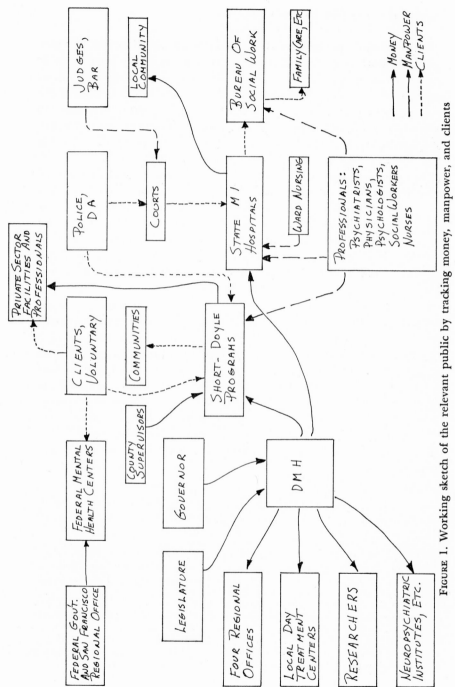

FIGURE 1. Working sketch of the relevant public by tracking money, manpower, and clients

operations of the larger system. To be more specific, they provide manpower to work in the hospitals and receive in return the benefits of the hospital's large payroll. To be sure, some method other than the use of tracer resources might have identified this feature of the system. But it is certain that a systematic procedure—any one, even a poor one—is an improvement on intuition and trial and error as a means of identifying the relevant operators in the policy system. Systematic procedure is a supplement to these latter means, not a substitute for them.

In some ideal sense it might be desirable to map the flow of all tracer resources among component units of the system, and then to ascertain the factors determining the rate of flow of these resources. Loosely speaking, these rate-determining factors would reflect the policies of the system—not all the policies, to be sure, but some very important ones.[2] In practice, however, such a thorough description of the system is, if not plainly impossibly, too time-consuming to be worthwhile. Ordinarily one would wish to examine only those policy features that seem to bear directly or indirectly on certain effects or system-produced outcomes. We shall now briefly examine the California mental health system with the aim of seeing who were its clients and how they were treated.

During the period studied, two principal administrative subsystems supplied treatment at public expense. One was the state mental hospital system, including nine separate institutions, six of which were located in the northern half of the state.[3] The other was the Short–Doyle system, which dispensed treatment at the community level. As of July 1, 1966, forty-one Short–Doyle programs were operating in thirty-eight of California's fifty-eight counties wherein lived 96 percent of the state's total population.[4]

2 I have borrowed the notion that these rate-determining factors are the policies of the system from Jay W. Forrester, *Principles of Systems* (Second preliminary edition; Cambridge, Mass.: Wright-Allen Press, 1969), pp. 4–8, 4–9.

3 A tenth, Atascadero, located midway between Los Angeles and San Francisco, was reserved exclusively for "the criminally insane." Unless otherwise noted, the discussion of the state hospitals excludes Atascadero and the hospitals for the mentally retarded. Nor have I included the Veterans Administration hospitals, since their financing and administration was completely in the hands of the federal government..

4 Two cities and one group of three cities set up Short–Doyle programs of their own. These three programs were independent of Short–Doyle programs run by the counties in which the cities were located. All forty-one programs included outpatient treatment, and about half administered inpatient facilities as well. Many of them also administered indirect services in the form of consultation to local police departments, school administrators, and other such agencies both public and private.

The state hospital system was financed almost completely by the state's General Fund, although, since early 1966, the federal government had contributed relatively small amounts authorized by the Medicare legislation enacted in 1965. Table 1 summarizes annual appropriations for

TABLE 1

APPROPRIATIONS FOR CALIFORNIA STATE HOSPITALS FOR THE MENTALLY ILL AND FOR SHORT–DOYLE, 1958–1968

Fiscal Year	MI Hospitals [a] (millions of dollars)	% Change from Previous Year	Short–Doyle (millions of dollars)
1958	67.5	26.8	0.0
1959	69.0	2.2	1.6
1960	73.9	7.2	2.5
1961	79.1	6.9	2.8
1962	80.5	1.9	3.1
1963	87.2	12.1	3.1
1964	99.0	13.6	5.5
1965	101.5	2.6	11.7
1966	111.5	9.8	15.7
1967	122.0	9.5	18.0
1968	112.0	−8.2	23.9

[a] Includes Atascadero. Excludes estimated reimbursements from patient fees, federal subventions, and capital outlay.

SOURCE: Annual budget acts, 1957–1966, passed by the legislature and signed by the governor. Source for fiscal 1968 appropriations, Department of Mental Hygiene press release, July 6, 1967.

the state hospitals for the mentally ill (MI hospitals) and for Short–Doyle programs for the decade 1958–1968. Short–Doyle was a state-county program initiated in 1957 on a 50–50 cost-sharing basis. In 1963 the matching formula was revised to the counties' advantage to 75–25. It applied only to services initiated after that date, whether by counties that were simply adding new types of services to ongoing Short–Doyle programs or by counties initiating Short–Doyle programs. In 1966–1967 Short–Doyle programs were authorized to spend $34 million in public money, about two-thirds of which was contributed by the state and one-third by the counties.

The California State Department of Mental Hygiene was the government agency responsible for administering the state hospital system. It was the largest agency of state government after the semiautonomous University of California, in terms of both General Fund expenditures and number of personnel employed. The DMH maintained its headquarters in Sacramento, the state capital, and four regional offices in San Francisco, Los Angeles, Fresno, and Sacramento. It had responsibility for the nine hospitals for the mentally ill, the four state hospitals primarily for the mentally retarded (MR hospitals), Atascadero, two neuropsychiatric research institutes (Langley Porter in San Francisco and the Neuropsychiatric Institute in Los Angeles), and a number of smaller specialized facilities in several large or medium-sized cities throughout the state. In 1966 these operations employed around 22,000 persons, or about one-fifth of all state employees. Appropriations for the department (excluding capital outlay) totaled $190 million in fiscal 1967.

Administrative responsibility for Short–Doyle was largely in the hands of local government officials. The DMH was nominally responsible for supervising the quality of the programs and for allocating state monies among the counties when allocation decisions were required by budgetary constraints imposed at the state level. Except for three programs operated by Berkeley, San Jose, and a three-city combine in the Los Angeles area, all the programs were controlled by the counties. In nearly every county Short–Doyle made extensive use of the county hospital's psychiatric ward, where it reserved a number of beds for its own in-patients. Each county board of supervisors appointed two officials, the Short–Doyle director and the program chief, to supervise the program. Until the third quarter of fiscal 1967, local expenditures for Short–Doyle never exceeded the amount the state had given in matching funds. Hence the only budgeting constraints were at the local level; whatever the counties contributed, the state automatically matched. Under these conditions the role of the DMH in overseeing Short–Doyle had been rather restricted.[5] The headquarters and regional offices of the department were limited to reviewing local standards, auditing local expenditures prior to authorizing reimbursement from state funds, and offering some limited staff assistance in coordinating the activities of local programs in the same geographical region.

The Bureau of Social Work employed some 400 psychiatric social workers to assist released state mental hospital patients in making a re-

---

[5] In the opinion of not a few Short–Doyle administrators, the DMH had been guilty of excessive interference in Short–Doyle affairs. I disagree, but excess is obviously in the eye of the beholder.

adjustment to life on the outside. These patients were technically "on leave" from the hospital. While on leave status they were eligible for the bureau's services in finding them employment, welfare assistance (in some instances), and living quarters. Prior to July 1, 1966, these social workers were organized as the Bureau of Social Work, under the direct jurisdiction of the DMH. After that date, the bureau was transferred to the state Department of Social Welfare, and the name was changed officially to the Division of Adult Protective Social Services. Since the functions and personnel of the bureau changed very little after the move, most people continued to refer to the organization as the Bureau of Social Work, a convention I too shall follow.

The public mental health system also incorporated a large number of private facilities. Under the immediate supervision of the bureau, numerous nursing homes, boarding homes, and family-care homes kept both leave and discharged patients. Since many of these persons were eligible for public assistance of some sort, mainly from state-federal matching programs, the bulk of the clientele in many of these facilities was made up of persons supported by public monies. The operators of these facilities were, therefore, quite sensitive to the programs of the public mental health system and based their own planning on expectations of what the public system would be doing. During 1966–67, pressure from these quarters caused family-care board rates to be increased from $130 to $150 per month. In limited ways they may even have attempted to influence the regulations, though not often the programs, designed and carried out by the public agencies. Thus they may be thought of as having been part of the public mental health system, although certainly a peripheral one.

Private mental health facilities were incorporated into the public mental health system through still another means, federal grants authorized by the two federal Mental Health Centers acts of 1963 and 1965.[6] The first of the two provided for construction funds for comprehensive community mental health centers undertaking a minimum of five specific program elements: inpatient treatment, outpatient treatment, emergency services, partial hospitalization, and consultation and education. The law authorized an appropriation of $150 million over a three-year period, the funds to be allocated among the states on the basis of population and financial need. It required applicants, which in California as

6 These were PL 88–164 and PL 89–105.

elsewhere were usually private and public general hospitals, to clear their applications through a single state agency. In most states this agency was the same one that administered the distribution of hospital construction funds under the Hill–Harris program, which financed hospital construction for general medical care and which was used as the model for the Community Mental Health Centers construction act. In California the clearing agency was the Department of Public Health, acting usually on the advice of the department's Advisory Hospital Council, a small group of public officials, representatives of private interests, and a few members appointed "to represent the public interest." Although the director of the department had the formal authority to override decisions of the council, in practice he rarely did so. Under the 1963 act, the federal government paid up to one-third of the construction costs, and the state and the applicant shared the rest; in California, this remainder was usually split 50–50. The staffing act, which followed the construction authorization by two years, did not explicitly count on state participation. It was essentially a seeding program which committed the federal government to paying a declining share of the staffing costs incurred by new program development over a period of three to nine years. As of May 1, 1967, twenty-four applications for either staffing or construction or both had been approved for California. Roughly 40 percent of these came from programs connected with Short–Doyle and the remainder from strictly private facilities. Some effort at coordination in planning between the departments of Mental Hygiene and Public Health was reflected in the ex officio membership on the Advisory Hospital Council held by the director of the DMH and in the informal consultations carried on between counterpart roles in both departments.

Short–Doyle formally linked the public and the private sectors through its authority to contract for treatment services with private hospitals (and similar institutions), clinics, and agencies. However, according to representatives of the California Hospital Association (CHA), which spoke principally for the interests of private hospitals, Short–Doyle administrators in practice had shown little enthusiasm for bringing private psychiatric hospitals into the public system. It is hard to assess whether this was generally the case; but it is certain that there were great variations among counties in this regard, and probably equally great variations among Short–Doyle administrators with respect to their reasons for utilizing or ignoring private hospitals in their counties.

In at least one county, Short–Doyle maintained contracts with a private psychiatric hospital administered by one of the physicians who sat on the Mental Health Advisory Board. In another county the main Short–Doyle inpatient unit was the psychiatric wing of a large and reputedly excellent general hospital. Not all psychiatric hospitals were of such high quality, though, and Short–Doyle administrators may have been loathe to channel their patients into expensive and perhaps inferior facilities. In at least one county, the Short–Doyle leadership was strongly committed to avoiding inpatient treatment whenever possible and had managed to reduce the number of hospitalized cases to the point that they felt the county hospital alone contained sufficient beds to handle them. Some interviewees claimed that administrative costs were too great to warrant extensive reliance on the contract procedure.

Through Medi-Cal, the state's conduit for federal funds appropriated under Title XIX of the 1965 Medicare amendments (concerning the medically indigent as opposed to the aged, who were covered in Title XVIII), a number of persons received treatment from mental health professionals in private practice. Often they received referrals to private practitioners from Short–Doyle staff who, for one reason or another, felt the patient could not be accepted by Short–Doyle.

During the fiscal year 1966, Short–Doyle programs treated over 115,000 persons and closed the year with a caseload of nearly 33,000, all but 10 percent in outpatient status. During that same period, the state MI hospitals handled 26,800 admissions, of which roughly 60 percent were first admissions and the rest were readmissions and court-ordered observation cases. These facilities began the fiscal year with 30,193 patients in residence and ended with 26,567, thus continuing the decline in the average daily patient population which had begun in 1960.

Throughout the period studied, there were two principal classes of state hospital patients, the voluntary and the nonvoluntary. Approximately three-fourths of the total admissions were in the latter category. Most of these persons were brought into the treatment system either through the provisions for a seventy-two-hour hold or through petitions for civil commitment. Both voluntary and nonvoluntary patients, however, were drawn disproportionately from the less affluent and less powerful strata of society. A one-day census of all inpatient psychiatric facilities in the state conducted on August 19, 1966, revealed that, at the time of admission, 10 percent of state hospital patients were welfare recip-

23

ients, another 24 percent earned under $3000 annually, and 19 percent earned between $3000 and $5000.[7] Twenty-six percent were designated unemployed-incapacitated, and only 7 percent were classified as business, clerical, or professional.[8] While whites composed a proportion of the state hospital resident population that was consistent with their proportion in the state's population, Negroes were overrepresented by about 33 percent in the hospital resident population.[9] Unfortunately, no published data could be found describing the socioeconomic characteristics of voluntary and committed patients.[10]

It was commonly assumed that Short–Doyle cases were, in general, of higher socioeconomic status and had less serious mental disorders. In light of the fact that Short–Doyle patients were primarily outpatients and that Short–Doyle administrators usually sent the hardest cases to

[7] California State Assembly, Interim Committee on Way and Means, "The Dilemma of Mental Commitments in California, Technical Supplement No. 4" (Sacramento, 1966), Table IX. This report was prepared by Social Psychiatry Research Associates of San Francisco under contract to the committee.

[8] Ibid., Table XI. Five percent were unknown. These figures were based on a 10 percent random sample of the 34,104 patients resident in the state hospitals for the mentally ill on August 19, 1966. At the time of the Assembly committee's survey, the Department of Mental Hygiene was collecting data on the socioeconomic status of patients which they used only for the purpose of ascertaining a patient's ability to pay for his hospitalization. These data were not available either to the public or to the department's Bureau of Biostatistics.

[9] California State Department of Mental Hygiene, Bulletin no. 41 (1963). Although Negroes went in disproportionate numbers to state hospitals—presumably because they could not afford psychiatric treatment in the private sector or because they did not know how to avoid being committed to state hospitals by the police and courts—they made up only about 7 percent of hospital admissions and the hospital resident population.

[10] Socioeconomic measures are not cross-tabulated against this characteristic in the Assembly committee's Technical Supplement. It is difficult to generalize about voluntary and committed patients anyway, because admission practices varied widely from hospital to hospital and commitment practices varied from jurisdiction to jurisdiction. An account by the superintendent of Mendocino State Hospital of his hospital's systematic reclassification of patients from involuntary to voluntary status indicates that prior to reclassification the involuntary population was substantially older than the voluntary population, had been hospitalized longer, and had a much more severe psychiatric diagnosis. (Ernest Klatte, "Summary of Mendocino State Hospital Involuntary-Voluntary Reclassification, 1967" [mimeographed].) As Klatte points out, these correlations are likely to be meaningless, since they refer to the resident population, not to admissions. Persons who entered the hospital in an earlier era—say, in the early 1950s—but still remained there in 1967, were, of course, more likely to show the characteristics described above, including a high proportion of legal commitments. Legal commitment was virtually the standard route to the hospital in that era.

the state hospitals, these assumptions seem plausible, though there were no data available to confirm or refute them.

MAPPING THE ATTENTIVE PUBLIC

If the entrepeneur is to succeed in changing the policies of the system, he must know who cares about them sufficiently to be mobilized either as potential allies or opponents. These various audiences we shall call in the aggregate, the attentive public. It is safe to assume that most organizations, groups, and individuals involved in operating the present system fall into this category, but there are many others as well. These others are, in the main, organizations, groups, and individuals who are overseers of one or more of the operating units of the system.

Just what they oversee, and with what degree of concern or attention, may be left as open questions; and in general it is advisable to think of the oversight function quite broadly. How can the system's overseers be identified systematically and thereby be mapped into the attentive public? First, consider elected public officials and their staffs. In the case of the legislature, look for the relevant subject matter specialists, usually found on standing legislative committees and subcommittees. Within the executive branch, there are usually specialists in the budget review units. Next, consider the citizen advisory groups which elected and appointed officials sometimes recruit either to act themselves as overseers or, as is more likely, to create a communications channel back to the parent bodies that play certain overseer roles. In the mental health area, these are typically professional associations. Although these two steps will usually identify most of the overseers who are part of the attentive public, there may be certain groups who have been ignored, like clients in a welfare system, or deliberately excluded, like those groups who oppose government participation in the policy area altogether. The clients of the California mental health treatment system were not usually part of the attentive public, which is not surprising in view of their generally low status and presumably low social and political skills. However, from time to time their associates, friends, and relatives were more involved, and an account of the attentive public excluding them altogether would be inadequate. Similarly, the anti-mental-health groups on the radical Right were occasionally attentive, though none of their representatives ever sat on any citizen advisory groups to DMH or Short–Doyle programs. Hence step three in mapping the attentive public is to consider

25

the clients of existing programs (both beneficiaries and sufferers), and enemies of the whole constellation of programs.

There were many indications that in the state legislature, at least through mid-1967 when my study ended, there was minimal routine interest in either the budget or the policies of the public mental health system. The most important evidence is the fact that veteran observers of mental health politics were not able, when asked, to name more than a few legislators who were either informed or active in the mental health field.

The principal reason for such widespread indifference in high places is that, like congressmen, California legislators, to the extent that they have policy concerns at all, become specialists in no more than a few areas. Nonspecialists, who almost by definition would be uninformed and relatively inactive, constitute the overwhelming numerical majority in any given policy area. Mental health policy was certainly no exception. In the 1967 legislature, there were only four state senators (out of forty) and only one assemblyman (out of eighty) who were informed and active in this issue area. (The number of informed senators is reached by a generous count.) In the 1966 legislature, the last elected before redistricting made "sure" contests into free-for-alls which returned an unusually high proportion of freshmen in each house, one could probably have added a second assemblyman to the total number of specialists. Even the specialists, though, did little in the way of routinely guiding legislative policy. There were no standing committees in either house with a juridiction uniquely, or even approximately, limited to mental health policy. The Senate Finance Committee and the Assembly Ways and Means Committee each had subcommittees that considered mental health along with all other matters of health, education, and welfare. In 1963 the assembly appointed an interim subcommittee of the Ways and Means Committee to recommend solutions to the inadequate number of beds in the hospitals for the retarded. Two years later, the subcommittee was reconstituted in order to study the problem of civil commitment to the hospitals for the mentally ill. In both cases the subcommittee's work was carried out mainly by two (and sometimes three) legislators (included in the enumeration above) and two or three full-time staff members.

A somewhat greater number of legislators took an interest in state hospital construction and payrolls. Like other public works, state hospitals are good for the local economy. Most of the fourteen state hospitals for the mentally ill and retarded were located in rural areas of the state, where they often constituted one of the two or three most important sources of income and employment in the county, with a payroll value of perhaps $5 to $10 million annually. Hence legislators liked to be assured that hospitals in their districts would not suffer budget cuts, layoffs, or attrition of the patient admission rate which would in time lead to budget reductions and job eliminations. The DMH had been under occasional pressure from some quarters in the legislature to phase out one or more "underpopulated" hospitals altogether in order to reduce the department's overhead costs. But the pressure was neutralized again and again by legislators with hospitals in their constituencies. For the most part these legislators influenced mental health policy only inadvertently.

The trend in annual appropriations for the MI hospitals reflected in Table 1 (p. 19) is still another index of the low level of routine interest in mental health policy in the legislature. Annual increments in appropriations fall into a feast-and-famine pattern. Extraordinarily large increments are followed in subsequent years by extraordinarily small ones, and generally the large increments occurred historically only when the system was confonting (sometimes belatedly) a crisis of unusual magnitude. As may be seen in Table 2, the resident population in the MI hospitals increased steadily throughout the 1950s, as it had since the end of World War II. Immediately after the war, the state purchased two army hospitals in northern and central California to hold the patient overflow from the seven existing MI hospitals. Nevertheless, the patient population quickly outgrew total bed capacity. According to one administrator, in those days patients often slept two to a bed. Surplus army cots were set up in all available nooks and corners, occasionally even in the outdoors and without adequate protection from rain. Ward nursing staff was far from sufficient to cope with the vast number of patients; and even the most rudimentary medical (but nonpsychiatric) care was neglected for lack of professional staff. While the Department of Finance (in the executive branch) was evidently planning to expand existing facilities and build new ones, a movement spread across the state, beginning in 1954, to redirect the growth of the treatment system into quite different channels. The cry was for community-based services, which would supposedly forestall the necessity for persons to go to or be sent to overcrowded, remote, and impersonal state hospitals. The first Short–Doyle legislation was introduced in 1955. It failed but was reintroduced in 1957 and passed. Proponents of the legislation moved very energetically during the three-year period prior to their success, dramatizing both the inadequacies of the existing system and promising great things for the new system they themselves envisioned. It was only on the crest of an extraordinary increase of public attention to mental health policy that the legislature provided the 26.8 percent increment recorded for fiscal 1958 in Table 1.

TABLE 2

RESIDENT PATIENT POPULATION AND ANNUAL ADMISSIONS, STATE HOSPITALS FOR THE MENTALLY ILL, 1950–1966

(including Atascadero)

Fiscal Year	Resident Patients at Year-End (June 30)	Total Admissions[a] During Previous Year
1950	31,944	12,406
1951	32,813	12,551
1952	33,719	14,204
1953	35,354	16,026
1954	36,205	15,917
1955	36,994	16,479
1956	37,182	17,268
1957	37,155	17,482
1958	37,076	19,517
1959	37,592	20,105
1960	36,853	21,407
1961	36,048	22,183
1962	35,743	22,733
1963	34,955	23,798
1964	32,622	25,027
1965	30,193	25,500[b]
1966	26,567	25,300[b]

[a] Excludes admissions for court-ordered observation only.
[b] Estimate based on substracting 1700 "observation" admissions from total admissions and rounding. The 1700 figure is obtained from the number of 1964 observation admissions.

SOURCE: All figures for 1950–59 from DMH 1959 *Annual Report*, Tables 1 and 3, pp. 15–16; 1960–1966 resident population from DMH mimeographed statistical summary, untitled, distributed at Assembly Ways and Means hearing, April 25, 1967, Table 13–A; 1960–1964 admission figures from 1965 *Report of the Legislative Analyst*, Table 2, p. 537; 1965 and 1966 estimates based on 1967 *Report of the Legislative Analyst*, p. 551.

After four more years of famine-type budget increments, the legislature was finally forced to recognize that low salary scales were preventing the DMH from recruiting psychiatric technicians (ward attendants) for the hospitals. In the three-year period, July 1957 to June 1960, 59 percent of all psychiatric technicians and psychiatric technician trainees resigned or were fired within the first six months on the job. A Senate fact-finding committee, established in 1960, reported the following year its recommendations that salaries in the department be raised by 25 to 30 percent in the psychiatric technician categories. At the time of the study, psychiatric technicians were earning $295 to $358 per month, wages lower than those received by state employees in most other manual jobs, almost all of which demanded less skill and dedication, threatened less physical danger, and imposed less personal discomfort.[11] The response of the legislature is reflected in the 1964 and 1965 budget figures. Possibly another reason for the high increment in 1964 was the dramatic exposé of patient abuse in one of the MR hospitals which the press carried only a few months before the beginning of the 1963 legislative session.

The two main reasons for the low level of even the legislative specialists' interest in the mental health system have to do with the ordinarily noncontroversial character of the system's operations and with the disjunction of such controversies as do occur from the standard ideological and political contexts familiar to legislators. Although from the inside the activities of state hospital administrators seem to raise highly political issues, from the outside—that is, from the perspective of the general public and the legislature—the operation of a state hospital is largely an administrative, and perhaps a somewhat technical, matter in which it would be unprofitable and inappropriate to intervene. Even when issues are raised concerning the very existence and function of state hospitals, as has been happening for well over a decade, legislators still define them narrowly: Will a community-based system save the state money? Do the doctors and other experts think it is a better way to help people?

To a certain extent the controversy preceding the enactment of the Short–Doyle program did agitate traditional ideological currents of opinion. The tempting opportunity, advertised by the bill's proponents,

[11] California State Senate, Report of the Senate Fact Finding Committee on Revenue and Taxation, "Salary Problems of the Department of Mental Hygiene" (1961), pp. 18, 20, and *passim*.

to brake rising needs for capital outlay and for large hospital payrolls drew some traditional conservatives behind the bill. Others opposed it on the basis of their usual antipathy to extending welfare programs of any kind. Other standard ideological disagreements involved the relative autonomy of the local jurisdiction vis-à-vis the state. Had the 1955 bill not been amended to give more autonomy to the counties, the bill would probably have failed again in 1957.

Historically, the states drifted into assuming responsibility for the care and treatment of the mentally ill when reformers like Dorothea Dix, in the 1840s, persuaded humanitarians that the local communities, which had theretofore borne that responsibility, could no longer do so. In California it was still the counties' legal obligation to provide public funds for the care of the socially and medically indigent, but the state had wound up with the obligation to look after the mentally ill. Thus, the state MI hospitals still retained their image as charity institutions, which combined with charity the social function of isolating the dangerous, unpredictable, or disagreeable members of society who happened not to have broken any laws and therefore could not be sent to prison. The population treated by the hospitals was viewed characteristically as needy but vaguely undeserving. Because the state had to provide facilities of some sort, the state hospital system became disengaged from the ideological debate over individualism *versus* statism which settles people's positions on so many issues in American politics. The ideological debate over welfare *versus* fiscal responsibility could perhaps have been engaged over the quality of the facilities; and the issue was indeed drawn between liberals who pressed for more commodious, more "therapeutic" facilities at greater cost and conservatives who preferred to guard the tax dollar. At the same time, though, the issue was drawn rather loosely, because both liberals and conservatives held somewhat convergent images of state hospital patients and not very distinct conclusions about their treatment: conservatives wanted *some* minimum level of decency in the hospitals, and liberals wanted *at least* a minimum level. If liberals and conservatives could agree on a minimum level, which it appears they did, this game had an obvious outcome—the hospitals got a minimum.

The ideological status of the debate had changed somewhat by 1966, however. Since about 1960, when the resident population in the MI hospitals began to taper off, the hospitals began to improve as treatment facilities, although in the opinion of many they were still quite poor.

The improvements in the hospitals created some disparity in liberal and conservative definitions of an acceptable minimum. In May 1966 while running for the Republican gubernatorial nomination on a very conservative platform, Ronald Reagan declared that if he were elected he would empower a committee of expert California hotel operators to inspect and recommend improvements in the state's mental institutions, "which are, in a sense, hotel operations." [12] The hospitals had arrived. They had entered into the mainstream of American politics, the Welfare State Question. Nine months later, when Governor Reagan announced that some 3,700 positions would be eliminated from the DMH in the 1968 budget, most from the MI hospitals, their new status was confirmed. Reagan spoke of them as excellent, progressive institutions providing helpful services to unfortunate patients. He lamented that owing to serious fiscal problems the public would have to forego the luxury of getting further improvements in the system for the present. [13]

The Office of the Legislative Analyst was the most persistent legislative watchdog over DMH expenditures and expenditure-related policies. Since 1949 the legislative analyst's job had been held by the same man, A. Alan Post; and during that period the legislature had come to rely heavily on the recommendations made by Post and his staff. These appeared in their most comprehensive form in the annual analysis of the budget bill, which is made public almost simultaneously with the governor's budget. In 1967 the analysis ran to 1,100 pages, and most of them contained recommendations for trimming the governor's requests or for changing policy or management practices so as to increase revenues or decrease costs. In 1967 the Analyst's Office, which employed around fifty professional and semiprofessional staff members, had two specialists with jurisdiction confined largely to the Department of Mental Hygiene and Short–Doyle. The high competence and reliability of the Legislative Analyst's Office in this policy area permitted elected representatives to divert their attention from it somewhat more than they otherwise might have.

Although mental health had few close friends in the legislature, neither did it have many dedicated enemies. Veteran observers of the men-

---

[12] *San Francisco Chronicle.* June 1, 1966.

[13] Reagan denied that the cuts were a step backward. Since the resident population could be expected to continue to decline, a corresponding decrease in staff would not amount to a cutback. The recommended appropriation would merely maintain current effort. See chapter 5 for a full description of this controversy.

tal health scene in Sacramento could name no one with an anti-mental-health stance of the kind associated with the radical Right. Thus, mental health programs were rather different from other programs in the health, education, and welfare area. Legislative interest in them was minimal, intermittent, and usually unemotional.

As for the executive branch of state government, again the mental health system was far from a central concern, at least until the Reagan administration took office. The first evidence of executive interest in the policy goals of the system came in 1949, when Governor Earl Warren convened a two-day Conference on Mental Health, which brought together some 900 interested citizens and officials. Although the conference participants intended to create a permanent organization, a semiofficial lobby, after two or three years it fell into desuetude. The last discoverable report of its executive committee (which was optimistically called "The Governor's Continuing Committee on Mental Health") was published in 1951. It took credit for "a significant increase" in the DMH budget for that year and suggested that it was having an impact on decisions about hospital expansion, the location of new hospitals, and the treatment programs within the hospitals. It is a plausible inference that the governor had convened the conference for just such ends. Both he and they could trade on each other's prestige to promote a cause on which all parties were generally agreed. Governor Goodwin Knight and the mental health activists repeated the same maneuver in 1956, with the mutually agreed upon aim of promoting support for the community clinic legislation (Short–Doyle) due to go into a second round in the 1957 legislative session. The administration of Governor Edmund Brown established a permanent Governor's Advisory Commission on Mental Health. According to one of its members in the later years of the Brown administration, it gave little advice but did much to lay the mantle of respectability on whatever mental health programs were currently operating. It was concerned mainly with protecting the administration and sympathetic legislators from the occasional but ferocious blasts from the anti-mental-health forces on the Right.

Governor Reagan earned the reputation among many mental health advocates of having a strong interest in the system, but one driven by values opposed to their own. Reagan's most contested action during his first term in office was the attempt to make deep cuts in the DMH budget, particularly in the support budget for the MI hospitals. In fact, he probably cared little one way or another about the system; he was simply casting about for a way to save the state money (or at least to *appear* to save the state money). In one installment in the serialized romance of Sir Ronald and his loyal servant Sancho Nofziger (the reference being to Lyn Nofziger, Reagan's press secretary) *San Francisco Chronicle* columnist Arthur Hoppe had Sir Ronald slay an innocuous creature called "the Mental Health." This act of specious courage he justifies to the alarmed Sancho by saying, "Fear not, loyal Sancho, I know somehow in my bones that around here it never will be missed." Hoppe's ironical implication was that Reagan mistakenly believed the beast to be as little visible to others as it was to himself.[14]

The relevant overseers for the Short–Doyle programs during the 1964–1967 period were mainly the residents of the several counties (or cities) in which the program operated, the board of supervisors of each of these counties, and the program's official Mental Health Advisory boards composed of seven persons appointed by the supervisors. During the first few years of the Short–Doyle program, strong opposition emerged in a number of localities from members of right-wing groups; but this opposition generally quieted down once the programs were launched. There was considerable variation from county to county in the degree of oversight of the program by the advisory boards. Some Short–Doyle administrators felt there was little participation but desired more; others felt there was much but desired less. It appears that the lay activists were generally attentive and also favorable to the programs. From interviews with both Short–Doyle administrators and California Association for Mental Health leaders, it appeared that the criticism of the programs was usually limited to specific areas of programming and performance, but that there was substantial consensus on the value of some sort of locally administered and state-financed mental health program. These informants also believed that there was substantial approval for Short–Doyle among the less aware or involved residents of the local communities.

Because of the limited statutory and revenue-raising powers of county governments, county supervisors are able to concentrate attention on those few program areas over which they do have power and responsibility. From my observations of County Supervisors Association meetings, it seemed there were greater interest and awareness in mental health programming among the supervisors than among state legislators. Much

14 *San Francisco Chronicle*, April 17, 1967.

of the concern, however, was limited to the fiscal aspects of the programs. Probably the main component of a county supervisor's definition of his political role is dedication to keeping the property taxes down.[15] Even the promise of equal matching funds from the state did not suffice to induce the majority of the counties to undertake Short–Doyle programs. The counties that did so in the first few years of the program were mainly the populous or wealthy ones. Only when the matching formula was changed in 1963 to three state dollars for every county dollar did the number of programs increase rapidly. During the period 1964–1966, the number of Short–Doyle programs grew from twenty-one to thirty-nine, almost doubling the growth rate of the preceding seven years. In fiscal 1965, eight new inpatient services—the most expensive, but optional, feature of Short–Doyle programs—were added, that is, as many as had been started in the eight years previous.

In a rather general way, several associations of mental health professionals also kept watch over the public mental health system. Their concerns were not so much budgetary as programmatic, and the program features that most concerned them were those that affected the experience of their respective professions within the system. Of these various associations—principally the three California branches of the American Psychiatric Association; the California Medical Association (CMA); the California State Psychological Association (CSPA); the California chapters of the National Association of Social Workers (NASW); and the California Nurses Association (CNA)—only the medical groups had managed to establish routine and formal access to policy makers in the DMH and Short–Doyle. (All, of course, enjoyed either informal or intermittent access, both to administrators and to elected officials.) At the county level, Short–Doyle found it advantageous to have leaders of the county medical society on the local advisory board. (By law three of the seven positions on each board were required to be held by physicians in private practice, one of whom was to be a "specialist in psychiatry.") During the 1964–1967 period, the DMH had a Medical Advisory Committee composed of nine or ten psychiatrists from diverse regions of the state and prominent in state or local professional circles.

There were three district branches of the American Psychiatric Association in California, with a total of about 1600 members (not all

15 The second important component is the desire to maintain county autonomy against encroachments by Sacramento.

34

practicing psychiatrists were affiliated). Over half resided in the Los Angeles area and were members of the southern California district branch. The northern branch claimed about 600 members, mainly in the San Francisco Bay Area; and the central branch accounted for about 100 members, located mainly in the large cities of the Central Valley. An Inter-District Branch Committee served to coordinate these three groups when the need arose. One such need was that of protecting and controlling the Mental Health Committee of the CMA. The committee was institutionalized only in the 1960s. It had been an uphill struggle for the psychiatrists to create this niche in the CMA, whose elderly and conservative leadership was suspicious of psychiatry's claims to being a branch of medicine. It was the CMA, indeed, that stalled the passage of the Short–Doyle Act for several years in the mid-1950s.[16] It goes almost without saying that the DMH's Medical Advisory Committee collected its members as much as possible from the Inter-District Branch Committee and from the Mental Health Committee of the CMA.

In legislative arenas the several professions were on somewhat more equal terms. Organized psychiatry had no lobbyist of its own in Sacramento. The CMA employed one of the most effective lobbyists in the capital, but organized psychiatry rarely if ever commanded his services. The CSPA employed a part-time lobbyist. The CNA lobbyist was employed full-time and had a reputation for effectiveness. Having no statewide organization, the NASW chapters employed no lobbyist; but their large membership, geographical dispersion, and their readiness to believe in the efficacy of political action partially compensated for this lack.[17]

Although the public mental health system was salient to its nominal clients, the general public, only infrequently, there were vocal citizen groups for which it was highly salient and which tried vigorously to persuade the public to support more and higher-quality mental health programs. The most active and energetic of these groups was the California Association for Mental Health (CAMH), which was a unit within the National Association for Mental Health. Given the population and

[16] William R. Vizzard, "An Outline and Analysis of the California Medical Association's Support of SB 244 (1957)—The 'Short–Doyle' Act" (unpublished manuscript, 1958).

[17] The California State Employees Association and the California Society of Psychiatric Technicians represented a large number of hospital employees with regard to matters like wages, working conditions, and general issues of personnel policy. Both groups employed full-time lobbyists.

wealth of California and the comparatively enlightened character of its public policies, it was natural that the CAMH should have been one of the most prominent units in the national group. During 1967, Earl Warren, Jr., a Sacramento lawyer and bearer of his father's famous name, was elected president of NAMH. State chapters could follow policies independently of the parent organization, to be sure; and in California the statewide organization permitted a similar autonomy to its thirty-three local chapters. These chapters were organized by county, conveniently coinciding both with Short–Doyle jurisdictions and with those of local medical societies. In 1966 these chapters enrolled some 28,000 members. The state division and the local chapters were spending, during the mid-1960s, around $800,000 annually. This money was spent on salaries for a few full-time and part-time administrators (one executive director with an office near the state capitol is included) and office expenses; communications and travel; and publications and the expense of distribution. The highest formal authority was its board of directors, made up of one delegate from each local chapter plus about a dozen at-large and ex-officio members. A statewide public affairs committee, constituted in a similar manner, developed an annual policy program which it then recommended to the board of directors. In addition, there were local public affairs committees that channeled recommendations to the statewide body. Each local chapter had relative freedom to undertake its own political action programs.

The CAMH membership resembled in many ways those of other organizations devoted to progressive causes. They were middle and upper-middle class, well educated, suburban, connected with additional cause-oriented progressive groups, and to a certain extent consciously identified with the ethos of public service and social responsibility. The data from our subsample of twenty-nine CAMH leaders (see Appendix B) are highly indicative. Seventeen lived in households with annual incomes above $15,000. Eighteen had at least one postgraduate degree. Fifteen were professionals of some sort, six were administrators of some non-profit organization, and eight (of twelve women) were housewives. Twenty had lived in California since before 1952 or had been born in the state. Three-quarters belonged to at least one organization other than the CAMH. Democrats outnumbered Republicans sixteen to seven; and only one respondent designated himself as a political conservative, with eighteen identifying themselves as liberals and nine as middle-of-the-roaders. All but five reported having voted for Governor Edmund Brown against Ronald Reagan in 1966.

The social and personal characteristics of the CAMH membership base in effect made the CAMH competitive with certain other groups like the League of Women Voters and the California Democratic clubs. From informal conversations with many CAMH leaders one could have been impressed by the frequency with which contingency determined that they channel their energies into mental health causes rather than, for instance, consumer protection or natural resources conservation. Some had become acquainted with problems of mental illness through having had instances of it arise in their own families or in the families of friends. Others had spouses who were professional mental health workers. (The CAMH encouraged mental health professionals to become members but discouraged them from entering leadership positions.) Still others were recruited at the urging of friends who happened to have a special interest in mental health policy. No matter how they arrived at it, though, once fully committed to the cause and the organization, CAMH activists did not drift away quickly. They persisted in their work with great zeal, though most of it, to be sure, involved efforts merely to mobilize the more passive members on behalf of the association's or chapter's goals and programs.

As an overseer of the public mental health treatment system the CAMH labored under two serious handicaps. First, it was obliged to stay on good terms with the DMH except under extraordinary circumstances. In the long run, the CAMH reasoned, administration rather than politics would be the way to reform and improve the system. Hence, the CAMH only occasionally could afford to stir up trouble publicly. Secondly, the CAMH recognized that in the long run politics could be extremely dangerous to the system. If the status quo was not good, politically inspired change was in any case not likely to improve it. Politicization meant threat—either from more economy-minded lawmakers or from the dark side of public opinion, the anti-mental-health movement on the radical Right.

2

Mapping Ideological Consensus and Cleavage

Existing programs and practices in the policy area and alternatives to them are recurrent topics of discussion and opinion within the attentive public. To gauge in advance how proposals for change will be received and to be able to promote them in a vocabulary familiar to the attentive public, it is useful for the entrepreneur to know which issues have been a matter of discussion at all, which issues are subjects of continuing controversy, and which opinions are presently widely shared. The entrepreneur can inform himself on these matters by reading the public statements of the leading organizations, groups, and individuals in the attentive public and by soliciting such information from veteran observers. There are few trustworthy shortcuts in this process. In the case of the attentive public of California mental health policy circa 1967, responses to a survey questionnaire support impressions I gathered over a period of many months prior to the administration of the survey. I would not have relied on the survey alone; nor should a political entrepreneur do so. The following material on opinions within the attentive mental health public is divided into three sections: propositions on which there was consensus; propositions on which there was politically relevant disagreement; and an examination of the underlying ideological reference axis which organized attitudes on the controversial propositions.

IDEOLOGICAL CONSENSUS

In view of the many ideological conflicts that divided the attentive mental health public, it is easy to lose sight of the attitudes and beliefs on which there was consensus. They were numerous, however, and provided significant reference points to which competing factions could repair when controversy became overheated and when the attentive public was obliged to stand united against threats from without. By "ideological consensus" something quite specific is intended: there was no dissent at all on the following propositions, some of which appear commonplace or so lacking in content that they seem hardly worth mentioning. It is probable, however, that propositions the attentive public took for granted enjoyed no comparable status outside it. If this is so, it is obviously worthwhile to list them. In any case, it is better to err on the side of caution, leaving no assumptions implicit that can easily be made explicit.

(1) "The system should give 'help' and 'care' to as many persons as want and need it."

(2) " 'Help' and 'care' should be given close to the client's home whenever possible." In 1962, a task force broadly representative of all sectors of the attentive mental health public put forth a "Long Range Plan for Mental Health Services in California," one major theme of which was that "the best way to give care to individuals is in local communities." The task force commented further, "We know of no responsible dissent from this proposition."[1] This was also the view of policy makers in Washington. The National Institute of Mental Health prepared a kit of documents, brochures, publications, and conference minutes concerning the two Community Mental Health Center acts in which the theme was constantly reiterated that local care was the wave of the future. The standard opening of many of these presentations was to quote President John F. Kennedy's words, "The time has come for a bold new approach." Local services were then identified as the bold new approach and state hospitals as the stale old approach that should and would be superseded. A recurrent analogy in the rhetoric supporting this aim was "the battlefield." Mental illness was the enemy. An army of dedicated if none too numerous mental health workers would oppose it. The community mental health programs would act as a "main line of defense" against mental illness, while the state hospitals would be the "back-up resources."[2]

---

[1] DMH, *Legislation to Implement a Long Range Plan for Mental Health Services in California*. Report of the Legislative Task Force Committee to the Director of Mental Hygiene (Sacramento: DMH, March 11, 1963), p. 2.

[2] Joint Commission on Mental Illness and Health, *Action for Mental Health* (New York: Basic Books, 1961), p. 263. See also minutes of the December 1966 meeting of

(3) " 'Help' and 'care' should be given promptly, when the client wants and needs it, not when it is convenient for the organization rendering the services."

(4) "Prevention is better than cure."

(5) As a client passes through the treatment system, "he should receive 'continuity of care.' " There should be no unplanned discontinuities, and a maximum of coordination among suppliers of treatment. Whether this principle implied that a single agency should take charge of the client's career through the system was a matter for some debate. No agency wanted to lose jurisdiction over its own particular administrative or treatment functions for the sake of such a principle. Since every agency in the system faced such a threat from at least one quarter, the principle was given little more than lip service. A second interpretation of the continuity of care principle was that programs for a defined population of potential clients, for example, in a given county or service area, should be administered by a single authority. Failure to apply the principle in this way would result, it was said, in fragmentation of services. Although the connection between jurisdictional continuity and treatment continuity is more metaphorical than logical or empirical, contending interests almost never took notice of the fact. It would almost certainly have served the interests of some groups, for instance, the Bureau of Social Work, to have supported one kind of continuity and ignored or damned the other. Why no interest chose to disrupt consensus on the slogan "continuity of care" is a bit of a puzzle, though probably the most important reasons are that few actors understood the essential vacuity of the slogan and that those who did felt no pressing need to clarify the matter.

(6) "If possible, hospitalization should be avoided." This ideological norm underlay the movement toward local services and community mental health centers. It also underlay the attempts by local administrators to treat clients on an outpatient basis or to provide whatever other

---

Short–Doyle administrators and program chiefs, that is, the Conference of Local Mental Health Directors. The Joint Commission was established by Congress in 1955 to carry out "an objective, thorough, and nationwide analysis and reevaluation of the human and economic problems of mental illness and of the resources, methods, and practices currently utilized in diagnosing, treating, caring for, and rehabilitating the mentally ill." *Action for Mental Health*, p. 303. Establishment of the Joint Commission represented a signal that political leaders were prepared to accept some sort of innovation in the mental illness field, and that a massive combination of professional and academic talents were prepared to spur them on.

services—welfare, social work, job placement—were needed in lieu of hospitalization even in local facilities. The consequences were thought to be more humane, more effective, and less expensive.[3]

TABLE 3

MALE FIRST ADMISSIONS RELEASED FROM MI HOSPITALS WITHIN FIRST AND SECOND SIX-MONTH PERIODS FOLLOWING ADMISSION

Fiscal Year of Admission	Percent Released in First Six Months After Admission	Percent Released After First Six Months but Before End of One Year
1949	52.4	8.0
1950	58.2	7.3
1951	56.2	8.4
1952	57.9	7.0
1953	59.9	6.2
1954	60.7	6.8
1955	59.5	7.2
1956	62.3	7.7
1957	64.3	6.7
1958	65.0	4.7
1959	64.3	7.5
1960	68.2	6.0

Source: Adapted from Tables 1 and 2, *Report of the Legislative Analyst*, 1965, pp. 526–527.

(7) "If hospitalization is unavoidable, it should be terminated as quickly as possible." Table 3 provides evidence of a very gradual but unambiguous trend toward earlier release from state hospitals during the 1950s, thus reflecting, at one level, the consequences of this consensus. An important auxiliary proposition, somewhat less widely held, was that prolonged hospitalization probably had distinctly adverse ef-

[3] See, for example, the address by Don Heath to a group of mental health professionals and lay activists in Texas, February 23, 1966: Texas Association for Mental Health, "Design for Community Care . . . from Concept into Reality" (Austin, Texas), 1966. Heath was the "demonstration officer" (public information and public relations spokesman) for the San Mateo County Short–Doyle program, which in 1967 was reputed to be one of the best community mental health programs in the nation under public auspices. Heath estimated that fifty to one hundred mental health professionals were visiting the program monthly. His office had also made a film of certain aspects of the program for public distribution. He spoke proudly of the fact that San Mateo admitted only four out of ten persons to inpatient beds. (Interview, November 2, 1966.)

fects. On the basis of his own research, the administrator of the psychiatric department of Los Angeles County General Hospital concluded,
"We have recognized that much of what was formerly described as the
clinical picture of the chronic schizophrenic is not at all the inevitable
outcome of the disease process. Rather, it is the inevitable outcome of
prolonged hospitalization. The chronic, deteriorated, alienated schizophrenic patient who vegetates in the back wards of our many state
hospitals is the final outcome of an iatrogenic condition resulting from
prolonged hospitalization superimposed on the schizophrenic illness."[4]
One could also infer from the data in Table 3, column 2, that early release policies lost their effect on patients who had been hospitalized for
over six months. There may have been disagreement over just how important the iatrogenic factor was in the whole process of illness, but there
was no disagreement that its effects were real. Exactly what factors lay
behind the trend toward earlier release reflected in Table 3 were not
reliably understood. One careful analyst in the DMH Bureau of Biostatistics conjectured that some of the more important factors might
have been the "fairly steady year-to-year improvement in the ratio of
staff to patients, the introduction of tranquilizers and other psychotropic drugs in the 1950's and the development of alternative psychiatric
resources in the community. Possibly there has been some increase in
public understanding and toleration of harmless, mild forms of mental
disorder."[5]

[4] Werner Mendel, "Effect of Length of Hospitalization on Rate and Quality of
Remission from Acute Psychotic Episodes," *Journal of Nervous and Mental Diseases*
143, no. 3 (September 1966): 226–233.

[5] Richard Morgan, "They Are Getting out Sooner," DMH Bureau of Biostatistics
Report (February 1967), pp. 16–20. This article was a follow-up of two previous technical reports by Morgan, "Trends in Hospital Population Movement, 1949–1961," and
"A Model for Estimating Cohort Residuals," published by the DMH Bureau of Biostatistics as reports nos. 23 and 24 (December 11, 1964, and December 13, 1965), respectively. One hypothetical factor that could be reliably disconfirmed, however, was
the possibility of a shift in the composition of the population of first admissions.
Morgan found essentially the same trend toward early release when patient characteristics were, in effect, statistically held constant. He gathered data on patient cohorts
admitted in each of the years 1949 to 1960 with the following characteristics: white,
male, age 25–44, diagnosed schizophrenics, first admissions, admitted by civil commitment. California State Legislature, *Analysis of the Budget Bill of the State of
California for the Fiscal Year July 1, 1965, to June 30, 1966.* Report of the Legislative
Analyst to the Joint Legislative Budget Committee (Sacramento: Office of State Print-
ing, 1966), pp. 526–527. These reports are hereinafter cited as *Report of the Legislative
Analyst.*

(8) "Symbolic and actual physical violence to patients as part of an approved treatment system are to be avoided." Lobotomies and sterilization had been eliminated from the state hospitals since at least the late 1950s. Electroconvulsive therapy (ECT, or "shock treatment") was still practiced, but much more infrequently with each passing year, especially as more varied and improved pharmacological agents were developed to pacify and restrain troublesome or hyperactive patients.

(9) "The public mental health system should reach out especially to those potential recipients of treatment who cannot afford to obtain it in the private sector." This applied mainly to the sorts of outpatient treatment provided by Short–Doyle programs. Short–Doyle employed a sliding scale of fees to consumers based on their ability to pay.

(10) "A serious obstacle to rendering service to all the people who need and want it is 'the mental health manpower shortage,'" a problem that was nationwide and not peculiar to California. A planning study conducted by the DMH in 1965 concluded that

> The problem is a severe one, as most of those in the mental health professions are aware. There are insufficient numbers of persons in each of the "core" mental health fields of psychiatry, clinical psychology, psychiatric social work, and psychiatric nursing. In addition, there are inequities of distribution, as in all the service professions. The shortage in public mental health personnel is far more extreme than that in private practice, and the shortage in rural areas is more acute than that in urban areas.[6]

Beyond the consensus that there was a shortage, there was little agreement on why or what to do about it. Some believed it was simply an aspect of a manpower shortage affecting all the professions; others, that it was especially severe in the mental health field. Some believed that the problem could be alleviated by higher salaries; others looked to more intensified recruitment into professional education programs; still others claimed that a redistribution of existing professionals among institutions and a redefinition of task roles would be the most important steps. Finally, some wished to blur the distinction between professional and nonprofessional in order to augment the manpower available for tasks defined hitherto as lying within the competence of professionals only.

(11) "More money spent on the public mental health system is bound

[6] Murray Klutch, *Mental Health Manpower: An Annotated Bibliography and Comment* (Sacramento: DMH, 1965), pp. ii–iii.

to improve it." No one considered whether or not there was some upper limit on the improvement that more money could produce, since there was also agreement that if such a limit existed there was no realistic hope of approaching it in the foreseeable future.

(12) "It is also possible to make improvements without money." Much faith was invested in the potential for improving techniques of psychotherapy, changing attitudes of treatment personnel and administrators, coordinating the programs of agencies serving the same consumer population, finding the right balance between centralized and decentralized administrative arrangements, involving consumers and ordinary citizens in political and administrative decision making, and so on. Naturally, there was little consensus about which of these specific improvements was workable, desirable, or deserving of priority.

(13) "Research helps," though there was disagreement on just how much.

(14) "Planning helps. It is better to think, talk, and negotiate in advance of investing scarce resources in new programs or institutional arrangements." Naturally, the cry for more planning was not infrequently an attempt to stall or sabotage an innovation of which one did not approve.

IDEOLOGICAL CLEAVAGE

Outside this core area of ideological consensus remained a sizable number of ideological controversies. To many professionals my treatment of these issues is bound to appear too simple. It should be borne in mind, though, that this is not a treatise on how to diagnose and treat mental illness. We are discussing politics, and for that purpose, it is sufficient to describe the sorts of issues that found political expression within the hospitals and clinics and within the broader public arena.

(1) "Does mental illness exist?" One point of view, often identified with academic sociology, and particularly with the phenomenological school, virtually denied that mental illness exists. The work of Erving Goffman is the intellectual foundation for this point of view. Ken Kesey, in *One Flew over the Cuckoo's Nest*, provided a literary vehicle for the argument. Virtually alone among psychiatric theoreticians, Thomas Szasz had flooded *Harper's*, the *Atlantic Monthly,* and the *New York Times* Sunday magazine with the very unpsychiatric view that mental illness is a myth.

Probably the most sophisticated published statement in 1967 of the sociological argument against the existence of mental illness was *Being Mentally Ill: A Sociological Theory* by Thomas Scheff.[7] While acknowledging that many persons exhibit symptoms of mental illness, Scheff insists that these are defined as mental illness only because they are labeled that way by "the culture of the group." These symptoms are, for the most part, only "instances of residual rule-breaking or residual deviance." Rule breaking is a concept drawn from the work of sociologist Howard S. Becker, which Scheff defines as "a class of acts, violations of social norms"; deviance is a subclass of these, namely, "particular acts which have become publicly and officially labeled as norm violations." Of residual rule breaking and deviance, he writes:

> The culture of the group provides a vocabulary of terms for categorizing many norm violations: crime, perversion, drunkenness, and bad manners are familiar examples. Each of these terms is derived from the type of norm broken, and ultimately, from the type of behavior involved. After exhausting these categories, however, *there is always a residue of the most diverse kinds of violations, for which the culture provides no explicit label.* For example, although there is great cultural variation in what is defined as decent or real, each culture tends to reify its definition of decency and reality, and so provides no way of handling violations of its expectations in these areas. The typical norm governing decency or reality, therefore literally "goes without saying" and its violation is unthinkable for most of its members. *For the convenience of the society in construing those instances of unnamable rule-breaking which are called to its attention, these violations may be lumped together into a residual category: witchcraft, spirit possession, or, in our own society, mental illness* [p. 34, emphasis added].

Residual rule breaking originates in diverse ways, including organic causes, psychological causes, external stress, and volitional acts of innovation or defiance (p. 40). Residual rule breaking is much more prevalent than the rate of treated mental illness, for most of it is " 'denied' and is of transitory significance" (pp. 48–49, 51). Some residual rule breaking, however, is stabilized: "The hypothesis suggested here is that the most important single factor (but not the only factor) in the stabilization of residual rule-breaking is the societal reaction. Residual rule-breaking may be stabilized if it is defined to be evidence of mental ill-

---

[7] Chicago: Aldine Publishing, 1966.

ness, and/or the rule-breaker is placed in a deviant status, and *begins to play the role of the mentally ill*" (pp. 53–54, emphasis added). Why does the deviant or rule breaker assume this role? First, he knows what the role is supposed to be, because "the stereotypes of insanity are continually reaffirmed, inadvertently in ordinary social interaction" (p. 67). Secondly, "labeled deviants may be rewarded for playing the stereotyped deviant role"—by psychiatrists, among others—and "are punished when they attempt to return to conventional roles" (pp. 84, 87). Moreover, "In the crisis occurring when a residual rule-breaker is publicly labeled, the deviant is highly suggestible, and may accept the preferred role of the insane as the only alternative" (p. 88). And finally, the key thesis of the book: "Among residual rule-breakers, labeling is the single most important cause of careers of residual deviance" (pp. 92–93).[8]

Scheff's theory, which he explicitly insists is only partial, fails to address the question of why certain residual rule breakers and deviants are labeled mentally ill and others are not. Nor does it deal adequately with the question of why some accept the labeling but others reject it. Finally, his phenomenological approach forbids even raising the question of whether or not some constructions of reality are more warranted, or even practical, than others. A related but differentiable sociological interpretation of mental illness, which also emphasizes the social definition of behavior and which indirectly suggests answers to some of these questions, we shall call "the social loser theory." This theory is more specific than Scheff's about the kinds of deviants and rule breakers that are most often labeled mentally ill. They are the persons who cannot, have not, or will not "make it" in a basically competitive, materialistic, and atomized society, even by the most relaxed and generous standards of social success and functional competence. They are the hoboes, the drunks, the homosexuals, the deteriorating aged, the penniless, the bohemians, the aesthetes, and a variety of others.

One incident was observed during a visit to a state hospital that illustrates the sets of facts to which the social loser theory is most sensitive. Following a staff discussion of the past week's behavior of patients on an "acute, therapeutic" hospital ward, which I was permitted to attend, I inquired about the prognosis of one young man (about nineteen) with whom I had previously conversed at some length. "Oh, my," said the leader of the ward's treatment team, "he's still in pretty bad shape, even

---

8 He is careful to stress that it is not the only cause, however.

after six months here. He says he feels better and wants to leave soon. But I don't think he will. He talks a lot about getting a job as a counselor in juvenile hall down in ———. But just the other day he told us that what he would really like is to sit under a tree on a mountain top and read and think. He has big ideas—but he has no power of execution."[9]

A rough index of the extent to which the cultural labeling theory had taken hold in the attentive public is provided by the distribution of responses to one of our questionnaire items, " 'Mental Illness' is nothing but a label we apply to people who happen to deviate from conventional social norms" (item 24). Only 5 percent strongly agreed and another 16 percent agreed without emphasis (Table 4). Sociological nominalism was clearly a minority viewpoint, although the critical thrust of its arguments was much more influential than the small number of its true believers would suggest. For instance, it led people to ask the following question, and to disagree on the answer.

(2) "Who is really the 'patient'?" Given that illness is real rather than imaginary, it still is open to question who or what is ill. If a man showed up in the hospital or the clinic for treatment, could one be sure that he

---

[9] A fascinating historical treatment of differing definitions of insanity in Europe from the Middle Ages to the nineteenth century may be found in Michel Foucault, *Madness and Civilization: A History of Insanity in the Age of Reason* (New York: Pantheon Books, 1965). (Originally published in French as *Histoire de la Folie*, 1961.) Foucault traces the practice of institutionalizing "madmen" to the leprosaria of the Middle Ages, the "ships of fools" of the Renaissance, and then to the first landmark in the period of "the Great Confinement," the founding of the Hôpital Général of Paris in 1656. In each period, the definition of madness seems to be the obverse of the most highly prized definitions of moral excellence of the time. In the seventeenth and eighteenth centuries, for instance, when "reason" was particularly exalted, institutionalization prevented the "contagion of un-reason." The "birth of the asylum" in the late eighteenth and nineteenth centuries, first in France and then in England, marked the insinuation of guilt into the definition of mental illness. The regimen of the asylum employed "moral treatment," expressed in the imitation of family life within the institution. Under the directorship of Samuel Tuke in England, a distinctively religious (Quaker) milieu was established. Unlike many present-day "progressives," who look back to the ideology and regimen of moral treatment as an exemplary instance of therapeutic success, Foucault suggests that the consequences of these reforms were, in the long run, negative. Some suggestion of the social loser theory may be found in various research pieces by Dorothy Miller. Dr. Miller was particularly influential in nurturing the commitment reform project described in chapter 4. See too accounts of her speech at the San Francisco State College symposium in the *San Francisco Chronicle*, February 28, 1967, and "Worlds that Fail: Part I, Retrospective Analysis of Mental Patients' Careers," Research Monograph no. 6 (Sacramento: DMH, Bureau of Research, 1965).

TABLE 4

FREQUENCY DISTRIBUTIONS OF SAMPLE RESPONSES TO TEN ATTITUDE ITEMS[a] (in percent)

Item	Question Number	Strongly Agree	Agree	Neutral	Disagree	Strongly Disagree	Total Percent	Total Number
The most important cause of mental illness is probably heredity	23	2	3	9	49	38	101	579
"Mental illness" is nothing but a label we apply to people who happen to deviate from conventional social norms	24	5	16	6	51	22	100	580
Someday we will probably be able to trace all mental illness to physiological causes	25	2	10	15	51	22	100	576
Most mental illness originates in people's immediate personal environment	26	12	55	13	17	2	99	575
It would probably cause more harm than good if state hospital patients were to become much more conscious of their legal rights	28	1	6	13	48	33	101	578
We could go a long way toward solving the mental health manpower shortage if each of the mental health professions would stop insisting on its traditional job assignments	29	16	41	21	20	2	100	571
All things considered, increased reliance on "non-professionals" in therapeutic roles would be a good thing	30	11	50	15	20	4	100	576
Even the best system of community mental health services will never do away with the need for large state hospitals	31	5	26	9	45	15	100	579
State hospitals don't get enough credit. They really do help people to overcome their mental illnesses and return to the community	32	10	59	18	11	3	101	578
Hospitalization for mental illness rarely helps the patient—and often it is downright harmful	33	4	11	9	57	20	101	578

[a] The questionnaire contained eleven items tapping ideological orientations. Many strands of evidence developed in the subsequent analysis led to the conclusion that the wording of item 27 meant quite opposite things to different respondents. This item was therefore discarded from the analysis.

was not merely the accidental victim of a pathological social environment? Perhaps his neighborhood was so crime ridden or deteriorated that his symptoms were in fact a healthy response to the difficulties of living in such circumstances. If his family life was the problem, perhaps it was his wife or children that really ought to have come for treatment.

(3) "What are the primary causes of mental illness?" If the individual who has appeared for treatment is indeed conceived of as the patient, how does one interpret the etiology of his illness? While most of the attentive public would have agreed that each individual case had to be diagnosed separately, most would also have been willing to theorize about the relative importance, in general, of personal traits as opposed to environmental circumstances. Two-thirds of our sample agreed to the proposition that most mental illness originates in the immediate personal environment, 19 percent disagreed, and 13 percent were neutral (item 26). At the other extreme, 12 percent of the sample believed that mental illness ultimately might be traced entirely to physiological causes (item 25). Although it would have been difficult to find many true physiological purists in the attentive public, there were many professionals and laymen who used a vocabulary almost as highly personalized as the vocabulary of such purists. In this vocabulary "the patient" is the single biological organism that has appeared for treatment. He is assumed to be afflicted with some sort of mental disease. It is the professional's task to restore him to a state of health. Because mental health is assumed to be a real and recognizable state of being, there is little doubt when success has been achieved. Because of the obvious analogy between physical illness and mental illness in this vocabulary, this particular etiological model was often referred to as "the medical model." It was also a view that happened to be more popular among medically trained professionals than it was among psychologists, social workers, or laymen. As one prominent Short–Doyle psychiatrist put it, "Until it is scientifically shown that mental illness is something *other* than 'illness' medicine should still hold on. I take a pragmatic view. You get *further* on the medical model. It is not an intellectual view being expressed here. It is just irresponsible to say, now, that it's not [an illness]."

It was equally difficult to find a pure environmentalist in the mental health public. One interviewee who leaned as far in this direction as any I met expressed the position roguishly: "Look. A rich businessman gets depressed about the boredom of his life. He goes to a fancy private psychiatrist. The psychiatrist says, 'Take a vacation; take the wife, go to

Hawaii for a month, get a suntan.' But a poor wage earner, suppose he gets depressed about the boredom of the assembly line, stops showing up for work, hits the bottle. *He* goes to the state hospital for a year and comes out (if ever) an 'ex-mental patient.' The vacation in Hawaii cost the businessman $2,000 and he felt much better afterward. The year in the hospital for the other one costs the state $5,000. We should send all the hospital patients to Hawaii. It would be cheaper."

(4) "What, if anything, is the role of 'personality' in the etiology of mental illness?" Most, though not all, mental health professionals and interested laymen conceived of individuals as being made up of mind and body. Although they may not have harkened back to the radical dualism of Descartes, they nevertheless postulated some functionally autonomous, or partially autonomous, entity that obeys natural laws independent of those governing either the physical organism or the social environment. There are many names for this entity—mind, psyche, emotions—of which "personality" is probably the most common. Typically, personality is viewed as an emergent or developing entity, shaped by both environmental and personal influences. Some theorists conceive of personality as a largely passive recipient of these influences; for others, it also acts, through "the ego," upon these influences, modifying them to accommodate whatever personality needs have already developed in the organism.

The principal opposition to the personality postulate came from two sources. One was the new wave of behavior therapists who were seeking to introduce the methods of classical and operant conditioning into treatment programs. The second was the old guard of nonpsychiatric physicians who refused to believe in an entity that was not amenable to direct observation. There was a certain quaintness and a hint of old-fashioned moralizing in the traditionalist's defense of physiological determinism, especially when it argued for genetic determinism as well. One state hospital superintendent with two decades of service in his post averred that heredity was the single most important cause of mental illness and added sadly that people were not willing to listen to his arguments any more. Since these views rarely surfaced, in order to capture the spirit of the extreme somatic view, we may refer to a 1908 report submitted by one Dr. King, the superintendent of Mendocino State Hospital, to the California Commission in Lunacy (as the DMH was then called):

Now, the same principle applies in the predisposing causes of mental diseases. A very large percentage of mental diseases is the result of a weak, unstable, nervous organization received from ancestors or acquired by dissipation or wasting diseases by the patient himself. Here we find the real cause of much of the crime and insanity that is the bane of civilization. The predisposing causes are deeply rooted in our civilization, in many cases reaching back to the second or third generation. . . . Every healthy, normal man who from any cause, either from serious disease, alcohol, or sexual excesses, or through a life of debauchery, lowers the tone of his vital forces and afterwards propagates the species is preparing the soil which will surely bring forth a class of degenerates, many of whom will be insane or criminals, and many of whose children will be feeble-minded, or perhaps idiotic.[10]

(5) "By what means, or techniques, should mental illness be treated?" Although there is in fact a correlation between preferred etiological doctrines and preferred treatment techniques, there is no strictly logical basis for the connection. To say, for instance, that the most important cause of mental illness is disturbance in the immediate personal environment might mean that this disturbance is a necessary but not a sufficient condition for the illness. Perhaps treatment should aim at removing the latter rather than the former. Neither logic nor science alone can determine a "correct" answer to the problem of how to treat mental illness in general or its manifestations in an individual case. Yet choices are made. How? The nature of the therapist's goals plays a role; so do the nature and extent of mundane resources like time and energy; perhaps, too, his orientation toward experiment and innovation, or toward research, is a guide. Certainly his sense of risks and probabilities becomes involved. As much as by anything else—and perhaps even more so—the actual choice as well as the grounds for it are determined by ideology. The ideology may, of course, have emerged from playing these instrumental considerations off against one another. On the other hand, the ideology may not be instrumental at all, but the product of indoctrination or wish. For convenience, we may begin by reducing the vast array of treatment methods and techniques to a three-part classification: somatic manipulation, environmental manipulation, and psychotherapy.

Somatic manipulation, which once included lobotomy and other surgical operations, was restricted largely to the use of pharmacological

---

[10] State Commission in Lunacy, *Sixth Biennial Report* (two years ending June 30, 1908), p. 10.

agents and to "shock treatment," effected either by ECT or by insulin.[11] A variety of psychotropic drugs have come on the market since the early 1950s that have proven their utility in counteracting states of anxiety, hypertension, depression, hyperactivity, and a number of specific symptoms of mental illness. In January 1967 the legislative analyst reported that the DMH in the previous year had spent $2.8 million for drugs, of which an estimated one-half was spent on tranquilizing drugs. It is difficult to do better than guess at the extent to which psychotropic drugs were used and for what purposes.[12] Interviews with hospital personnel, however, suggested that at any given time drugs were being administered to more than half the patients in the hospital and that nearly all patients who spent more than a brief time in the hospital were at some point given drugs. Although again it is impossible to do much better than guess, reliance on drugs was probably less common in Short–Doyle inpatient facilities and, within Short–Doyle, still less common in the treatment of outpatients. The large proportion of the total drug budget spent on tranquilizers suggests that the most common use to which drugs were put was to maintain social peace on the ward.

Opposition to the use of drugs had been gradually declining, although it was still occasionally strident. One interviewee called them "insidious substitutes for the straitjacket," and one ex-patient who testified at a legislative hearing on an unrelated matter plaintively objected to the regularity with which he had been "doped up." My impression is that nonphysicians, who were barrred by law from prescribing or administering drugs and who therefore could not conceivably make use of this treatment technique, were more skeptical about the use of drugs than were the physicians. Those who were most closely wedded to the medical model of mental illness found them less objectionable; and those who did object were less likely to do so on grounds of principle than of practicality.

Environmental manipulation could occur at one or more of several points in the patient's passage through the system. Environmental manipulation at the prehospitalization stage (which it was hoped would

[11] At one time germicidal agents were also used, most notably in the (often successful) attempts to cure mental disorders connected with syphilis by inducing a mild malarial fever in the patient. In fact, Stockton State Hospital developed one of the best strains of malaria virus for this purpose known in the country.

[12] Probably the DMH could do little better than guess either, for record keeping at the ward and hospital level was not particularly reliable. *Report of the Legislative Analyst, 1967,* p. 566.

forestall hospitalization) could involve visits by mental health professionals to the patient's home for consultation or for counseling with members of his family. It could involve referral to a public or private agency which the mental health professional felt was better equipped to deal with the patient's problem (or, in the case of a public agency, had "jurisdiction" over the category of problems into which it fit). Posthospitalization, or "after-care," programs included helping the former patient obtain welfare assistance, boarding-home placement, and placement with family caretakers.

Environmental manipulation within the hospital was usually known as "milieu therapy" or "creating a therapeutic community." In California, as elsewhere, it took many forms. The nationally known San Mateo Short–Doyle program advertised the success it was having with group therapy techniques and "open wards." "We don't believe in lock-and-key therapy," the director often used to say. The national Joint Commission on Mental Illness and Health, in *Action for Mental Health*, described the "new trends and programs" aimed at reducing or eliminating "the negative consequences of hospitalization associated with traditional institutions" as "breaking down the barriers between the hospital and community through open-door policies and strengthened volunteer activities; individualizing care and treatment by reducing the size of hospitals and orienting personnel to treat each patient as an individual rather than as a case or a number; and developing therapeutic milieus where the therapeutic potential of all persons in the hospital is recognized and used" (p. 178).

An enthusiastic account written by the administrative assistant to the superintendent of Mendocino State Hospital, often said to have been the most progressive of California's MI hospitals, illustrates the main features of the milieu therapy ideology in more detail:

> For a mental hospital, one of the first tasks is creating an atmosphere where things can happen. When that's done, you let them happen—even if it sometimes means jumping out of the way!
> The hospital's setting . . . is beautiful, by any standard. Since most of the units are open, the patients are free to explore the grounds, dotted with great oaks, Douglas firs and madrones. . . . The hospital is not only attractive but relatively small. . . .
> . . . At Mendocino, therapeutic efforts involve not only psychiatrists, psychologists, and social workers, but also plumbers, carpenters, typists, food service people, and all other employees.
> Among nonprofessional therapists, one of the largest and most

successful groups is that composed of the patients. Some of the best programs have been suggested or inspired and often implemented by patients.

Patients not only help entertain other patients but encourage the quiet ones to talk, at least a little, and help orient newcomers to the hospital. In many cases, they show both sensitivity and empathy when one of their friends is disturbed or agitated. . . . [The author then describes a few instances of outstanding success.]

The Patient Staff Advisory Council is hospital-wide. This is a hospital equivalent of self government. Area PSAC representatives meet regularly to discuss joint problems.

. . . Such discussions have ranged from minor problems (more coffee or more privileges) to major innovations—the choice of a meaningful research program, for instance.

That the ideology of milieu therapy found much favor in the DMH is reflected in the fact that this account was the lead article in the March 1963 issue of *California Mental Health Progress*, the department's monthly public relations offering. That month the issue was subtitled "Patients Helping Patients." Although milieu therapy had been demonstrably successful in many cases, and although the editor's introduction implied that the activities described were "typical of programs at other state hospitals," it was not clear that the ideology had caught on very widely among state hospital staffs or that its practice was very prevalent.

Some advocates of milieu therapy had recognized that it was not a new technique. Indeed, it does bear more than a passing resemblance to the method of "moral treatment" which flourished in American asylums before the Civil War.[13] This was a form of treatment that sought to encourage the patient to restore his capacity for autonomy and self-determination by providing him with a sheltered environment, peopled by other patients similarly motivated and by a warm-hearted staff. Ideological disagreement on the appropriateness of this sort of treatment usually involved questions of prudence rather than principle. The dispute turned on the question of whether or not it was reasonable in *most*

---

[13] See, for example, California Commission on Staffing Standards, *Staffing Standards for Public Mental Hospitals* (Sacramento: DMH, 1967), 1:8; Joint Commission, *Action for Mental Health*, pp. 25ff; and Dorothy Miller and Esther Blanc, "Concepts of 'Moral Treatment' for the Mentally Ill: Implications for Social Work with Post-hospital Mental Patients," *Social Service Review* 41, no. 1 (March 1967): 66–74. The standard reference work on the history of moral treatment in America is J. S. Bockoven, *Moral Treatment in American Psychiatry* (New York: Springer Publishing, 1963).

cases to seize on environmental manipulation as a treatment modality of first resort.

Obviously, both environmental and somatic manipulations are in some sense intended to be psychotherapy. Nevertheless, we need some classificatory label to cover a method of treatment that is rather distinguishable from the two described above. Psychotherapy involves a one-to-one relationship between the patient and the mental health worker. It can range from in-depth psychoanalysis to casual counseling. Use of the term in *Action for Mental Health* is indicative. "In recent years, increasing efforts have been made to treat schizophrenics with the aid of psychotherapy; an attempt by a professionally trained therapist to gain cooperation and insight through verbal or nonverbal communication with the patient at regular intervals over some extended period of time" (p. 35). One might add to the goals of "cooperation and insight" aimed at by psychotherapy only one other: behavior modification. Since 1960, when *Action for Mental Health* was essentially completed though not published, techniques of behavior therapy had made a limited impact on the field. Though not widely used up through 1967, it had achieved demonstrable success in limited areas (like training the mentally retarded, de-sensitizing phobic reactions, curing some alcoholics) and had certainly crossed the threshold of acceptance. Although some of its practitioners might object, it fits the connotations of psychotherapy we have suggested.

Probably owing to the large caseload in the state hospitals, one-to-one psychotherapy was the least common treatment modality in these institutions. It was somewhat more common in the Short–Doyle system, particularly in the outpatient services. When it was employed, its goals were necessarily limited to restoring the patient's ability to cope minimally with daily problems of life in the community or in the family. Full scale psychoanalysis was unheard of. As a consequence of the relative impracticability of psychotherapy, particularly its more intensive and time-consuming forms, there was scant ideological commitment to this treatment technique. Because the convinced adherents of psychotherapy could do little to promote its use (at least in the short run), they resorted to second-best techniques. They then had to defend the efficacy of what they *were* doing. Thus, while there may have been and probably were (there is no accurate way of telling) many whose ideal treatment modality was one-to-one psychotherapy, the impact of the ideal was visible only indirectly. It probably served to make them less ardent advocates of

55

other techniques, and perhaps less aggressive in searching for new ones, than others would have been. Strong belief in the ideal of one-to-one psychotherapy probably dissuaded psychiatrists and clinical psychologists from entering the public sector. If they did enter, they either modified their ideal or they left hospital practice as soon as their residency or training period was concluded. While associated with the hospital, they found ways to "make do." Anselm Strauss and his colleagues observed such coping strategies even in a private psychiatric hospital they studied. The most frequent concession to the hospital's rules and physical constraints made by psychotherapeutically oriented psychiatrists was the substitution of the therapeutic ward for intensive contact with the therapist himself. These practitioners would "chart the hospital's interior space according to the therapeutic consequences that may follow from placing patients upon various wards. The hospital's interior space is not pictured in the same way by each psychiatrist, but all do picture various wards according to *therapeutic* qualities and possibilities."[14] The practitioner would construct this map by gathering both explicit information and more subtle cues, and would assess his patients' progress by reading nursing notes, conversing with ward personnel, and talking to the patients during therapeutic sessions. Strauss and his collaborators conclude:

> On general ideological grounds, these physicians would insist to a man that psychotherapy is far more important than ward setting. They would deny that they are *milieu* therapists. They believe that there can be no basic change in a patient without adequate psychotherapy. But what is true in theory is not entirely relevant to their kinds of hospital practice. . . .
> This style of hospital practice can be visualized as if it were an elaborate chess game: The therapist seeks to gauge his patient's therapeutic movement and relates that movement to various therapeutic strategies of his own; whether in shaping the environment, in transferring the patient from one environment to another, or in managing his therapeutic sessions with the patient. The analogy with the chess game, of course, is most striking when the therapist moves his patient around the hospital according to some overall therapeutic plan.[15]

[14] Anselm Strauss, Leonard Schatzman, Rue Bucher, Danuta Ehrlich, and Melvin Sabshin, *Psychiatric Ideologies and Institutions* (Glencoe, Ill.: Free Press, 1964), p. 190 (italics in original).
[15] *Ibid.*, p. 195 (italics in original). The authors found five "individualistic psychotherapists" who did not fit the above descriptions.

(6) "What are the rights and duties of providers and recipients of treatment toward each other?" In civil society, most adults participate in a large number of role relationships which entail the reciprocal acknowledgment of rights, duties, and privileges by the participants in the relationship. These range from casual exchanges of courtesies to highly elaborated legal relationships. Most adults have full membership in civil society and a correspondingly full complement of such entailments. There are those, of course, like recent immigrants, homosexuals, and felons, who have less than full membership. Persons institutionalized in mental hospitals also enjoy less than full membership, it being denied them by a combination of legal prescription, social stigma, and often certain doctrines concerning the etiology and treatment of mental illness. Mental patients are often treated as the merest shadows of civil persons. The substance of civil personality has been eaten away, supposedly, by the individual's mental illness. Both professionals and laymen hold such beliefs, though usually in quite different degree and for different reasons. They may refuse to believe, for example, that the mentally ill have the capacity for *any* kind of voluntary or purposive behavior, for self-control, for rational thought, or even for experiencing physical pain. As Erving Goffman has shown in *Asylums*, the standard admitting procedure in some mental hospitals deliberately strips the patient of his sense of personal identity. He is deprived of such important tools in his identity kit as his personal clothing, combs, needle and thread, and shaving sets. The undercutting of the patient's capacity for "self-presentation," and the consequent unraveling of the patient's sense of selfhood Goffman terms part of a "mortification" process.[16]

There is no question but that the official and professionally approved ideology today is to minimize mortification, and conversely to maintain and augment whatever degree of self-esteem, ego strength, or sense of identity the patient still possesses when entering treatment. In our sample of the California mental health public, for instance, fully 81 percent disagreed with the proposition, "It would probably cause more harm than good if state hospital patients were to become much more conscious of their legal rights," and 33 percent disagreed strongly (item 28). But there was less consensus over the details of how to accomplish this and over whether, or which, risks would be run (by the mental health worker

---

[16] Erving Goffman, *Asylums* (Garden City: Doubleday, 1961), pp. 14–48, especially pp. 20–23.

and the patient alike) if this humanism were "carried to an extreme." Naturally, there were even wider variations in the practice of humanism than in its theory. Probably the most agitated theoretical controversy in this area involved the laws that permitted (and some said encouraged) the judicial commitment of persons alleged to be mentally ill. Should society and its agents be permitted to send a harmless but disturbed individual to a mental institution against his will? May he be "forced to be free" by physicians or judges who claim to act in his true interest, which he himself cannot, nevertheless, perceive? The medical profession, generalizing from its experience treating physical illness, had traditionally answered affirmatively. It had gone even further: not only had the physician a right to prescribe involuntary treatment, but for the sake of the patient, he had a duty to do so.

Within the psychiatric profession, Thomas Szasz has been the most vocal opponent of these doctrines. Szasz claims that psychiatrists seriously underestimate their patients' capacity for autonomous (and intelligent) choice. He considers psychiatry presumptuous in its claim to superior understanding of the patient's true desires and, at best, irresponsible in usurping the patient's right to make moral choices which, by Szasz's lights, belong properly to none but the patient himself. He upholds the doctrine, for instance, that any person, even someone who is supposedly mentally ill, has exclusive jurisdiction over whether or not to continue living. Szasz's most important contribution on the whole issue, prior to 1967, was his book *Law, Liberty, and Psychiatry: An Inquiry into the Social Uses of Mental Health Practices*.[17] It is flamboyant, self-righteous, polemical. The author clearly sees himself as lone hero, dragon slayer, and Old Testament prophet all in one. It is also, in the view of a representative of the mental health and psychiatric establishment, "irresponsible, reprehensible, and dangerous." Bernard L. Diamond (professor of law and of criminology at the University of California, Berkeley; assistant chief of psychiatry at Mount Zion Hospital, San Francisco; fellow of the American Psychiatric Association, and one-time chairman of its committee on law and psychiatry) made this judgment in a review published in the *California Law Review*.[18] He was so outraged by the book that his lengthy review consisted mainly of summarizing and quoting

---

17 New York: Macmillan, 1963. However, it addresses principally the problem of commitments for criminal insanity rather than for civil breaches. The former was not especially salient to the mental health public, though the latter was.

18 *California Law Review* 52 (1964): 899–907.

Szasz's own words, on the theory, no doubt, that Szasz would be justly and adequately hanged by the rope he himself wove. My impression from interviews was that Szasz's work was strongly disliked and often feared by most psychiatrists, though also adjudged definitely worthwhile by a large minority. A clever "Psychiatric Career Game" (called "Scramble") published in the *SK and F Psychiatric Reporter* adds weight to this interview evidence. The player who lands on space number seven on the board is told: "You've been highly praised in Tom Szasz's latest book. (Lose 1 turn.)" This is one of the more severe penalties in the game.[19]

In 1967 California changed the laws governing civil commitment to accord persons accused or suspected of being mentally ill much more judicial and even professional protection against "inappropriate, involuntary, and indefinite" hospitalization. The change had the support of the great majority of the mental health public, including that of a substantial number of psychiatrists. Indeed, fully 87 percent of the psychiatrists in our sample (N=99) disagreed with the "greater legal consciousness is harmful" item. Yet, many also felt that the proposed change in the laws had "gone too far" and opposed it vigorously.

(7) "To what extent is it worth preserving 'professional standards' if the cost is a serious manpower shortage and great administrative inflexibility?" Although mental health professionals—psychiatrists, social workers, nurses, and psychologists— disagreed among themselves about the appropriate division of power, status, and financial rewards among the professions, they all had common stakes, albeit of varying sizes, in the ideology of professionalism per se. In order to understand the nature of the debate over the validity of this ideology, it is necessary first to describe the legal and institutional supports for professionalism in the mental health system.

First, all positions in the state civil service were under the limited jurisdiction of the California State Personnel Board, which published specification sheets for each position. The specification sheet set forth the details of the job definition, typical tasks, minimum qualifications, salary range, and the nature of the work week. These, of course, were the minimum specifications for the position. The employing agency could add to them if it wished, provided it did not violate equal oppor-

---

[19] *SK and F Psychiatric Reporter* 26 (May–June 1966): 16–17. The magazine was a kind of *Esquire* for psychiatrists by Smith, Kline, and French, drug manufacturers.

tunity codes. The agency directors could advise the board, but in practice it was difficult and time-consuming to get job specifications changed once they had been operating for some time. State hospital administrators frequently complained that the personnel board-DMH specifications were too rigid and that authorized positions remained vacant when effectively qualified recruits were in fact available for them merely because the recruits did not meet the specifications. Occasionally, too, one could find DMH headquarters officials who thought the board's specifications too rigid in regard to hiring for positions at their own level or higher. Being under local jurisdiction, Short–Doyle positions did not fall under the state board, but they did come under the control of county personnel boards in counties where such boards existed. The DMH also had limited statutory authority over job specifications in Short–Doyle programs.

The job specifications for top administrative posts and for a large variety of positions on the treatment staffs in both the state-administered and the Short–Doyle systems included minimum levels of professionalization. These requirements could be met by credentials alone, by experience alone, or by some combination of both credentials and experience. For the most part, the acceptable credentials were obtainable only from private professional societies, like the Committee on Certification of Mental Hospital Administrators of the American Psychiatric Association, the American Board of Psychiatry and Neurology, the American (or California) Medical Association, and so forth. The degree to which public authority intervened in the accreditation practices of these private bodies varied from profession to profession. If semiprofessional postgraduate courses were sufficient credentials, the university departments, which in turn were linked informally to the professional group, held unencumbered power and responsibility. During the period 1964–1967, psychologists were licensed in California by the Board of Medical Examiners acting through its Psychology Examining Committee, all of whose members themselves had to be licensed psychologists, except for one "public member."

Line-item budgeting (for most departments) at the state level was another constraint on flexibility in recruiting workers. If there were two positions authorized for psychiatric social workers but only one could be found, the second position remained vacant. This was especially irritating to an administrator if the nature of the tasks he would have assigned to the second psychiatric social worker were such that a psychiatric nurse or perhaps an especially able psychiatric technician could have performed them satisfactorily.

Underlying this legal and administrative system of minimum job specifications were a number of currently contested premises: (1) members of a particular profession had a "distinctive competence" to deal with certain kinds of tasks;[20] (2) nonmembers of that profession were not competent to perform them; (3) the need of the system (and its various subsystems) for functional inputs of certain kinds and in certain quantities could be projected fairly accurately; (4) it was possible to translate the functional needs of the system into structural needs ("authorized positions") by known, workable rules of correspondence; and (5) it was desirable to codify the system's structural needs in an authoritative manner that could not be changed in the short run (say six months to a year). The last three premises raise issues that are more managerial than ideological and may be omitted from our discussion here.[21] The heat in the debate over the validity of the first two premises was created principally by the competition among the mental health professions for status, power, and money and was intensified by the different treatment ideologies which the various professions wanted the system to emphasize. The mental health manpower shortage, however, which all the professions recognized, made the debate more continuous and the common goal of finding some generally acceptable resolution more urgent. At stake in the debate was not only the allocation of benefits among the various professions, but also the survival of professionalism itself.

Of all the proposals circulating through the attentive public to solve the problem of the manpower shortage, two in particular presented the greatest threat. One proposal was to blur the job assignments traditionally allocated to one or another of the mental health professions. The second was to recruit treatment personnel from the untapped reservoir of "indigenous leaders," sometimes called "indigenous nonprofession-

[20] Philip Selznick, *Leadership in Administration* (Evanston, Ill.: Row, Peterson, 1957), chap. 2, especially pp. 41ff.

[21] These issues were raised implicitly by the report of the Commission on Staffing Standards (n. 13, above) which employed systems analysts from the Sacramento plant of Aerojet General to measure the staffing needs of the state hospitals in functional, or program, terms. According to sources in the DMH, the state legislature had resisted attempts by the department to prepare program budgets because the legislature did not wish to take responsibility for the inadequacy of staffing in the hospitals. As usual, the ostensibly managerial issue of choosing between program budgeting and line-item budgeting reflected an underlying political issue.

als." In our sample of the mental health public, 57 percent favored the first, and 61 percent favored the second (items 29 and 30).

In February 1967 the California Commission on Staffing Standards reported the results of its eighteen-month study of staffing patterns and requirements in California mental hospitals. The commission endorsed both proposals. It observed that the DMH currently recruited employees from a restricted base: "It can't, because of minimum requirements, hire the so-called 'indigenous leader'; it sets up barriers against hiring the high school dropout who might have potential; the Department cannot hire the average college graduate, simply because it has created no appropriate job which, for instance, the holder of a Bachelors Degree in Sociology can qualify for; neither can it hire 'Surrogate Mothers.'" The commission also recommended "consideration of a new personnel series, to be called 'Mental Health Services Worker Series' or some other appropriate title, which would represent progressive pay grades ranging upwards to include all levels—from unskilled trainees to program administrators—and to which all disciplines and all persons whose primary job role is direct or indirect services to patients would be assigned." It then noted some potential (and actual) criticisms: "You just can't test for the kinds of abilities the single class series requires and thus you would probably wind up with some very bad promotions. The proposal does not suggest a step forward, but rather suggests regressing to a day when there were no quality standards. Though not the end all in quality determination, requiring licensure and academic degrees was an improvement over prior times of no quality determination."[22]

The commission did not shrink from addressing the problem of the manpower shortage and proposing its radical solution. It did, however, tuck the proposal into an appendix. Those private and public discussions of the report that I heard entirely ignored the proposal. After March 14, 1967, the day the governor's office announced its intended staffing cuts in the MI hospitals, any attention to the report naturally focused on the section on quantity, rather than quality, of personnel. Since the report appeared only six weeks earlier, and within the first few weeks received only limited circulation, it is impossible to say whether the attentive public ignored this appendix accidentally or deliberately.

(8) "What kind of institutional structure, or combination of structures, can best meet the needs and demands of the client population?" In particular, what ought to be the role of the present state hospitals in

[22] California Commission on Staffing Standards, pp. 145–151.

a system that more and more tends to treat people within the community? In the following discussion, we shall assume that the ideal-typical adherent of any of the orientations we describe believed that there is such a thing as "mental illness," that it can be treated reasonably effectively, and that government ought to play some role in providing treatment. Anyone who disbelieved in any one (or more) of these propositions would logically oppose state hospitals, so we shall omit consideration of such viewpoints. Several of the attitudes listed below are not only compatible but mutually reinforcing. It was often quite difficult in individual cases to identify which beliefs were present and which absent.

First, there was a generally anti-institutional viewpoint: any kind of "total institution" is dehumanizing at best and genuinely destructive at worst. The anti-institutionalist not only dislikes state mental hospitals, he also dislikes prisons and nursing homes. There were very few who took this extreme position, but there was a much larger number who, while believing that institutions were necessary, would have liked to minimize their role in society and, perforce, in the treatment of mental illness.

More often, one found persons who could tolerate institutions in general but who objected to mental hospitals in particular. Hospitalization, they argued, was an inappropriate treatment modality for all or most mental illnesses. Some prominent figures even expressed this viewpoint. Werner Mendel, for instance, chief of inpatient psychiatric services at the Los Angeles County Hospital, upset his medical and psychiatric colleagues on more than one occasion by announcing that even for schizophrenia, the most prevalent and one of the most resistant disorders classed as major mental illness, hospitalization was not indicated. He defended this conclusion by referring to the results of an intensive longitudinal study of schizophrenics admitted to his unit and assigned arbitrarily to different terms of hospitalization. During a two-year follow-up period, the researchers found that the rates of rehospitalization did not vary by the duration of the original period of hospitalization. He concluded from these results that hospitalization did no good; and since it did no good, it should be eliminated.[23]

Those who had no objection in principle to total institutions or to

---

[23] Mendel, pp. 226–233 (n. 4, above). Rehospitalization rates were about 20 percent for all schizophrenic patients followed for two years after discharge, and the rate of readmission did not vary with the length of hospitalization during the index period. Mendel's strong conclusions were not part of his research report. I heard him state them in a public speech.

mental hospitals might, however, have objected to state mental hospitals as they were. They were understaffed, they said, too large, too far from population centers, too burdened by custodial or otherwise antitherapeutic traditions. Like the adherents of the two previous views, they considered hospitalization undesirable. But they felt that enough money, training programs, and other resources could improve the hospitals to the point where they might be effective and beneficial. Their principal rationale was that hospitalization was occasionally necessary: 31 percent of the sample agreed there was an inevitable need for large state hospitals. If the mentally ill had to be sent there, and perhaps reside there for some lengthy period, it was desirable that the facilities be humane and effective. They ought to become genuinely therapeutic and cease to be merely custodial institutions.

A special version of the improvement doctrine prescribes improvement through radical transformation. In this view, the hospitals will persist into the foreseeable future independently of whether they are actually desirable or necessary; for institutions that have persisted for generations have inertia on their side. They will survive despite the trend toward community mental health and despite the continuing shrinkage in the resident patient population. The prospects for improvement, however, are doubtful unless the role and mission of the hospitals change drastically. This view begins to transcend the definition of the alternative roles of the state hospitals as custody *versus* therapy. Mendocino State Hospital, for example, attempted to transform itself into the administrative headquarters of a regional mental health center, coordinating treatment services of many different kinds for a large and sparsely populated region of northern California. Dr. James V. Lowry, the director of the DMH, wrote in 1964 of the state hospitals becoming "one element in mental health service area programs. Their functions will be in partnership with community services operated by local agencies. All mental health services (state and local) will be part of one service area program."[24] The department's long-range plan, published in 1962, recommended "more emphasis on intensive treatment . . . and eventually, with the help of other resources, they will change from treatment to other functions, i.e., demonstration and local operations."[25] Others saw the future of the state hospital as a back-up resource to han-

[24] James V. Lowry, "The Mental Hospital" (paper presented at a meeting of the San Francisco Association for Mental Health, November 21–22, 1964).
[25] DMH, *A Long Range Plan for Mental Health Services in California* (Sacramento: DMH, 1963), p. C–3.

dle the overflow from local programs. Some felt that whatever else they might do, the hospitals should concentrate primarily on education, training, and research.[26]

In the short run, most of our sample would have defended hospitals: two-thirds agreed that the hospitals "don't get enough credit," and two-thirds also disagreed that the hospitals were useless or harmful. Yet, 60 percent believed that large state hospitals would eventually disappear.

THE MEDICAL MODEL AS AN
UNDERLYING REFERENCE AXIS

Attitudes regarding the eight above issues were not independent of each other. Although the interrelationships among the attitudes were far from perfect, knowing a man's attitude on one issue would have enabled our

TABLE 5
THE COMMON IDEOLOGICAL REFERENCE FOR
SPECIFIC DISAGREEMENTS

Sources of Disagreement	Orientations Consistent with Medical Model	Orientations Inconsistent with Medical Model
Nature and etiology of mental illness: Does mental illness exist Who is the real patient Primary causes	Emphasizes traits of the person	Emphasizes circumstances in the environment
Role of "personality"	No distinctive orientation	No distinctive orientation
Preferred treatment methods	Somatic manipulations and psychotherapy	Environmental manipulations
Rights and duties of treatment providers and recipients	Expert diagnoses and prescribes for passive, obedient patient	Active reciprocity between treatment recipient and sources of help in environment
Worth of professionalism	Competency tied to formal credentials or training	Indigenous leaders may be as helpful as formally certified professionals
Worth of hospitalization	Hospitals can be beneficial	Hospitals of dubious value, perhaps even harmful

[26] See, for instance, the minutes of the California Conference of Local Mental Health Directors, December 1966, p. 3, The minutes contain a summary of a workshop session, in which both state hospital and Short–Doyle administrators participated, called the New State Hospital.

hypothetical entrepreneur to predict his attitudes on most of the others with a probability of success better than chance could afford. This was especially so—it appears from interview evidence—for persons whose attitudes were unusually strong or intense. The underlying principle that organized these attitudes around a single reference axis we shall call "the medical model," a term in common parlance among the attentive mental health public. Its basic features are summarized in Table 5, where each row refers to one of the eight sources of disagreement already discussed and each cell contains the attitudes consistent with other attitudes in the same column. Column 2 contains attitudes consist with the medical model, and column 3 contains attitudes generally inconsistent with this model.

Data from our survey of the mental health public permit us to buttress these conclusions about the existence and the substance of ideological consistency reached originally from interview and documentary evidence. The ten items in the questionnaire that tapped attitudes toward these issues were combined into a single measure, the validity of which could be evaluated statistically.[27] When the item-index gamma coefficients were computed, the evidence favoring the single axis interpretation was impressive. Not only were all the signs as predicted, but the magnitudes of the coefficients were also high, the range being from .39 to .61 in absolute magnitude (Table 6). Since attitudes strongly

TABLE 6

TRADITIONALISM INDEX AND ITS TEN COMPONENT ITEMS
(gamma coefficients) [a]

Item	Question Number	Gamma	Item	Question Number	Gamma
Heredity	23	+.46	Job roles bad	29	−.51
Label	24	−.50	Nonprofessionals	30	−.51
Physiology	25	+.39	Large state hospitals	31	+.52
Environment	26	−.45	Too little credit	32	+.58
Legal consciousness	28	+.61	Hospitals harmful	33	−.60

[a] Gamma assumes values between +1.00 and −1.00, with a coefficient of .00 implying that the variables are completely independent. The gamma statistic is an appropriate measure of association for our data, in which the levels of measurement for both variables are ordinal and there are a great many tied pairs. See William L. Hays, *Statistics for Psychologists* (New York: Holt, Rinehart and Winston, 1965), pp. 655–656.

[27] Item 27 was, of course, omitted. See the footnote to Table 4, p. 48.

TABLE 7

CORRELATES OF TRADITIONALIST MENTAL HEALTH IDEOLOGY

(percent across)

	Percent High [a]	Percent Low	Total Number
Party Identification:			
"Independent Democrat"	32	52	59
Democrat	38	42	356
Republican	54	26	132
Self-Designated Political Outlook:			
Liberal	29	50	345
Conservative and Middle-of-road	58	25	218
Religious Identification:			
Major denomination (Prot., Cath., Jew)	42	38	526
"Other"	28	61	57
Age:			
Under 34	25	60	85
35–44	33	45	188
45–54	47	37	185
55–64	51	27	97
Over 65	76	12	25

[a] High and low are defined by sample norms, that is, scoring ranges of the highest and the lowest 40 percent, respectively. The total percent is therefore less than 100.

favorable to the medical model were associated with a long tradition still more or less dominant in 1967, I called this measure the "traditionalism index."

Why should these attitudes cluster as they do? Unfortunately, we can only speculate about the answer. Historical continuities in professional education, particularly in the training of psychiatrists, have something to do with the phenomenon. Yet acceptance of the medical model was by no means uniform among psychiatrists, nor was it confined to them. A more fundamental organizing impulse may have resided in certain individuals' preferences for seeing phenomena as relatively closed rather than open systems. In some diffuse metaphorical sense, the medical model is after all populated by closed systems: a patient housed within the individual person; a relatively structured therapist-patient relationship; a known body of expert knowledge for effecting cures; professional groups insulated from lay participation and influence; hospitals with an interior living and working space sharply separated from the space outside. In any event, Table 7 makes it clear that "traditionalism" is not a bad name for our index, since those who identify least with traditional religious and political orientations also score much lower on our mental health traditionalism index. There is also a strong negative correlation with age, though it is open to question whether this reflects a generational difference or the typical conservatizing force of aging per se.

The attentive public was very loosely divided into a traditionalist faction and a contervailing and rather more fragmented progressive faction. Both factions, however, cut across numerous other factions, which also cut across each other, according to the standard patterns called by political scientists "multiple and overlapping memberships" and "cross-cutting cleavages."[28]

[28] See, for instance, David B. Truman, *The Governmental Process* (New York: Knopf, 1951); V. O. Key, Jr., *Public Opinion and American Democracy* (New York: Knopf, 1960), esp. pp. 153–181.

3

Mapping Factions, Interests, and Alliances

Ideological disagreements are only one source of controversy in an attentive public. Other significant competitive stakes are prestige (or status), hierarchical power, jurisdictional scope, and money. These may not be the only important nonideological "sources of faction," in James Madison's words, but they are probably the most prevalent. The rational entrepreneur would wish to identify as many such factions as exist, including even single-individual factions. But this would be a Herculean task; and in general it is necessary to employ certain simplifying procedures. The most economical procedure is to begin with those factions that have some formal or semiformal collective expression. Initially, each organization within the attentive public can be assumed to be involved in the competition for greater authority and jurisdiction, money, prestige, and, with lesser frequency perhaps, hierarchical power. Similarly, one can assume, at least initially, that factions within an organization will be competing for these same stakes. Starting with these provisional assumptions, the entrepreneur then canvasses the organizations and groups identified by the methods of previous chapters. He asks, in effect, which if any of these stakes each values (and if there are additional ones), with what intensity, with what degree of success they are pursued, and the conditions that have typically affected their success.

The same sorts of questions can be posed concerning factions within organizations and groups, although such information may be difficult to obtain without reliable informants within the organizations and groups themselves. It is probably useful to look within organizations initially for a split between a majority and a minority faction—although there is probably no good systematic method for identifying intraorganizational factions in greater detail.

Factions that cut across two or more organizations or groups can be thought of as alliances, following the conventional meaning of that term. A discussion of how to map such alliances must be postponed, however, until we have mapped the principal nonideological factions within the California mental health public.

THE MENTAL HEALTH PROFESSIONS
AS A SOURCE OF FACTIONALISM

The nonideological stakes for which the mental health professions competed most were the four named above: prestige, money, hierarchical power, and jurisdictional scope. The gross parameters of the contest were set by the fact that medical men, usually psychiatrists, enjoyed a good deal more of these valued goods than any of the other professions.

An accumulation of historical contingencies initially entitled the medical profession to dominate both the treatment and the personnel policies of the public mental health system. Once successfully endowed with legitimacy and vested with effective control of the system, though, the medical profession then consolidated its power over the system by ensuring that guarantees of its continued dominance were written into law and administrative regulations. Statutes prescribed that at least one of the top two Short–Doyle administrators be a psychiatrist, and that state hospital superintendents be physicians. Other restrictions on eligibility practically ensured that the superintendents would be psychiatrists as well. The California State Personnel Board restricted a number of administrative posts in the DMH and in the state hospitals to physicians. Although the director of mental hygiene was a political appointee of the governor and was exempt from eligibility restrictions of any kind, there has been only one instance of an appointment going to anyone other than a physician. For the past several decades, moreover, the appointees have also been psychiatrists.

Until recently the effort to define mental disorder as a medical problem, rather than as a problem properly dealt with by law or other means of social control, was seen as an unqualifiedly progressive, humane, and liberal cause. In the general public, this perception probably continues, only mildly abated by the impact of Szasz's crusade. The public view is that doctors on the whole are humane, knowledgeable, dedicated, and competent; and that, within the confines of medical knowledge on the subject, which the public agrees are rather narrow, psychiatrists' treatment of mental patients partakes of the same beneficence to be found in the medical profession as a whole.[1] Within the attentive rather than the general public, however, there was much more skepticism about many of these beliefs. Although one cannot be certain, it is likely that the attentive public had more faith in the competence of psychiatrists than did the general public but less faith in their superior competence relative to other professionals. There was probably a greater readiness, also, to question, in specific instances, their humanitarianism, dedication, and knowledgeability. Skepticism was nowhere greater than among the most recent arrivals to the list of mental health professionals, the clinical psychologists.

In America, psychology originated and for many years flourished in an exclusively academic setting. In contrast to the great theorists of early psychiatry, Freud and his disciples, the early theorists of American psychology were experimentalists who were more concerned with research than with treatment. Nor did their theoretical work lend itself easily to therapeutic application. It deemphasized the special qualities of human behavior in favor of illuminating the laws of behavior applicable to all members of the animal kingdom; it was suspicious of theories postulating the independence of mind from body; and it focused much more intensively on the influence of environmental stimuli in shaping behavior than on the nature of the behaving organism. In 1960 *Action for Mental Health* reported that only about one-third of all psychologists were engaged in any clinical work.[2] In California during the mid-1960s, only a minority of clinical psychologists worked in the state hospitals or in the Short–Doyle system. The absolute number of clinical psychologists who at some time did work in the public mental health system was steadily increasing, however, and their experience in the public system could only aggravate their resentment toward psychiatry.

Inequalities of income and prestige compounded inequalities of power and aggravated disagreements on points of doctrine. Within the state hospital system, the salary scale in 1964–65 for a senior psychiatrist was

---

[1] Jum C. Nunnally, Jr., *Popular Conceptions of Mental Health* (New York: Holt, Rinehart, and Winston, 1961), chap. 5.

[2] Joint Commission on Mental Illness and Health, *Action for Mental Health* (New York: Basic Books, 1961), p. 149.

71

$1,351 to $1,724 per month; for a senior psychologist, it was $914 to $1,008, about two-thirds that of the psychiatrist. When the two did similar work, as occasionally happened, the salary differential rankled even more. This situation reflected a similar inequality in the private sector. Although the somewhat higher age level of our Northern California Psychiatric Society (NCPS) sample and the marginally greater prevalence of high professional degrees (M.D., Ph.D.) might account for part of the disparity, the average income of NCPS psychiatrists was much higher than the average of psychologists in the California State Psychological Association leadership sample: 78 percent of the psychiatrists earned over $22,500 annually, compared to 46 percent of the psychologists. Psychologists also ranked behind psychiatrists in prestige and status. The nonprofessionals in our sample (N=174), for instance, indicated greater willingness to take advice on mental health issues from psychiatrists than from psychologists (item 38), 70 percent as against 56 percent. The difference in attitude was greater still in the more explicitly attentive segment of the public, the California Association for Mental Health leaders (N=29): barely half said they would be "most likely" to take advice from psychologists, but three-fourths would have been this open toward psychiatrists.

If competence were any criterion for reward, many psychologists argued, they would have received more money, status, and power than psychiatrists, not less. Their training was better, they said. Whereas the psychiatrist had done no more than take a few courses in psychiatry in medical school, the clinical psychologist had devoted virtually all his years in graduate school to the study of mental illness and its treatment. Moreover, many psychologists regarded the quality of the psychiatrists' psychiatric training as being definitely inferior to their own. The psychologist had been trained in research methods, including experimental design and statistical analysis. He had received a broader theoretical base than the psychiatrist, for he had studied Freudianism, learning theory, interactionist theory, neo-Freudianism, sociological and anthropological theories of the family, and so forth. As for the psychiatrist, it was conceded that he knew more about physiology and body chemistry —but the psychologist had also taken courses in these subjects. Besides, he was willing to let the psychiatrist write out prescriptions, so long as he, the psychologist, had equal status in all other areas in which the two professions made parallel claims to competence.

A psychologist's frustrations were never so exacerbated as when ward psychologist and ward psychiatrist came to loggerheads over an issue of patient care and treatment. To a degree largely dependent on the personal relations between the parties, the ward psychiatrist might have acknowledged the operational competence of a psychologist on the ward treatment team by allowing him to have his way with a number of patients or to make decisions about the ward as a whole in certain limited spheres. Technically, the medical chief had responsibility for the ward, and the psychologist legally practiced psychotherapy only under his medical supervision. But tacit spheres of actual influence were often acknowledged and generally respected. If an equilibrium acceptable to both parties could not be reached, however, it was nearly always the physician who won. The physician would be backed up by the medical hierarchy, up to the hospital superintendent himself. The psychologist would either give in or transfer to another ward.

Psychologists in the Short–Doyle system generally received more tolerable treatment from their medical superiors. Los Angeles Short–Doyle's three-page circular, "Guidelines in Regard to Medical Responsibility," written in 1966, is as notable for what it omits as for what it says. It recognized explicitly that nonmedical personnel would have to do screening and implicitly that they would practice some sort of therapy. It said nothing about the exclusive right of psychiatrists to practice psychotherapy or their ultimate authority over decisions that were "properly medical in nature." Whether despite its basic liberality or because of it, the circular opened with a short reminder of how, for the time being at least, the staff should "define the nature of the medical facility" (Short–Doyle) for which they worked:

> Psychiatric disorders are conceptualized in multiple frames of reference, in contrast to physical disorders which tend to be viewed from primarily a single frame of reference. One consequence of this *multi-ordinality* of the concept "psychiatric disturbance" is that help for those with such disorders is provided by people from varying disciplinary backgrounds and in widely differing settings.
> *Whatever may be the future developments in this field*, administrators of programs must concern themselves with the present. It thus becomes important to *define the nature of the medical facility* which provides treatment, and to distinguish medical agencies from non-medical ones. The prime determinant of a medical facility is that it offers services in a context of health and illness, to *those who see themselves as "patients" by those who see themselves as "physicians" or "physicians' agents."* In practical terms, this "medical" quality of an

agency is expressed by the rubric "medical responsibility." [Emphasis added.]

Since the cold war between psychiatry and psychology was often fought with semantics and tokens of victory were captured definitions rather than hostages or fortresses, the emphasized words and phrases indicate this was a relatively dovish statement. "Multiordinality" should be read: psychiatry does not claim that there is only one correct theory of mental disorder; other disciplines might find good theories too. The "whatever" clause speaks for itself. Defining the "nature of the medical facility" is an alternative to defining the nature of the tasks its staff may legitimately perform or the "nature of mental disorder." It permits greater ambiguity in the definition and thus greater flexibility. Finally, tying the definition of "medical facility" to patients and staff "who see themselves" in these roles is another useful loophole.[3]

The ideological differences between psychiatrists and psychologists were also considerable, as can easily be seen in Table 8. In addition to being more progressive in their attitudes toward mental health and ill-

TABLE 8

TRADITIONALISM SCORES OF MENTAL HEALTH PROFESSIONS
AND SELECTED LAY GROUPS

(percent across)

	Percent High[a]	Percent Low	Total Number
Physicians	69	19	42
Psychiatrists	48	29	99
Psychiatric social workers	36	41	111
Psychologists	18	74	50
Judges	67	8	12
CAMH leader sample	28	38	29
ACLU members	25	65	20

[a] High and low are defined by sample norms, that is, scoring ranges of the highest and the lowest 40 percent, respectively. The total percent is therefore less than 100.

[3] In contrast, a slightly more hawkish move in the definitions game is evident in the definition of aftercare formally adopted by the Short–Doyle directors at their December 1966 conference: "Aftercare [which, in practice, was the domain of the bureau] is the continuing medical supervision, treatment, and rehabilitation of patients in the community following an episode of intensive treatment for mental illness." This move was directed at the Bureau of Social Work which had irritated Short–Doyle some months earlier by rejoicing at its transfer from the DMH to the state Department of Social Welfare.

ness, psychologists were also more liberal politically. Of the psychologists in our sample, 71 percent identified with the Democratic party, 70 percent called themselves political liberals, and 84 percent voted for Governor Brown in the 1966 gubernatorial race with Ronald Reagan. Comparable figures for the psychiatrists in the sample were 56 percent, 59 percent, and 77 percent. Another indicator of strong ideological differences between the two professions is the difference in the degree of recognition paid Thomas Szasz's work. Whereas the psychiatrist playing the Smith, Kline, and French "Psychiatric Career Game" lost a turn for being praised by Szasz, the presidential address to the CSPA appearing in the June 1967 *California State Psychologist* declared, "As members of a younger professional group on the outside of organized medicine's attempts to pre-empt all 'medical' fields (including and especially mental health) and the historical, social and philosophic reasons for society's views on mental health, I think psychologists find themselves in a philosophic position very close to that of . . . Szasz. (Maybe as an emergent group we even secretly gain solace and sustenance from these views. . . .)"

The more than 400 psychiatric social workers who worked for the Bureau of Social Work or for the DMH (there were still a number who worked on the wards and were directly employed by the DMH) were caught in a squeeze. They were higher in status and power than the nurses and psychiatric technicians, were clearly lower than the psychiatrists and general physicians, and were running behind the psychologists by a slight margin. Probably the most important factor in explaining the attitudes of psychiatric social workers toward ideological issues and the other professions was their uncertainty, perhaps even insecurity, about the legitimacy of their claims to a distinctive professional competence. Within the social work profession as a whole the psychiatric social workers were regarded as an elite corps. Compared to their nonpsychiatric co-professionals, their training was a little more intellectualized, a little more demanding; the nature of their work, a little more interesting and a little more rewarding. But within the hospital or clinic setting—surrounded by psychiatrists, physicians, and psychologists, from whose professional ranks, no doubt, came most of the authors of the books they read in graduate school—they were nowhere near the top of the totem pole. From Table 8 it is clear that they were less accepting of the medical model than the psychiatrists but more accepting than the psychologists. Indeed, they scored closer to the position of the psychiatrists on eight of the ten index items than to that of the psychologists.

Rank-and-file social workers might have aspired to higher status and to an enhanced sense of professional identity, but most of them were content to rely on slightly environmentalist modifications of the medical model in order to further these aspirations.

Within the attentive public were a small number of strategically placed laymen—in the CAMH, in some of the lobbies, and in the environs of the legislature, for the most part—who treated skeptically the rhetoric of professionalism no matter from which of the mental health professions it emanated. In their view, one of the most profound troubles of the entire system was that it was designed for the convenience and emolument of the administrators and professionals that operated it rather than for the clients that ought to have been served by it. They were also annoyed at the rigidity of the traditional method of allocating tasks among the professions and at the barriers to communication and cooperation which arose from it. Although they tended to oppose the medical model in all its dimensions, they were especially intent on introducing more indigenous nonprofessionals, undermining the traditional professional jurisdictions, and gaining a stronger voice in policy making for those who would "represent the public interest." They tended also to want to expand the opportunities for the client to exercise choice among different treatment services by giving him more cash grants that would permit him to exercise consumer sovereignty through the market mechanism.

As of 1967, those who articulated this point of view were not numerous. They did not appear with any statistical frequency in our sample. But the professionals and administrators were obviously sensitive to these new currents of opinion. Some were vaguely defensive, others vaguely supportive, though in neither case had they crystallized programs or tactics to give force to their feelings. One psychiatrist connected with Short–Doyle administration confided:

> It used to be thought that the citizens committees spoke for the community; but they really speak for the experts. . . . [The citizens committee that speaks for the community] is the future though. Dr. ——— [another Short–Doyle psychiatrist] just returned from a trip across the country in which he found interest in this. But it has not become noisy enough to be threatening to the experts and professionals. Those psychiatrists schooled in "the tradition of the nervous breakdown" will not like this.[4]

4 See also the summary of the workshop session, Community Mental Health Services, of the December 1966 meeting of the California Conference of Local Mental Health

The California Association for Mental Health was by no means limited in its policy goals to undermining professionalism or to developing the concept of consumer sovereignty, but to the extent that there was any significant pressure at all for these developments one found much of it coming from that source. The twenty-nine leaders in our sample overwhelmingly agreed (72 percent) on the desirability of introducing more indigenous nonprofessionals, for example (3 percent strongly agree and 69 percent agree).

BUREAUCRATIC INSTITUTIONS
AS A SOURCE OF FACTIONALISM

The state Department of Mental Hygiene performed principally managerial functions. It was, therefore, not the sort of organization that stimulated warm loyalties on the part of its workers; there was no dedication to the role or mission of the organization that Selznick declares is necessary to turn a mere organization into a genuine institution.[5] This is no special reflection on the administrators of the department, for its functional role in the mental health system was determined by factors partly beyond their control. It was mainly a holding company for other people's stocks. When those stocks did well, the others got the credit; when they did poorly, the blame was readily passed to the DMH. A mental health bureaucracy that does not give direct services to clients necessarily has a difficult time claiming credit for good works, and no clients appeared for treatment at DMH headquarters in Sacramento or at any of the four DMH regional offices. When its managerial functions were carried out smoothly, there was likely to be little notice taken. When they were botched, no matter whether DMH responsibility was operational or merely formal, the blame piled high. Over the past few decades the DMH has taken unto itself some relatively novel, and slightly more creditable, tasks, like planning, training, and the direction of research. Yet these were either not so intimately tied to the DMH, or

---

Directors (Short–Doyle), p. 4. The group foresaw the eventual development of "a buyer's market." Comments on the prospect were more anxious than optimistic. The anxiety was exacerbated at that particular meeting by the publication a few days earlier of a legislative report recommending radical revision of the commitment laws along with what then appeared to be a new community mental health system paralleling and competing with Short–Doyle. See below, chapter 4.

[5] Philip Selznick, *Leadership in Administration* (Evanston: Row, Peterson, 1957), chap. 5.

else not so effectively performed, that the department could actually claim much credit for them.

There were two principal reasons for the failure of the DMH to expand its sense of mission beyond the strictly managerial. One was that the legislature expected the department to concentrate principally on narrow management problems, and consequently did not readily provide the funds to enable the department to expand its mission. The second and more important reason was that the long-term historical development of the department had established in the culture of the institution itself a narrowly bounded conception of what was appropriate. The historical prototype of the department first came into existence in 1897 as the California State Commission in Lunacy, established by the legislature "to provide for a uniform government and management of the State Asylums for the Insane, and to provide for the care, custody, and apprehension of persons believed to be insane." The first biennial report of the commission makes it clear that the two principal purposes of establishing more centralized control over the five state hospitals then operating were to effect economies, by increasing revenues and cutting costs, and to establish the institutional machinery to clean the asylums of aliens and residents of other states who were seen as an unfair burden on California taxpayers. The commission stressed the humanitarian reasons behind this latter effort, but not very convincingly:

> A large number of these foreign born patients have expressed a desire to return to their native countries, and in many cases it is the opinion of the medical authorities having them in charge that if it were possible to send them home, where they would be environed by the surroundings of their youth and the mode and manner of life to which they were accustomed before coming to this country, they would undoubtedly, if not entirely recover, at least be very much improved. With this object in view, to improve the health of the patients, as well as to relieve the taxpayers of this State from the burden of caring for so many aliens, the majority of whom are not taxpayers and have paid nothing toward the support of the State government, the Commission has been actively engaged in trying to arrange for their return to the countries whence they came. The prospect for the return of the Chinese, particularly, is favorable. . . . [Many Chinese had been imported to California in the late nineteenth century as a source of cheap labor for the mines and railways.] However, the disturbed state of China for the past year, and the fact that there is not a single insane asylum in the Chinese empire, has occasioned an embarrass-

ment on the part of the Commission which has not yet been over-come.[6]

Of the 5,001 patients in the hospitals, said the commission, only 605 were native Californians, and the expected savings to be had from being rid of the other 4,396 were evidently worth the few hundred dollars the commission spent for its yearly budget. In order to justify even further its operating expenditures, the commission listed its additional activities: (1) collecting examination fees and transportation charges for non-indigent patients; (2) "discovering a number of patients who could, but who were not paying"; (3) collecting payments from the counties for the board of certain classes of patients; (4) determining ability to pay and protecting patient estates; (5) securing guardians for the estates of the patients; (6) procuring federal pensions for patients entitled to them, which, by implication, could then help to reimburse the state for the costs of hospitalization.[7]

The early records of the commission's activities also reveal a highly detailed interest in the revenues earned by the hospitals' dairies and farms. It published the complete annual reports of the boards of managers of each hospital (local notables charged with oversight of the hospital), which described at length the decisions to purchase more cows, kill more hogs, cure more bacon, and so on.[8] The first report by the commission ran forty-one pages, but only one page was required to describe the nature or effectiveness of treatment programs for the patients. Not until after World War II did the department's reports begin to discuss the treatment programs at any length. Indeed, the war's end also marked the beginning of a new epoch for the public mental health system. After 1922, the Lunacy Commission was dissolved into a new Department of Institutions, which was to administer the state's prisons, the mental hospitals, and a number of smaller institutions. In 1945 the Department of Institutions split into (principally) the Department of Corrections to administer the prisons and the Department of Mental Hygiene to administer the mental hospitals. The first neuropsychiatric institute was completed in 1946, and the state purchased two army hospitals to at-

[6] State Commission in Lunacy, *First Biennial Report* (two years ending June 30, 1898), p. 30.
[7] *Ibid.*, p. 33.
[8] *Ibid.*, pp. 117–118.

tempt to relieve the overcrowding that had occurred during the war. The department also received a legislative mandate to proceed with a program to establish community-based outpatient clinics. By 1963, change in the institutional self-image of the DMH had proceeded far enough so that the department was publishing a series of monthly public relations magazines attempting to promote a reputation for itself as a progressive treatment-minded organization.

Change was slow, however, and occurred more swiftly in the domain of rhetoric than in the domain of action. According to one prominent Sacramento lawyer who was familiar with the department's operations, the DMH in 1967 still put an exaggerated emphasis on collecting payments from nonindigent patients. In some cases the department had deliberately ignored a 1964 ruling by the state Supreme Court which prohibited it from assessing charges against the children of patients in the state MI hospitals. The department's Bureau of Biostatistics (employing fifteen persons) still, in 1967, collected very little data that would have been useful in evaluating the effectiveness of different modes or programs of treatment. Although the Bureau of Patients' Accounts recorded information about the economic and occupational status of patients, none of this information was shifted down the hall to analysts in Biostatistics. Not more than one or two of the special analyses of the patient population movement which the bureau had made public up to 1967 had even attempted to answer the question of why after 1960 the resident population had declined so strikingly. The attempted answers, moreover, based on Biostatistics data, were more heroic than successful.[9] Not until 1964, when Dr. Lowry acceded to the directorship, did the department establish a full-fledged Office of Program Review to deal with just such questions as these. Of our total sample, only 29 percent listed the DMH as a group from which they would be "most likely to take advice," and 16 percent said "least likely."

In one sense, the department was trapped between constituencies with somewhat incompatible demands. The economy-minded men in the Department of Finance and in the legislature wanted it to manage the hospitals efficiently, minimize costs, and avoid troublesome incidents like patient escapes or mysterious deaths. They wanted the hospitals to be decent, clean, and humane, but they lacked any strong desire to fit

9 See, for instance, Richard Morgan, "They Are Getting out Sooner," DMH Bureau of Biostatistics Report, February 1967, pp. 16–20 and the discussion above, p. 42.

them out in the latest fashions in psychotherapy. The professionals and lay activists in the attentive public, on the other hand, wanted more progressive and usually more costly staffing ratios, treatment facilities, and so on. If the entrapment was classic, so was the department's adaptation to it. In arming themselves for the annual series of budgetary encounters, DMH administrators necessarily became spokesmen and representatives of the several institutions funded through the department's budget. During budget season, which in most years became a public spectacle only between February and May, the DMH was permitted to assume credit for all the good works carried out by the system. It was a useful fiction for all concerned, and a certain halo effect persisted even after the drama was over. The economy-minded financiers were grateful that the DMH had been a good spokesman and that they themselves, therefore, did not have to make difficult and time-consuming decisions about individual treatment institutions. The professionals and activists were grateful that they had in the DMH an able, or at least adequate, spokesman. In most years, the department was able to endure the year-round on its seasonal accumulation of gratitude from all quarters, minimal though it surely was. In an exceptional year, like 1967, when the DMH failed to perform adequately as budgetary spokesman in the eyes of many in the attentive public, the upward spiral of appreciation turned in the opposite direction.

Among its own personnel, there was no evidence of any particular loyalty to the DMH. Yet, if there was little heartfelt loyalty, there was much bureaucratic tenacity. It was justified, in the eyes of those who worked there, first of all by the belief that the DMH was necessary. Beyond that, the DMH had been around for a long time; and any institution that had persisted that long must surely have had a presumption on continuance.

Many larger and older Short–Doyle programs were administered by forceful individuals who regarded themselves as leaders within the medical or psychiatric profession, accomplished fighters for a worthy public cause. They took much personal pride in what they considered the many achievements of Short–Doyle in general and of their own programs in particular. Short–Doyle was reputed to be one of the best community mental health programs in the nation, and a constant flow of professionals from other states eager to learn from the California experiment made them conscious of their reputation. The San Mateo program had gone so far as to budget at least one full-time "demonstration officer" in order to meet the demands for information that came from hundreds of interested groups and individuals both from within and from without the state. At least one speaker from San Mateo was virtually standard equipment at nearly every national or regional symposium on community mental health services. The director of the program, Dr. Harold Chope, won the 1962 Bronfman Prize of the American Psychiatric Association, given for distinction in bringing together the fields of public health and mental health. Other Short–Doyle administrators believed that success such as San Mateo's was a realistic goal to set for their own programs.[10]

In general, the Short–Doyle programs appeared to command a relatively high institutional loyalty from their professional staffs. The most striking evidence—apart from the claims made by the top administrators about their own programs and the reports of many informants—is that many staff members in the Short–Doyle system were willing to work for lower salaries than they could obtain in private practice or even in the state hospital system.

This high level of commitment to Short–Doyle rested on several foundations. First of all, Short–Doyle could claim to be in the ideological vanguard of public mental health administration: not only was it located in the community, it was controlled by the community. Short–Doyle administrators harbored a deep suspicion of any efforts to increase "state intervention." They were concerned, for example, lest the DMH's growing capacity for electronic data processing would eventually subject their own operations to closer scrutiny and possibly control. The principal item on "the hidden agenda" of any meeting among local and state administrators, according to one interviewee, was strengthening the coalition of the former to fend off attacks by the latter. Although Short–Doyle's problems with the DMH were not imaginary, the stakes in the conflict were perhaps less significant than the contestants believed. The DMH never challenged the existence of a local program; and unless state funds were so scanty that the department had to make decisions about how to allocate them among the several programs (which rarely happened), it lacked the effective capacity to resist local proposals

10 Like front runners in all fields, San Mateo also had its detractors. One DMH administrator alleged that San Mateo Short–Doyle had weak links to the community. Toward the end of the controversy over the commitment bill, San Mateo Short–Doyle assumed a relatively prominent role at the head of the opposition forces. Its prestige dropped somewhat as a consequence.

for continuing any ongoing service or for adding a new one. The omnipresent fear of the state, however, helped to keep Short–Doyle solidarity high and ideological sensitivity acute.

Secondly, the prevailing ideological climate also rewarded the Short–Doyle professionals' commitment to local treatment services, outpatient services, preventive services, and the treatment of patients who sought it voluntarily rather than by court order.

Thirdly, they were pleased with the opportunities for upgrading and expanding teatment services that Short–Doyle provided. In private practice, the professionals had to wait for the patients to come to them. In the state hospitals there were too many patients to begin to think of upgrading treatment in a serious professional sense. Through Short–Doyle, however, the imaginative professional could experiment with new types of consultation services, home-visit emergency psychiatric teams, storefront psychiatry in remote satellite facilities, working with indigenous nonprofessionals, and the like.

Furthermore, because the county encompassed a relatively small target population (Los Angeles being the significant exception) and because Short–Doyle often held a near monopoly on publicly administered and financed treatment services within a county, the growth and the achievements of any county's Short–Doyle program were highly visible. The sense of accomplishment was immediate and tangible.

Finally, more intensive therapy was possible in a Short–Doyle setting than in a state hospital. Under such conditions, results were easier to achieve, and the professional could more readily satisfy his humanitarian impulses. The only fly in the ointment was that most Short–Doyle facilities concentrated on the "easy" cases—"the pretty co-eds with interesting sex lives," as one administrator chided his colleagues—and sent the "hard" ones off to the state hospitals. Probably most Short–Doyle professionals found a means to avoid recognition of the fact, however, or else managed to make their peace with it.

Although Short–Doyle was afflicted by internal problems of interprofessional competition, personal rivalries, and administrative confusion, it probably had no more than the normal quota of troubles that one would find in most complex organizations. It experienced its unusually hard problems with the community, particularly in those areas where the radical Right, or what was called the anti-mental-health movement, was strong. Usually, these problems would be most severe in the early years of a program's existence. Once the program was established and the county supervisors had continued its budgetary support for a few years, the opposition admitted defeat and left it alone.

Because the anti-mental-health movement was based in the fluid congeries of groups and ideologies known as the radical Right, it is as difficult to describe and explain the former as it is to describe and explain the latter. The whole problem is further complicated by the occasional rapport between the radical Right and the traditional, conservative Right. Both factions opposed the expansion of government welfare programs altogether, no matter what their content. Both were especially opposed to government participation or intervention in the area of health care or medical services. Yet these attitudes still do not account for the special hatred that the radical Right reserved for mental health. It was probably exceeded only by their hatred of fluoridation. I would attribute the intensity of the movement to three principal beliefs: that the naturalistic view of deviance taken by mental health professionals undermined traditional criteria of moral judgment; that the degree of professional knowledge about how to change personality (or "character") was extraordinary and the techniques insidious; that involuntary commitment was usually unjust at best, politically inspired at worst, and in either case very probably directed against their co-believers, their friends, or perhaps even themselves.

One of a number of anti-mental-health pamphlets and leaflets being distributed in a radical Right bookshop in Orange County was written by Matt Cvetic, the former FBI counterspy. It is fairly representative of the literature:

> We have been under a constant barrage of warnings by professional fund raisers that the mental health of the nation is bad, and getting progressively worse.
>
> . . . .
>
> [M]uch of the false propaganda concerning the mental health status of the nation has a . . . bizarre purpose.
>
> Much of the fear engendered in the minds of the American people has an ulterior Communist motive behind it. This "phony" concern about our so-called declining "mental health" has been planted by Communist agents, fronters and sympathizers for the purpose of demoralizing the American people and spreading defeatism. As a part of the Kremlin's psychological warfare, this negative propaganda is calculated to destroy our morale, thereby rendering us ineffective, and making us easy prey for the Red vultures.
>
> . . . .

The Communists' psychological warfare is a typical Communist technique of demoralization devised by Lenin and Stalin. This systematic and diabolic scheme to destroy the moral fibre of people and nations is being carried on right now. . . . Very coyly these Red vermin and their sympathetic allies are inculcating in the minds of the American people, especially our students, the idea that belief in God, love of country, family, and the American way of life denotes something radically wrong, psychologically speaking.

In 1956 the Congress passed the Alaska Mental Health Enabling Act, which permitted the U.S. Public Health Service to establish mental hospitals in Alaska as an alternative to the then current practice of transporting persons from Alaska to Oregon for confinement or treatment. The parallel between Alaska and Siberia was obvious, and the anti-mental-health movement has hammered away at its implications. In 1962 the *Santa Ana Register* editorialized:

> In the kind of world we are living in, where political wishes are constantly being substituted for private incentives and objectives, the rise of this type of mental depression [frustration, melancholy] has a more than ordinary incidence. In consequence, there is some ground to suppose that mental illness, in general, is more prevalent than at any time in our past.
>
> . . . .
>
> . . . We can surmise that our monstrous state has already gotten into the mental health business with a vengeance and with our money. And it follows that persons it frustrates with its endless ukases may well end up under the care of Public Health Service attendants who may decide to ship them off to Alaska, the American version of Siberia.
>
> . . . .
>
> So long as men adopt the government as a sort of pagan deity, so long will government enlarge and seek sacrifices for its insatiable appetites.[11]

---

[11] *Santa Ana Register*, October 11, 1962. There was perhaps a measure of substance to some of these beliefs. The psychiatric and the "judgmental" views of man are not compatible in many contexts. Some professionals do have reliable knowledge about how to change some aspects of personality (or behavior). Even if not insidious, treatment methods often entail manipulations for which the patient does not give explicit consent, and which he may scarcely recognize as even taking place. Many, perhaps most, legal commitments are unnecessary, undesirable. and unjust. One or two may even be inspired by broadly political motives: General Edwin Walker, Ezra Pound, "uppity niggers" in some southern states. But the response of the radical Right has been characteristically melodramatic. In their approach to the world, there is no

Short–Doyle administrators usually dealt with less exotic groups in the community than the radical Right. They turned to the county board of supervisors for their budgets, to community planning councils, charitable organizations, and Mental Health Association chapters for political support and occasionally for help in coordinating certain services that required joint administration by the private and public sectors. The few identifiable Short–Doyle administrators in our sample expressed generally favorable opinions of the mental health advisory boards and of county supervisors, which they probably interpreted as those in their own county. (It appeared from interviews that there was a near-perfect correspondence between the generosity of a supervisor toward Short–Doyle and how favorably he was viewed by the administrator.) Quite independently of how individual supervisors and the local administrators got along with each other, Short–Doyle administrators as a body had cordial relations with the collective group of supervisors, the County Supervisors Association of California (CSAC). As the logic of interorganizational relations would have it, the advisory group on mental health issues to the CSAC was made up of five of the top leaders from among the Short–Doyle administrators. The significance of this connection with the CSAC was that it enormously magnified the influence of Short–Doyle with the state legislature. Unless it would entail greater expenditures by the counties, the CSAC would support the position of its advisory group regarding mental health bills pending before the state legislature. The CSAC, moreover, was one of the most effective and weighty lobbies in Sacramento.[12]

Short–Doyle had a statutorily based forum from which to lobby the

---

boundary between what they perceive and what they experience. Senses and sensibilities are all of a single piece. Whatever facts might actually be found to give point to their criticisms form the merest skeleton for a ponderous body of doctrine that they cannot sustain. Predictably the Communist menace is invoked for added support. It is tempting to speculate about the reasons for constructing such an elaborate and inappropriate doctrine. One prominent California psychiatrist has advanced the hypothesis that the ethnocentric syndrome described in *The Authoritarian Personality* by T. W. Adorno et al. (New York: Harper, 1950) is at the root of the phenomenon. See Alfred Auerback, "The Anti-Mental Health Movement," *American Journal of Psychiatry* 120, no. 2 (August 1963): 105–111. My own interviews with adherents of the anti-mental-health movement in Bircher-populated Orange County lead me to be skeptical of this thesis. Although there are no doubt many instances of its validity, I encountered too many "little old ladies in tennis shoes," all firmly opposed to "mental health," who scarcely fit the ethnocentric-authoritarian stereotype.

12 John C. Wahlke, Heinz Eulau, William Buchanan, and Leroy C. Ferguson, *The Legislative System* (New York: John Wiley and Sons, 1962), p. 315.

DMH, the Conference of Local Mental Health Directors. It was not so useful as other more informal means, but it did provide the administrators themselves with a semiannual ritual for expressing solidarity among themselves and dramatizing it to the DMH personnel in attendance. The conference was also a vehicle for elevating certain of the Short–Doyle directors to official preeminence. (The second in command in each program, the program chief, also attended the conference but was not eligible to vote or to hold office.) The principal importance of holding a conference office was that it provided good access to the higher powers in the DMH, the CSAC, the press, and the state legislature. Officials of the conference were also in a better position to maneuver the conference into endorsing their own preferred policy positions. Observations of three Short–Doyle conference meetings confirmed the reports of interviewees that there was something of an old guard–Young Turk split within the conference. The old guard was composed of the directors of the larger programs, the more senior directors in terms of both age and length of connection with Short–Doyle, and the more conservative directors, that is, those who tended to prefer administrative stability to administrative experimentation. By no means was the old guard a uniformly cohesive or self-conscious clique. Nor did it completely dominate the elected offices or the rare hours during a two-day conference when there was open-floor debate. It was a collection of men with similar background, experience, and probably disposition, who had mutual regard for each other. Many younger members and many of those who represented counties with relatively small populations stayed in the background because they too held them in high regard.

Like the larger Short–Doyle programs, the nine state hospitals for the mentally ill were given over to the spirit of autonomy. Unlike Short–Doyle, each one made its own defense against pressures from DMH headquarters largely independently of the others, notwithstanding informal collaboration and occasional formal meetings of the superintendents arranged by the DMH. Serious budgetary struggles between a hospital superintendent and the department or among the superintendents themselves for preferred treatment by the department were very rare. The system had developed routines to minimize these forms of competition: reliance on incrementalism as a decision-making rule in capital budgeting, and allocations for operating expenditures automatically tied to indices of patient population movement, for example the average daily resident population or the monthly rate of admissions. The hospital superintendents had only limited freedom to approach either the legislature or the Department of Finance on budgetary or other policy matters. The norms permitted them to appear at the side of the DMH spokesman stating the case for new capital outlay or other unusual expenditures in their own hospitals if the department had approved the request itself. But superintendents did not ordinarily approach the financiers as a court of appeal when the DMH had itself returned a negative verdict.

When the hospital superintendents did represent themselves to the financiers independently of the DMH they generally went to their own assemblymen or state senators, who were liable to be sensitive to the potential voting bloc strength of the hospital's employees. Occasionally the superintendent could mobilize some members of his hospital's board of trustees, who more often than not had some degree of political prominence in the community. They might lobby the local state legislators or the hierarchs of the local political parties, if such existed, on the superintendent's behalf. The DMH looked somewhat askance at these sorts of activities, particularly if they threatened to put the department in a bad light. Since it would have been almost impossible to curtail them completely, though, given the long tradition of hospital autonomy, the DMH had instructed all its employees, including the hospital superintendents, to emphasize that they did not represent the department but spoke as private citizens.

Since no one realistically suspected the hospital superintendent was speaking for the DMH, rather than for himself or for his own hospital, this restriction should have been fairly easy to tolerate. Some of the hospital superintendents, however, especially the (very) old guard left among them, viewed restrictions of this kind as part of a long development of centralized control over the hospitals. And, indeed, it was. Stockton State Hospital was founded in 1851, and four more like it were founded and operated completely independently of each other over the next half century. Within his own fiefdom, the superintendent was then, as he remained in 1967, virtually omnipotent with regard to medical decisions like moving patients or staff from ward to ward. Yet he had lost virtually all direct control over finances, construction, and major personnnel practices. Many of the higher administrators in the hospital system in 1967 had been recruited during or just after World War II. Even then they surely were hearing golden age legends from their elders; and by 1967 they had been around long enough to have tasted the gall

TABLE 9

THE RELATIVELY LOW STATUS OF STATE HOSPITAL
SUPERINTENDENTS IN EYES OF PSYCHIATRISTS, CAMH
LEADERS, AND TOTAL SAMPLE[a]

(in percent)

	NCPS	CAMH leaders	Total Sample
As a Most Likely Source of Advice:			
Hospital superintendents	27	21	21
Short–Doyle[b]	42	35	34
Psychiatrists	85	76	72
As a Least Likely Source of Advice:			
Hospital superintendents	13	10	19
Short–Doyle	2	3	6
Psychiatrists	0	3	9
Total Number	52	29	558

[a] Status is indicated by responses to item 38, about groups the respondent would be most likely, and least likely, to "trust and take advice from."

[b] The questionnaire named Short–Doyle only, and some respondents may have been thinking of the programs rather than their administrators.

of increased control from Sacramento themselves. This attitude was not nearly so strong among the younger men in the system.

Declining rule-making autonomy was in part an expression of the declining viability of the state hospitals as treatment institutions. The superintendents and lower-ranking administrators whose careers and in some cases self-respect had been linked to the institutions suffered the changes in silence. On the one hand, they too shared the ideology of treatment close to home, therapy is better than custody, and so forth. They were pleased to see treatment humanized. Yet they could not help resenting the cultural definition of their work as mere ripples in an ideological, institutional, and professional backwater. The SK and F "Psychiatric Career Game" mentioned above suggests the complex nature of this definition and the equally complex response that top hospital administrators had to fashion to it. A player is permitted to move three spaces forward if he is appointed superintendent of a state hospital, but four spaces if he is asked merely to help design a community mental health center! If the player has the misfortune to land on the last space,

number fifty-one, he is credited with having "become the nation's leading advocate of custodial care in large state hospitals" and told to "give
up." It was the rare hospital superintendent (in California) who had
much interest or involvement in the local or statewide medical societies
or psychiatric associations. His colleagues in private practice or in community psychiatry undoubtedly missed his presence but little. Table 9
shows that hospital superintendents evoked fewer positive responses and
more negative responses than both Short–Doyle and psychiatrists, not
only from other psychiatrists but also from CAMH leaders and from the
attentive public as a whole.

The hospitals' morale problem was probably caused, to a large extent,
by the invidious comparison made between the relative rates of progress
of the state hospitals and other methods of distributing treatment services. Those who were identified with the hospitals stressed the absolute
rate of progress in hospital care, while the antagonists of the hospitals
stressed its relative sluggishness. Moreover, it was not always easy for the
defenders of the hospitals to shift the blame for their relative backward-
ness to factors outside their control. As we saw in the case of the DMH,
the ideological culture of the institutions, accumulated over many years,
had definitely set limits on innovation and optimism. Most importantly,
the ideology in this case seems to have been self-fulfilling. While I know
of no explicit research proving this point to my satisfaction, there are
indications that the ideological climate of the institution as a whole (not
merely an experimental group or ward) made a considerable amount of
difference in how the patients fared. Although it was not stressed in the
official propaganda of the department and was probably not fully recognized by professionals or administrators either in the DMH or elsewhere,
hierarchically legitimated change in the official line—amounting to "Get
the patients out early!"—which occurred in the very late 1950s was probably a key factor in the drastic population decline that began in 1960.[13]
A study of death and discharge rates of patients admitted to Stockton

[13] It was only one of several factors, of course. Drugs were most often credited with
the change. But they were introduced in 1955–56. Although it took a few years for
them to become widely used, the relatively late onset of the population reduction be-
lies the almost exclusive causal role that some persons imputed to them. Short–Doyle
did not begin operating until 1958 and, most importantly, did not lower the overall
number of annual admissions to the hospitals. Changes in federal eligibility requirements for certain forms of public assistance for aftercare patients did not occur until
1962.

TABLE 10

DEATH RATES AND RETENTION RATES OF COHORTS OF MALE
FIRST ADMISSIONS, AGES 25-34, TO STOCKTON STATE HOSPITAL,
1852-1954

Period of Admission		Cumulative Percent Dead Within				
		3 mos.	6 mos.	1 yr.	2 yrs.	3 yrs. and over
I	1852-1870	4.0	7.5	10.7	13.5	29.2
II	1875-1890	3.1	7.0	10.0	15.5	42.5
III	1900-1910	3.1	5.4	7.7	14.6	38.5
IV	1920-1930	2.0	3.1	6.6	10.7	25.0
V	1954	0.5	0.6	0.7	ND	ND
		Percent Still Retained at				
		3 mos.	6 mos.	9 mos.	1 yr.	2 yrs.
I	1852-1870	70.7	53.1	43.4	38.5	29.1
II	1875-1890	75.5	60.3	50.4	47.6	38.0
III	1900-1910	80.0	66.9	59.3	56.1	40.0
IV	1920-1930	86.7	68.8	56.6	48.9	32.6
V	1954	59.3	27.3	21.5	18.6	ND

SOURCE: Adapted from Michael T. Savino and Stuart A. Brody, "Discharge Rates in California State Hospitals, 1852–1954," *Archives of General Psychiatry* 15 (November 1966): 478–479, Tables 5 and 7. (Reprinted with the kind permission of the author and publisher.)

State Hospital between 1852 and 1954 reveals a clear coincidence of change in both death and discharge rates and changes in officially sanctioned ideologies of etiology and treatment. Table 10 reproduces some of the findings. The researchers describe the patient cohorts in period I as having been admitted during the moral treatment phase, cohorts II and III as having been admitted during the custodial phase, and cohorts IV and V as having entered after the beginning of the phase of renewed optimism.[14]

Although the phase of renewed optimism began many years earlier, the state hospital superintendents and many of the staff were, in 1967, still suspected of being "confirmed bughousers," in the words of one brash young hospital psychologist. Former hospital staff members some-

14 Michael T. Savino and Stuart A. Brody, "Discharge and Death Rates in California Hospitals, 1852–1954," *Archives of General Psychiatry* 15 (November 1966): 475–484.

times claimed they left work there principally because they felt themselves becoming institutionalized in the same unfortunate way as the patients. It is not unlikely that many of the top administrators and professionals, men and women who had built careers in the state hospital system, were also vulnerable to such feelings. For them, however, the time had passed to do much about them. Before the era of renewed optimism, it might have been possible to accept the limitations of the hospital culture and to take some pride in the fact that one did what one could. By 1967, however, this was not enough. By that time, administrators and professionals were supposed to exude optimism. They were supposed to create or at least sustain a milieu of optimism. "Making do" was no longer quite sufficient. For the older administrators and professionals in the hospital system, the discrepancy between what they had come to feel was possible and what, at some level of consciousness, they believed was required undermined their sense of self-esteem. Without this important resource, the hospital superintendents and deputy superintendents were unable to bring themselves to defend the integrity of their institutions from threats that they saw originating in the political or administrative environment.

During 1966–1967, the Bureau of Social Work employed over 400 full-time psychiatric social workers to look after more than 20,000 leave-of-absence patients from the state hospitals for the mentally ill and retarded. It had a central headquarters in Sacramento, two regional offices (San Francisco and Los Angeles), and service-area headquarters roughly corresponding to the service areas of each of the state hospitals. There were also a number of district offices, usually two to four within each service area. The bureau offices housed clinical as well as administrative functions. Convalescent leave psychiatrists held office hours there during the week, where patients could come for consultation and have drugs or medications dispensed to them. The bureau kept an eye on about 4,000 family care placements for former MR and MI patients. In addition, it supervised another 4,000 extramural placements that were independent of the family care program, for example, sheltered workshops and work placements. Its workers visited these former patients at varying intervals to make sure that they were managing satisfactorily on their own.

These statistics reflected a twenty-five-year history of which the bureau's founders and its present administrators were quite proud. All the professional staff were social workers with master's degrees in social work, most of whom had specialized in psychiatric social work. Thus, they could contrast themselves favorably with all county welfare departments and with not a few private agencies. Their history paralleled the period of the increasing professionalization of social work, a development that the bureau both reflected and helped to foster.

The leadership of the bureau had been fairly uninterrupted during its quarter century of activities. The first chief was Nathan Sloate. He personally groomed his successor, William Wilsnack, who was chief during the period covered by this study. Throughout its history, the leadership of the bureau had alternated between positions of relatively great and relatively little power within the Department of Mental Hygiene hierarchy. Much depended on the personal relations between the bureau administrators and the particular medical administrators at the helm of the department. Sloate was brought into the department by a psychiatrist, Dr. Aaron Rosanoff, when Rosanoff was appointed DMH director in 1939. The two men held each other in great esteem and mutual respect, and the new program prospered. The extramural care program, as it was then called, was the first of its kind in the nation and was credited by its founders and others with having forestalled a far worse wartime deterioration in the hospitals than that which actually occurred. During the sixteen years following the death of Rosanoff in 1943 the bureau had to fight harder to maintain its institutional integrity and to initiate new programs for "breaking down the walls between the hospital and the community." Its stock rose again under the directorship of Dr. Daniel Blain, a celebrated figure in American psychiatry. Blain, who took office in 1959 (the choice of Governor Brown in his first term), excelled at infusing enthusiasm for progressive therapeutic ideologies into the hospital staffs and at convincing lay activists to take a more vigorous role in supporting the department's new direction. His attention to administrative detail, however, was minimal. Indeed, he was not even a full-time resident of Sacramento. He had left his family and many professional connections in Philadelphia; and while he shuttled back and forth between Sacramento and Philadelphia, effective control of the department was largely in the hands of his administrative assistant, Philip Sirotkin, another energetic and innovative personality. Sirotkin, Sloate, and the DMH deputy director of community services (Short–Doyle), Dr. Edward Rudin, formed the nucleus of a powerful policy-making bloc within the department. It was practically inevitable that such a group would alienate the more traditionally minded DMH and hospital administrators.

When Lowry replaced Blain in 1964 (after about a year of interim directors), it was widely and correctly believed that he had been named to increase administrative control over the sprawling operations of the department. (Lowry arrived in Sacramento after some twenty years' experience with the United States Public Health Service's tightly controlled Washington headquarters and was appalled to find twenty-eight separate officials reporting to him directly.) The bureau leadership and its allies were systematically displaced from their positions of preeminence. Lowry created new division layers immediately under his control and made the bureau subordinate to one of them. He then began to develop a program to break the bureau into regional units corresponding to hopsital service areas, each of which would be responsible to the superintendent of the hospital in that service area. According to Lowry, he found the bureau an "ossified, twenty-five-year-old dynasty," which had lost its original zest and vitality. The struggle that ensued between Lowry and the bureau spreads itself across two of the five policy controversies in this book.

MAPPING INTERESTS AND ALLIANCES IN THE ATTENTIVE PUBLIC

Once the entrepreneur has identified the principal factional interests in the attentive public, he will wish to sort out the historical patterns of mutual sympathy and assistance among them, that is, their alliances. Naturally, it is impossible to survey all possible combinations of interests (or individuals) to gauge their valence for each other as allies. Even though the entrepreneur will be interested primarily in the more powerful alliances, which are usually few in number and relatively prominent, a systematic scanning procedure can do no harm and might prove quite useful. First, the entrepreneur should identify any interests that are clear front-runners in the competition for stakes of whatever kind.[15] Have they any allies who help them, in any way, to retain their superior position? Next the entrepreneur should identify interests who consistently

[15] An interest may be defined formally as any group of individuals with similar goals and a similar competitive position with regard to achieving them politically. An interest is, therefore, what we have called a faction plus the individuals who are outside its organizational structure but who meet the criteria of having similar goals and competitive position.

must (or believe they must) struggle to protect their position against an identified adversary. Who, if anyone, helps them in their struggle? Using this method, we can identify five major alliances within the California mental health public:

1. The medical echelons of the DMH headquarters hierarchy; the mental health committee of the CMA; organized psychiatry (and its individual practitioners) in California; certain Short–Doyle administrators, typically of the old guard.

2. The entire mental health public against the anti-mental-health movement on the radical Right and against attempts from either the state legislature or the executive branch to reduce appropriations for hospitals for the mentally ill.

3. Top leaders from the CAMH; certain community welfare groups at the local level; organized psychology and social work; state assemblymen and staff with a special interest in mental health and mental retardation; the Bureau of Social Work; and certain Short–Doyle administrators, typically of a more progressive persuasion.[16]

4. The Bureau of Social Work and many local chapters in California of the National Association of Social Workers.

5. The Conference of Local Mental Health Directors (Short–Doyle) and the County Supervisors Association of California (CSAC), identifiable through their liaison committee.

The first alliance is identified by the clear front-runner test. In program administration and content, treatment ideology, money, and prestige, "medicine" was far in the lead. The other four alliances are all identifiable by the common-enemy test. For each of these alliances, respectively, these enemies were: total-system antagonists; forces of whatever kind resisting progressively oriented changes in policy; detractors of the social work profession; and centralizing forces emanating from Sacramento or other sources.

It should be emphasized that these long-term alliances among interests in the attentive public are not necessarily very strong. Allies manifest mutual sympathy and assistance most readily when it costs them little to do so. But no two allies' interests are ever perfectly congruent, and the concrete circumstances surrounding any given contro-

16 One may think of this alliance as linking individuals who would have scored unusually low on our traditionalism index.

versy inevitably prevent an alliance from being activated completely or for very long. In none of the five controversies described in Part II were any of these alliances mobilized fully. As we shall see presently this slack in the system has highly significant consequences for a would-be entrepreneur. Before we can elaborate on these consequences, however, we need to acquaint ourselves with the controversies described in the next five chapters.

FIVE MENTAL HEALTH CONTROVERSIES

Part II

4
Civil Commitment and
the Medical Model

Until a few years ago the opening lines of the petition initiating civil procedures against each of the 13,000 persons whom the state annually committed to its hospitals for the mentally ill declared the will of "the people" to act "for the best interest and protection of an alleged mentally ill person as respondent." About halfway down the page the petition modified the claim of the people to be acting with such complete benevolence. The committing judge was obliged to state his belief that one of these two conditions had been satisfied: the person is "(a) Of such mental condition that ——he is in need of supervision, treatment, care, or restraint, or (b) Of such mental condition that ——he is dangerous to h——self or to the person or property of others, and is in need of supervision, treatment, care, or restraint." On the one hand, the state might exercise its police power to protect the life and property of its citizens by committing allegedly dangerous persons to places of confinement. Alternatively, it might exercise its role as *parens patriae* to protect persons incapable of making or executing responsible decisions concerning their own well-being. These were quite different legal doctrines with quite separate philosophical and sociological foundations. No matter which clause the judge struck out as inapplicable, however, the outcome was the same. The "mentally ill person" was sent involuntarily to a state mental hospital, there to remain for a legally unspecified period of time.

In August 1967 the legislature acted to repeal this section of the Welfare and Institutions Code.[1]

Nine months earlier the Subcommittee on Mental Health Services of the Assembly Ways and Means Committee had issued a 200-page report entitled "The Dilemma of Mental Commitments in California" which documented the abuses of the commitment procedure and the failings of the state hospitals. "The basic dilemma," as the subcommittee viewed it, was the practical incompatibility of "the two basic objectives of California's mental health system—individual health and public safety," which forced those responsible for administering its policies "to choose between the medical objectives of treating sick people without legal delays and the equally valid legal aim of insuring that persons are not deprived of their liberties without due process of law."[2] The report, furthermore, proposed a radical change in the design of the present system, the most important features of which were: (1) repealing the present commitment law; (2) permitting involuntary commitment for observation and treatment for up to, but no more than, seventeen days (even in the case of allegedly dangerous or suicidal persons); (3) instituting a guardianship system for the gravely disabled, which would provide more individualized custodial care for patients who needed it, possibly in state hospitals but more likely in nursing homes or other such sheltered environments near their communities; and (4) creating "Emergency Service Units" (ESU's) in each county that would (a) evaluate the medical, psychological, social, and financial needs of all persons "who believe themselves to be mentally ill or whom others believe to be mentally ill" (that is, both voluntary and involuntary admissions), (b) give short-term treatment when necessary, and (c) make referrals to appropriate outside agencies when necessary and possible.

The subcommittee had given ample publicity to its research efforts, but it had written its conclusions and recommendations in relative

[1] SB 677, which was the principal vehicle for repeal, passed the legislature in August 1967, but the date it was to go into effect was July 1, 1968. During the 1968 session of the legislature, the effective date was moved forward to July 1, 1969. In the 1967 session, also, a second bill was passed, AB 288, which dealt with civil commitments. The provisions of AB 288 went into effect immediately. They were very similar to the provisions of SB 677 with regard to the commitment laws, but they ignored the administrative, fiscal, and treatment problems covered by SB 677. AB 288 was three pages long; SB 677 was over forty pages long.

[2] California (State) Legislature, Assembly Interim Committee on Ways and Means, Subcommittee on Mental Health Services. "The Dilemma of Mental Commitments in California," November 1966, pp. 6–7. Hereinafter cited as Dilemma Report.

secrecy. Publication of the report, on November 27, 1966, triggered a small explosion both within and outside of the attentive public. The printed media gave it front-page coverage: "Treatment of Mentally Ill Scored. Revolutionary changes . . . were proposed today . . ." (Oakland Tribune, November 28, 1966); "Assembly Report Attacks State Mental System. 'Thousands Locked Up Erroneously' " (San Francisco Examiner, November 28, 1966); "State's Mental Health System Hit as Legally, Medically Weak" (Los Angeles Times, November 29, 1966).[3] The item that struck home to all the newsmen was the finding of the subcommittee, based on a statewide survey of commitment court hearings, that the average courtroom proceeding took only 4.7 minutes. One-third of the hearings lasted less than two minutes.[4]

INTELLECTUAL AND POLITICAL ORIGINS

In 1965 California enacted a pioneering program in the field of mental retardation. It authorized and funded the first two regional service centers of a projected statewide system, intended to minimize the role of the state hospitals in caring for the retarded. This success marked the first legislative triumph of the newly created Subcommittee on Mental Health Services. Encouraged by this victory, the subcommittee members—particularly Jerome Waldie, who was also the (Democratic) majority leader of the Assembly, and Waldie's staff assistant, Arthur Bolton—were keen to press their reform efforts into the area of mental illness. Convinced though they were that the mental health system and the Department of Mental Hygiene were due for reform, they needed, first, a concrete issue around which to coalesce a large number of interests and, second, a feasible reform program. As a first step toward finding an issue they sent a mail questionnaire to persons on the subcommittee's mailing list, which they had taken care to create as a by-product of their efforts to mobilize support for the regional mental retardation centers bill. They explained their general aims in a covering letter and asked the recipients to indicate the problems in the area of mental illness that they believed ought to receive immediate attention.

As this first step was being taken, another staff assistant, with ties to

[3] The only major newspapers to give the story less than front-page coverage were the Bee papers in the major cities of the Central Valley. I do not know why the Bee chain gave the story less prominence.

[4] Dilemma Report, p. 43.

the academic community, arranged for Bolton to read a research report prepared by a student of Erving Goffman's. It described the author's observations of "a county lunacy commission" in California, that is, the work of a commitment court in a single county.[5] Bolton was much impressed by the findings: the average length of the commitment hearing was 4.1 minutes; the examining physicians recommended commitment "in nearly all cases"; "spouses were likely to be released, while those who filled the family role position of a relative and those who were living outside the family were likely to be committed"; "those who could not or would not defend themselves were not defended." The author conjectured that the medical examinations preceding the hearings were "as summary as the hearing itself." During the next few months Bolton and Waldie obtained two more pieces of graduate student research. One was by a law school student summarizing the mental commitment laws in California and in other states, and the other was by a student of Thomas Scheff's at the University of California at Santa Barbara. The latter documented the perfunctory nature of the prehearing medical examinations in the psychiatric observation ward of one county hospital. In this particular unit, the researcher reported, the average psychiatric interview lasted four or five minutes.[6] Bolton and Waldie concluded that they had found their issue.

A relatively small proportion of the returned questionnaires suggested an especial concern for reform of the commitment laws. Largely because of decisions taken that year at the national level, many members of the California Association for Mental Health assigned a high priority to improving the (desperately bad) state of public mental health services for children. Recognizing this, Waldie and Bolton concluded that they ought not to be bound by this particular sampling of public opinion. Besides, it was quite likely, in their eyes, that public opinion was peculiarly ill-equipped to understand the extent of the tragedy of civil commitment. Like many others, including themselves perhaps, the respondents to their questionnaire had had little first-hand experience of or knowledge about the commitment process. The conditions of the

5 The report was subsequently published by Dorothy Miller and Michael Schwartz as "County Lunacy Commission Hearings: Some Observations of Commitments to a State Mental Hospital," *Social Problems* 14, no. 1 (summer 1966): 26–35.

6 Karl W. Kreplin, "Mental Illness Commitment: A Study of the Decision-Making Process" (M. A. thesis, University of California at Santa Barbara, January 1966). Cited in Dilemma Report, pp. 29–30. The source is incorrectly cited at the bottom of p. 30, but correctly listed in the Bibliography, p. 203.

state hospitals were relatively enduring, to be sure, and visible even to the solid middle-class citizens who comprised the bulk of their sample. But these conditions were only the end product of the commitment process. The process itself was barely visible. Waldie's and Bolton's particular conception of the role of the legislature, particularly the role of the state legislature, implied a responsibility to lead public opinion as well as to follow it. If the attentive public did not see the problem as clearly as they did, it was their obligation to point it out to them. Most important, though, was their recognition of the great leverage they could gain on the whole mental health system by manipulating the commitment laws. As Bolton put it, "We saw that if we could lodge a huge boulder in the center of that over-used road to the mental hospital, the patients would have to be sent somewhere else, to more appropriate facilities. The system would *have* to move off dead center." Putting together enough support would not be easy, they guessed. But even if they were to fail in the first round, they would be in an improved starting position when they launched any subsequent effort.

In retrospect it is easy to see that they initially underestimated their potential support. Most of the attentive mental health public, when they thought of ways to ameliorate the follies of the commitment system, assumed that the legal features of the system were fixed stars in the firmament. They had been fixed in place, after all, by generations of legislators, by the legal profession, and in a sense by the strong desires of the public for protection. Though many professionals both in and out of the Department of Mental Hygiene and Short–Doyle had expended much energy on the whole problem, they never really imagined possibilities beyond patching up the treatment system alone. In December 1965, the DMH published its thirteenth planning study, in a series begun several years earlier under a grant from the National Institute of Mental Health, entitled "Screening the Mentally Ill Before Court Commitment." It was one of the best studies in the series, certainly one of the most inspired and most timely. Yet it granted no more than a footnote in the foreword to the consideration of "the basic legal framework," and went on from there to talk about the possibilities of "using . . . Short–Doyle . . . to assist the court" and "the role of the Mental Health Counselor in pre-commitment screening." Legal professionals, for their part, focused on patching up the legal system while assuming relative constancy in the system of delivering treatment. Earlier that year the state Senate Subcommittee on Commitment Procedures, whose parent committee was the Special Fact Finding Committee on Judiciary, had produced a lengthy report showing the state of disarray of the commitment statutes, which were at that time scattered throughout the Welfare and Insitutions Code. After receiving testimony from numerous lawyers, jurists, and hospital administrators, it concluded that existing legislation ensured sound medical practice and adequately protected the fundamental legal rights of the patients. It limited its recommendations to recodification of existing statutes and certain minor reforms having to do with procedures for jury trials, periodic reviews of the patients' needs for further confinement, penalties for maliciously instituting commitment petitions, and so forth. It raised no questions at all concerning the fundamental organization of treatment services. From its limited perspective, only the design of the legal system was at issue.[7]

Bolton and Waldie in effect capitalized, even to their own surprise, on a state of affairs sociologists call "pluralistic ignorance." The legal professionals were in fact quite ready to accept extensive changes in the treatment system; and the mental health professionals were in fact ready to accept equally far-reaching changes in the legal system (although they rejected some that Waldie and Bolton eventually proposed). Moreover, they were prepared, up to a point, to accept the same changes. Neither group, however, fully understood the readiness of its counterpart. Given the traditional tension between the objectives of the two groups, it was unlikely that a change in the total system proposed by either group would have met with favor in the other one. It required generalists in and around the legislature to bridge the gap between the two groups of specialists.

After gaining the consent of the other two members of the Assembly subcommittee, Waldie and Bolton scheduled hearings for December 1965 and January 1966, the proclaimed purpose of which was to gather information about the problem of commitment. In fact, of course, this series of hearings, like most legislative hearings, served many additional functions, some intended and some not. First, it served notice on the attentive mental health public that something revolutionary was afoot and that it principally concerned commitments. Second, it created a valuable public record which Waldie and Bolton could mine intensively for material that would make good reading in the Dilemma Report.

[7] In June 1966 the Midpeninsula Chapter of the American Civil Liberties Union of Northern California issued a call of its own for changes in the legal system. It gave no more than cursory attention to the treatment system.

Finally, it revealed to the members of the attentive public, as well as to the Assembly group itself, who was likely to be on whose side.

As far as the stated purpose of the hearings was concerned, they fulfilled and overfulfilled. Psychiatrists, judges, public defenders, social workers, hospital administrators—they followed each other to the witness stand and, moved either by their own spirits or encouraged by insistent probing from Chairman Waldie, revealed the sequence of abuses that hounded the alleged mentally ill en route from the county psychiatric observation ward, through the courtroom, and finally to the state hospital. Waldie himself seized every opportunity to insert in the record accounts of his own observations of prehearing psychiatric examinations in the crowded wards of San Francisco General Hospital. "It would clearly be a desirable thing, would it not," he asked one psychiatric examiner, "to hold an examination were there to be privacy?" Psychiatric examiner: "It would very much, yes." Waldie: "The examination I saw conducted—there were three or four patients listening in and watching and observing the one being examined."[8]

During the winter and spring of 1966, the subcommittee staff devoted itself to gathering more and more information about the legal disabilities and the social stigma that flowed from hospitalization and commitment. A committed mental patient, they discovered, suffered more legal disabilities than the worst violator of the criminal law. They also turned to the journals of the legal and mental health professions for descriptions of programs that had worked in other jurisdictions and that California might profitably emulate. They touched base with a number of important organizations whose support they knew they needed and with others whose support might be less important but also might be relatively easy to obtain. In the first group there was the CMA, the DMH, and the CAMH; in the second, the American Civil Liberties Union (ACLU) and the California Hospital Association (CHA). They initiated correspondence with legal and mental health experts in far-flung places like Cameron Village, North Carolina. Bolton managed to recruit the full-time staff assistance of Karsten Vieg, a recent graduate of the University of California Law School at Berkeley, who had drifted toward the state capital after graduation with little in mind except avoiding the practice of law and finding a temporary job that would challenge his many extralegal talents.

[8] Quoted in Dilemma Report, p. 28.

The Assembly group's approach to the CMA during this early phase of its work was executed with particular skill. A few years earlier the CMA had conducted an evaluative survey of the state hospitals.[9] Bolton now approached the association's Committee on Mental Health to request it to carry out a similar survey of Short–Doyle facilities. Here was a task the CMA Committee on Mental Health had accomplished successfully once, that it could execute successfully again, and that would turn up few results that could not be used advantageously by the subcommittee. The CMA report on the hospitals had been thorough, reliable, and surprisingly free of efforts to whitewash the system. Useful criticism of Short–Doyle might also be brought to light. If the survey did turn out to be a whitewash, the legislators could simply ignore it.

The real significance of the survey, though, was in the act of doing it. If the CMA invested its efforts on behalf of the subcommittee in a project they wanted to do anyway, would they not also develop a stake in the success of the legislation that would presumably be based on their work? It would help, too, to spread the word around that the CMA was working hand in glove with the Assembly group. The CMA would contact the Department of Mental Hygiene in order to secure their cooperation in the effort. The department would of course be unable to refuse, even if they wanted to; and they too would become directly involved in the subcommittee's efforts. Although they were considered a much more likely ally than the DMH, the same would apply to Short–Doyle. Moreover, the very presence of CMA inspection teams would put Short–Doyle on notice that the revolutionary changes planned for the system as a whole would certainly not leave them untouched.

In June the subcommittee contracted with Social Psychiatry Research Associates of San Francisco to carry out a survey of the commitment courts and to construct a patient profile of the state MI hospitals and several non-state-supported psychiatric hospitals. The director of this private research group was Dr. Dorothy Miller, the same researcher whose paper on the "county lunacy commision" had one year earlier attracted Bolton's attention. The research group that she headed was at that time nominally affiliated with the Research Bureau of the DMH but was in fact largely supported by grants from the National Institute of Mental Health (NIMH). By their own definition, they were "a group

9 "Observations and Comments, Based on a Survey of California State Mental Facilities by the California Medical Association" (submitted to the California State Department of Mental Hygiene, January 18, 1965).

of researchers . . . engaged in a series of social surveys generally focused on the community careers of persons *labeled as deviant"* (emphasis added). Their independent source of funds permitted them to generate research projects the nature of which, to say the least, caused some discomfort within the medical sections of the DMH. One major project, for instance, was a five-year longitudinal study of ex-hospital patients in one Bay Area county.[10] The conclusions were unsettling: 40 percent of the patients had returned to the state hospital within the first year out; 70 percent had returned by the end of five years.[11] DMH officials and a number of Short–Doyle administrators privately disputed the validity of these findings and, indeed, considered their publication an unambiguous attempt to subvert the system. Linking the subcommittee's research effort to Dorothy Miller's group surely alienated some officials in the DMH, but it is doubtful that Waldie and Bolton were aware of this prospect.

As with the CMA survey of Short–Doyle which the subcommittee requested, the political payoff would be in the doing. CAMH members were to become involved as volunteer observers in the commitment court survey. The observers would see for themselves how the beast appeared at close quarters and would perhaps spread the word among their fellow members and others. Involvement in the preliminaries, moreover, would hopefully commit the association to follow the issue through to its conclusion.

In May 1966 Waldie won a special election called to fill the congressional seat vacated by the death of the incumbent representative. The other two members of the subcommittee, a liberal Democrat from Oakland, Nicholas Petris, and a conservative Republican from Pasadena, Frank Lanterman, directed Bolton and Vieg to continue the project and to assume operational responsibility. Both Petris and Lanterman had diverse political obligations and interests aside from mental commitment reform that, in their view, deserved priority. Among other things,

[10] This project was completed shortly before they incorporated themselves as a private research laboratory. As a group attached to the DMH research program, they would have had access to NIMH research funds, but these funds would have had to have been processed through regular DMH procedures. The DMH would probably not have supported such an obstreperous research group for very long, however—not, at least, in a very open-handed way. Hence the group employed the device of legal incorporation in order to obtain NIMH (and other) funds without having to go through the department.

[11] Dorothy Miller, *Worlds that Fail: Part I, Retrospective Analysis of Mental Patients' Careers*, Research Monograph no. 6 (Sacramento: DMH, 1965).

only a few months remained before election day, and Petris was planning to run for a seat in the state Senate created by statewide reapportionment and redistricting that affected seats in both legislative chambers. Lanterman was a senior member of the Ways and Means Committee, which faced a flood of appropriations bills that would accumulate into a deluge as the legislative session neared conclusion.

Still more important than the fact that Lanterman and Petris needed to turn the field captainship over to Bolton was the fact that they felt they could afford to do so. During the three years Bolton had been on the Assembly staff, he had built a considerable store of credit with the legislators, both liberals and conservatives, Democrats and Republicans. Under the aegis of Waldie and Jesse Unruh, the powerful Speaker of the Assembly, Bolton had risen rapidly in the staff hierarchy. By May 1966 Bolton held the position of senior consultant to the assembly, one of the few staff posts serving the body as a whole rather than a particular committee or legislator. Bolton's own policy views endeared him more to the liberals and the Democrats in the Assembly than to the conservatives and Republicans; but even among the latter he had a reputation for intelligence, integrity, and "straight talk." In early 1967 the Assembly, at Unruh's urging, created for itself an Office of Research and named Bolton its head.

On November 24 the Dilemma Report was sent by messenger to the Department of Mental Hygiene and by mail to members of the state legislature. Three days later the report was given to the press and mailed to over 1,200 persons on the subcommittee mailing list and to Short–Doyle administrators. Lowry had not seen it, however, when reporters sought him out for comment on Tuesday morning, November 29, just as he was concluding an on-site inspection of Porterville State Hospital. Angry at having been caught with his guard down, he fired off a press release indicating the department's endorsement of the report's recommendations, which were redefined in the telling so as to make it appear that the department had been striving for the same goals all along.[12] Petris, the new chairman of the subcommittee, responded quickly with

---

[12] The Dilemma Report unambiguously recommended establishing community-based emergency service units to *"replace the commitment court"* (p. 85, emphasis in original). Lowry stated the department's support for what he chose to interpret as the subcommittee's "recommendations that would result in a reduction of court procedures associated with obtaining treatment for persons with mental disorders and make more treatment available in the local community on a voluntary basis." Then Lowry took the offensive: "The Department of Mental Hygiene will propose legisla-

a statement acknowledging the past efforts of the DMH to encourage voluntary as opposed to involuntary hospitalization and recognizing the noncomplicity of the department in the administration of commitments. For the next several months the department kept its silence about the report, admitting nothing but denying nothing. Within the first few weeks after the report appeared, the subcommittee staff held three or four lengthy discussions with DMH representatives whose attitude was cooperative but at the same time cautious.

On December 1 the semiannual Conference of Local Mental Health Directors opened in San Diego. Although the formal agenda did not call for a discussion of the Dilemma Report, it was a brooding presence. Nearly all the old-guard leaders of the conference expressed emotions ranging from pique to uninhibited anger that they had not been consulted about the report. One speaker suggested that the title of the workshop session that he was chairing should not have been "Where Are We Going?" but "Where Are We Being Taken?"

After an hour of increasingly heated discussion about what they took to be the report's slighting references to Short–Doyle, Bolton was invited to take the floor to present the legislative view. His unexpectedly candid remarks ("Frankly, I'm disappointed in you gentlemen . . .") were disarming. Tempers cooled. But the hush in the audience, punctuated by occasional laughter, suggested that tensions still ran high. Here, after all, were assembled the pioneers and leaders in the state and in the nation of the community psychiatry movement. Here were the professionals, the psychiatric experts, the progressively minded vanguard—and they were being lectured in print and in person by a youthful staff assistant, without medical credentials, without clinical experience, and without apparent deference for those who had them.[13]

The source of tension was deeper than wounded egos. If the Short–

---

tion at the next Legislature which would require that a person for whom commitment procedures are initiated must be referred by the local court to the local mental health facility, wherever there is one." Lowry evidently did not perceive. or did not wish to admit, the distinction between his own proposal and the subcommittee's. Experience interviewing mental health professionals over the next several months convinced me that many of them (not necessarily including Lowry) never understood the clear intention of the Dilemma Report and AB 1220 to abolish court commitments, rather than merely to effect "a reduction in court procedures associated with obtaining treatment." This was striking evidence of the imperturbability of established cognitive frames of reference.

[13] Bolton was actually thirty-nine but appeared much younger. Nor was he without credentials or experience of some kind. He had a master of social work degree which

Doyle leaders had found the substance of the subcommittee recommendations less distasteful, there is little doubt that Bolton would have been welcomed with applause. But they were concerned about the emergency service units (ESUs).[14] The report stipulated that "the various E.S.U. services need not be provided by a single local agency, and any community may incorporate several agencies in applying for an E.S.U. contract, provided they can offer a coordinated program." The local Short–Doyle program might be "one useful base" for the administrative direction of the new ESUs, but, said the report, "it does not appear as if *reliance* on the mechanism will be sufficient. 'Community Mental Health' and 'Short–Doyle' are not synonymous. Rather the Short–Doyle program must be viewed in historical perspective as one early step in the proper direction."[15] Thus, the Short–Doyle administrators envisioned a new community mental health system, providing more services than many of them were then providing, which would compete with Short–Doyle for clients. Worse still, the ESUs were to be financed in large part through Medi-Cal funds, half of which, under Title XIX of the 1965 Medicare amendments, came from the federal government. Since Short–Doyle's capacity to offer services to the public was limited by the fiscal conservatism of the county supervisors, the ESU's would have an unfair advantage over Short–Doyle in any competition for access to the client population. Indeed, many of the Short–Doyle administrators were inclined to see any sort of competition as unfair. The Dilemma Report took the opposite view: "Whereas people with their own funds or Medicare and welfare recipients are now able to select and purchase services from a variety of 'vendors,' other low income people now have no choice but to use the state hospitals (or in some communities certain local services funded primarily by the State through the Short–Doyle formula)."[16] The result, from Short–Doyle's viewpoint, would surely be "the

---

he did not go out of his way to publicize. Before coming to the Assembly, Bolton had been assistant director of the Sacramento Community Welfare Council. Whereas Bolton saw himself as a tough-minded, intellectually critical professional staffer, with a high sense of calling and responsibility, many of the Short–Doyle leaders and apparently some persons in the DMH viewed him as something of a juvenile delinquent. Bolton half understood that they saw him in this way, and he even used this image to gain certain rhetorical advantages.

14 Dilemma Report, pp. 85–86, 91.

15 *Ibid.*, p. 170.

16 *Ibid.*, p. 87. The word *vendors* caused particular irritation. Short–Doyle did not like to see itself as just another vendor of services, even though the term *vendor* was

fragmentation and duplication of services" and disruption of "the continuity of care."

Probably a majority of the Short–Doyle directors and program chiefs at the meeting were more favorably disposed to the report than otherwise, but the effective power in the legislative committee of the conference was in the hands of the administrators of the large established programs who felt a particular threat to the programs they had worked so long and hard to build. The consensus of a special caucus of the legislative committee held in the late afternoon of December 1 was that either the subcommittee's recommendations should be drastically modified or the entire reform project should be killed. They would make their views known to the department, to the CSAC, and to key members of the state Senate who they believed would be both willing and able to stop any bill which they opposed, regardless of the support mobilized by the subcommittee in the assembly.

During the first two weeks of December, the subcommittee held two public hearings on the report, one in Oakland (for northern California) and one in Los Angeles (for southern California), at which time organized psychiatry registered its own ambivalence toward the report. On the one hand, the spokesman, Dr. Warren Vaughan, praised the report's emphasis on community services and voluntary admission, and even alluded favorably to the report's emphasis on multidisciplinary evaluation procedures. He set the stage for psychiatric dissent, though, in his opening remarks summarizing the report's proposal "to do away with archaic and discriminating legal and administrative procedures now used for involuntary admissions." Of this, psychiatry could wholeheartedly approve. Who, after all, could favor the continuation of "archaic and discriminating legal and administrative procedures"? But the limitation on the period of involuntary confinement to seventeen days (three days of observation and evaluation by the ESU plus fourteen days of certification for certain classes of patients) was unacceptable. "Perhaps 80% of individuals in Emergency Service Unit care will be able to decide whether or not to follow recommendations of the professional staff or attending

---

quite common among planners in the public health field. One reason was that they were, in fact, more than vendors of direct services. Short–Doyle also performed educational, consultative, and coordinative services in the communities. The report did not actually recommend that Short–Doyle lose these functions or that the ESU's also perform them.

psychiatrist within a 14 day period. But a significant number will not."
There are

> agitated patients, driven by emotions with reason overwhelmed, often
> deluded or hallucinated, unable to perceive and interpret their reality
> in a normal fashion, for whom judgement is impaired and insight is
> lacking. . . . Some mentally ill persons have not the faculties for
> making such basic decisions due to the nature of their illness. One
> expects that—with all regard for civil liberties and due process—so-
> ciety will provide the machinery for protecting such individuals from
> harmful experiences while in states of impaired judgement and rea-
> soning.

Furthermore, "Custody and control can be seen as one of the most valuable tools for treatment of some patients. To rid ourselves of the inappropriate use of custody-control on a mass, sociological level should not
also mean that we deprive ourselves of its use on an individualized level
in a clinical context within the framework of an individualized treatment program." When asked by Vieg to explain how the English managed to handle these treatment problems without resorting to the use
of legal commitments, Vaughan replied that the English had different
cultural mores, means of inducing conformity and social control, and
ways of expressing hostility.[17]

The issue between psychiatry and the subcommittee centered around
the report's recommendations to divide the ESU population entering its
screening and evaluation section into three segments. The report projected that most of this population, which would include both those
persons who were brought in for evaluation under the existing seventy-
two-hour-hold law and the voluntary admissions, would be cared for
and released within three days (seventy-two hours). For the minority
there would be the possibility of fourteen-day certification to an appropriate treatment facility. Certification would be permissible only if the
evaluation suggested that the patient was a danger to himself or to
others or gravely disabled. Of this certified population, those who had
been hospitalized as potentially dangerous would have to be released
after a maximum of fourteen days unless they voluntarily sought to re-

17 Vieg's assumption about the English system was generally correct. England did,
however, maintain the statutory possibility for involuntary commitment, which was
used for under 5 percent of the patients hospitalized. Vaughan's reply evoked a
chuckle from one sociologist in the audience, who remarked in a stage whisper, "Well,
there's a new nosological category for you; 'English schizophrenia'—it's not the same
as our own 'American schizophrenia!' "

main for further treatment. For the gravely disabled, who were defined as "incapable of carrying on transactions necessary to survival and otherwise providing for such basic needs as food, clothing, and shelter," the courts, acting on the recommendation of the ESU staff, could appoint a legal guardian with specific powers detailed by court decree and "tailored to the disabilities of the ward." The powers of the guardian could include the right to send the ward to the state hospital. The ward would have the right to appeal to the courts for restoration of competency at least once every six months.[18] On questioning by Bolton, Vaughan recommended that "gravely disabled" be defined more broadly and that the potentially suicidal be included in the class of persons "incapable of carrying on transactions necessary to survival."

Representatives from the California membership of the American Civil Liberties Union raised opposite kinds of objections. There was potential for great abuse in the certification procedures, they said, if ESU administrators decided to "play yoyo" with the patient. Technically, they could release him, then have him detained immediately on a seventy-two hour hold, certify him for another fourteen days of detention and repeat this process indefinitely. They voiced skepticism, too, about the failure of the report to require mandatory court hearings before the ESU instituted certification for even fourteen days and to require the assistance of a public defender during the court hearing. Although the report recommended guarantees of a court hearing within four days after certification if the patient requested it, ACLU spokesmen thought it unlikely that most patients would actually be able or willing to make effective use of such guarantees.

Spokesmen for the California Hospital Association warmly endorsed the report, perceiving an opening for private hospitals to gain access to more paying patients than Short–Doyle had been willing to provide them through its contract authority. Testimony by psychologists and social workers endorsed the ideological and administrative aspects of the report and warmly praised the multidisciplinary features of the proposed ESU evaluation units. The CAMH spokesman "commended the committee on a stimulating and creative report," and quickly proceeded to state the case against Governor Reagan's already visible intention to hold the line on the budget for the state hospitals. Support was also voiced by representatives of the Alameda County Welfare Planning Council, the California Council for Retarded Children (CCRC), the

18 Dilemma Report, pp. 133–135.

California League of Senior Citizens, the Retail Clerks Union, and the Bureau of Social Work. The CCRC also took the opportunity to lodge its complaint against commitment procedures for the mentally retarded; the Senior Citizens, to plead for more state funds for nursing homes and rest homes; the Retail Clerks Union, to remark the success it had enjoyed with its pioneering group psychiatric insurance plan; and the bureau, to rehearse the variety of progressive programs operating then under its auspices.

Two Short–Doyle administrators appeared at the Oakland hearing to praise the report, buttress the document's criticisms of the hospitals and the commitment system with more of their own, and urge greater attention to the role Short–Doyle would have under the new system. Judge Joseph Karesh of San Francisco, whose liberal views were well known in the state and who had had several years of experience on the commitment court bench, hurled a fistful of thunderbolts at the commitment laws, recounted his shame and guilt at ever having been a party to their administration, and commended himself and the San Francisco County Short–Doyle program chief for having created the geriatric screening unit, which virtually eliminated the commitment of "nonpsychotic seniles" to the state hospitals from San Francisco. One Claudia Walker of P.O. Box 3189, San Francisco, spoke as "an ancestral American who has been here since before the Constitution." Although she had not yet read the report, she had read the Constitution and, as "a conservative political thinker," assured the committee that it forbade mental treatment "unless law or precept has been transgressed." The last speaker at the Oakland hearing was a Mr. Simpson, ninety-one, of Santa Cruz. He had spent seven months once in Agnews State Hospital "as a political prisoner" and had suffered physical abuse at the hands of the attendants. He rapped lightly on the cast around his chest to prove it. As Mr. Simpson recounted his unhappy story, he gradually gained the initially reluctant attention of both legislators and audience. At the conclusion of his lengthy narrative, which came at the end of a lengthy day, he raised over his head a paperback copy of Ken Kesey's *One Flew over the Cuckoo's Nest* and commended it to the subcommittee as "the truth about the mental hospital." The audience erupted in applause, and the legislators looked as though they wished they could join in. All in all, the subcommittee and staff considered the public hearings a great success.

The witnesses at both hearings who spoke for the Department of

Mental Hygiene reaffirmed the identity of the department's and the subcommittee's goals and objectives and stressed the "need [for] further discussion and clarification . . . of the structure, organization and administration of the ESU services." How would it mesh with Short–Doyle, which already, they observed, "gives attention to the multifaceted aspects of problems associated with mental disorder because it has a diversity of professions (social work, nursing, psychology, medicine) in its staff group and because it utilizes the services of other agencies—welfare, health, education"? The DMH was not raising criticisms, they emphasized, but "suggestions for . . . careful consideration of all aspects of the report as will lead to success in achieving the objectives." Thus, the public position of the department was essentially neutralist. In private, however, the objections of high-level administrators were much less guarded. One memorandum prepared by three top DMH administrators attacked the report from cover to cover. It pointed out that the report "recommends sweeping social reforms to take place within an 18-month period," but failed to take into account "the three most important factors that make it ineffectual . . . Time, Manpower, and Money." Moreover, "the general tone" of the report evinced "a strong bias against (and occasionally unjustifiably attacks) the very groups who could give the greatest support to the objectives of the report—namely, the judiciary and the psychiatrists."

It denied the validity of the report's general premises. Very often, individual health and public safety were not at all in conflict: "A contagious illness is both a matter of individual health and public safety. Public safety requires that the individual not be contagious." Custody and treatment were not necessarily in conflict either. The report showed "a naive concept of psychiatric treatment in assuming that voluntary patients should be treated in open hospitals and involuntary patients in 'secure' sections of the hospital . . . [for] it is not uncommon for voluntary patients to require some secure environment for a period of time; nor is it uncommon for an involuntarily confined patient to be able to utilize an open unit." The report had mistakenly argued that mental illness was "a catch-all concept."[19] It had utilized this premise to conclude that ESUs should be established under nonmedical supervision, which "would appear to be merely recommending change for the sake

19 The authors of the report had been influenced by the residual deviance construction of Scheff and other sociologists. See Dilemma Report, pp. 9–14, and chapter 2 above, p. 45.

of change." The memo conceded "the obvious fact that [medical examinations and court hearings are] perfunctory," but argued that this was
due to the insufficiency of judges, defense attorneys, and qualified medical examiners. The solution was not "to do away entirely with the commitment courts," but "to obtain the necessary trained manpower and
to establish the *appropriate place* for the commitment court." Neither
legal disabilities nor stigma were actually related to commitment per se
but to "the individual's mental illness. . . . The document offers no assurance that the stigma and legal disabilities will not be transferred to
the voluntarily hospitalized patient."[20] The ineffectiveness of the state
hospitals in providing treatment, which the report had abundantly demonstrated and the memorandum implicitly conceded, could be remedied
by more funds for staff.

The memorandum also found fault with many of the report's recommendations for administrative reform. Short–Doyle was already set up
to carry out the same functions as the ESUs; and if the high quality of
treatment services envisioned for ESU patients was to be realized, they
would need to solve the "very manpower shortage that is responsible for
the ineffectiveness of our current system." Secondly, it was "administratively and organizationally inconveivable that the Division of State
Services [the hospitals] would provide contractual services to the Division of Local Programs [Short–Doyle]." Thirdly, Medi-Cal funds were
already in such short supply that it was highly unlikely that the state
would extend eligibility to consumers of mental health services.

A noteworthy addition to the catalogue of criticisms that had theretofore been voiced publicly concerned the report's proposal to establish
a Program and Standards Board to "formulate policy and adopt standards for the operation" of the ESUs. The report deliberately left ambiguous the proposed relationship between the jurisdictional authority
of the board and that of the Department of Mental Hygiene, which the
report named to "administer the proposed program." But it left no
doubt about the ideological significance of the board, on which would
sit "at least one psychiatrist, social welfare expert, psychologist, legal

[20] At least with regard to legal disabilities, the report implicitly recommended the
elimination of the disabilities that attached to all patients and explicitly attacked the
single most important legal disability that befell the involuntarily committed, namely,
"loss of liberty" (Dilemma Report, p. 53). Concerning the loss of liberty, the memorandum commented that this was less serious than "the loss of the ability to use one's
liberty," apparently meaning that psychological freedom was a precondition for the
use of civil freedom.

expert, social research methodologist, and representative of the public."
It was "important to avoid the old error of casting all [mental illness]
problems into a single narrow pattern of service," stated the report; and
no one, least of all the Department of Mental Hygiene, could doubt that
the "single narrow pattern" meant "medical model."[21] The DMH
memorandum rebutted: the jurisdictional disputes that would be institutionalized in the composition of the board would be the surest way to
bring about its failure.

Following the hearings, Bolton and Vieg began anew their support-
gathering activities: reinforcing old supporters, finding new ones, getting supporters on the record, stimulating allies to greater exertions, and
neutralizing potential opponents. They also began efforts to improve
the technical quality of their proposal and to clarify details that would
need to be written into the bill. They solicited comments from all interested parties and accepted numerous invitations from groups all
around the state to speak about the subcommittee's proposals. Their
first meeting was with some twenty-five officials and other members of
the Northern California Psychiatric Society. The cordiality of the meeting, perhaps aided by the steak dinner provided by the NCPS, surpassed
anyone's expectations. Bolton and Vieg implicitly demonstrated their
concern for the psychiatric viewpoint by reeling off titles of books and
articles written by well-known psychiatrists. They cited impressive quantities of statistics about mental illness and the results of psychiatric experimentation in trying to cure it.[22] For their part, the psychiatrists
found as much as they could—which was actually a great deal—to praise
about the report. Bolton suggested that perhaps the subcommittee had
indeed not attached the ESU system firmly enough to Short–Doyle; the
psychiatrists willingly admitted that there was much to be said in favor
of some sort of legal safeguard against indefinite or inappropriate commitment. Perhaps the certification period might be extended for up to
thirty days; or perhaps there might be two fourteen-day periods back-to-
back. Lawyers, said Bolton, do not mistrust psychiatry in general, but
they do "object strenuously to anybody having any of his liberties re-

---

21 Dilemma Report, pp. 92–93.

22 In addressing lawyers, they quoted legal experts. It is difficult to gauge what they
believed they were doing in making this kind of presentation. It appeared to me they
were demonstrating concern for the professional viewpoint and giving evidence that
they had done their homework. Bolton's own description emphasizes the notion of
educating the profession (psychiatric or legal) about its own best, most progressive
trends.

moved." Bolton intimated that he had already pushed his libertarian backers about as far as they would go on the duration of any involuntary treatment period. "The ship we are trying to float can sink very easily with too much weight on one side or another." In the interests of affability as much as principle, a Short–Doyle program chief in attendance interjected that he was not particularly concerned about the fourteen-day limitation. The issue was what happened in the fourteen days—perhaps psychiatry had to change.

The discussion shifted to topics of lesser moment. Inevitably, the fourteen-day issue reappeared toward the end of the meeting; but again the spirit of accommodation was saved by the intervention of a recent past president of the society with claims to long experience in state mental health politics. "You can't be too specific in urging policy," he warned, "especially now with the right wing coming to power [that is, Reagan]. If you want this passed, keep it simple." Vaughan concluded the meeting by inquiring of Bolton, "How can we help further?" The key issue remained unresolved, but the focus of disagreement between psychiatry and the committee had been considerably narrowed—at least for the time being.

In late December Bolton and Vieg were joined in their full-time efforts by David Roberts, another member of the legislative staff, whose special competence was public finance. Roberts had been part of the staff group (along with Bolton) that two years earlier had designed two very complex systems of state-supported medical services, one of which became Medi-Cal and the other of which (Cal-Med, a program with more generous benefits) was defeated. Roberts was an undemonstrative but highly persuasive public speaker. Whereas Bolton and Vieg would deliver their points with maximum authority, Roberts was all humility. Authority in the tone of Bolton or Vieg, as they were themselves aware, could sometimes sound like arrogance. They would plan, therefore, to be followed on the podium by Roberts the velvet tongued.

Table 11 summarizes Bolton's and Vieg's activities for the six weeks between January 4 and February 10, when Vieg turned to full-time work at drafting the bill later introduced as AB 1220, and Bolton became occupied with administrative problems of managing the new Office of Research, of which he had lately been named director. It should be emphasized that Table 11 is at best an approximate depiction of the extent of their activities during this period. It probably under-reports by at least 25 percent the actual number and diversity of their personal contacts during that period. This distortion comes from the imperfections of the sources from which this schedule was reconstructed. I began by studying the very sketchy appointment calendars kept by Bolton and Vieg for those weeks. I supplemented this information with my own field work, interviews, and retrospective accounts provided several month later by Bolton and Vieg themselves. One of the most important channels of communication, the telephone, does not appear at all in this chart. I have attempted to indicate, in column 3, what were probably the primary—though not the only—purposes or functions of the approach: gathering endorsements and activating allies (E); seeking technical advice (A); and gathering feedback and political intelligence (F).

Although it does not appear in the table, there was fairly constant communication between the staff and Lanterman and Petris. Although Petris, having won his bid for the Senate seat, was by this time no longer in the Assembly, he still consulted frequently with Bolton and other Assembly staff members. Both he and Lanterman were pleased with the results of the staff work so far and strongly encouraged the staff effort. Staff work, however, was quickly approaching its limits. By late January it was important for the group to settle on a strategy for dealing with the legislature itself, and clearly some legislator had to take the responsibility for introducing the bill then in draft and acting as its floor manager. Petris was willing, but it seemed a poor strategy to launch the legislative career of this "delicately balanced ship" in senatorial waters. The leadership were known to be crusty old-timers, at least some of whom would have torpedoed the bill simply on the grounds that it was too sweeping and too complicated. Moreover, Petris was a freshman in the upper house, and practically none of the leadership had yet begun to notice his existence—or approve of it if they had. Lanterman, on the other hand, was the ideal sponsor. He was the dean of the Assembly Republicans, having first been elected in 1950, having been vice-chairman of the Ways and Means Committee, and being known for his strict sense of legislative duty. He was not so much admired for his political beliefs as liked and respected for his personal qualities. Ideologically, he styled himself "a conservative curmudgeon." It was no doubt his "conservative" respect for individual privacy that interested him in the commitments issue. He was also known as a long-time advocate of improvements in the public mental health system. He enjoyed himself greatly when at subcommittee hearings he could berate the ACLU witnesses for having ignored the mental commitments problem "for so many years," when

TABLE 11
POLITICAL COMMUNICATIONS OF SUBCOMMITTEE STAFF,
JANUARY 4 THROUGH FEBRUARY 10
(in approximately correct sequence)

Communication With[a]	By	Primary Purpose(s)
1. DMH legal expert, discuss guardianship (Sac.)	Vieg	A
2. DMH medical administrator believed sympathetic (Sac.)	Bolton	A, F
3. Berkeley psychiatrist, with interest in civil liberties (Berkeley)	Vieg	A
4. Continuing Education of the Bar (Berkeley)	Vieg	A
5. Tour through San Mateo Short–Doyle; discussion with Dr. Richard Levy, head of inpatient services and highly critical of report (San Mateo)	Both	A, F
6. CAMH annual meeting of local chapter presidents (Sac.)	Both	E
7. Director and program chief, Los Angeles Short–Doyle (L.A.)	Both	F, A, E
8. Two high-prestige psychiatric researchers and public hospital administrators (L.A.)	Bolton	E, A
9. Superior Court judge with experience on commitments bench (L.A.)	Both	A, ?
10. Los Angeles County Office of Public Guardian (L.A.)	Both	A
11. Los Angeles County Counsel's Office (L.A.)	Both	A. E
12. Los Angeles Welfare Planning Council special meeting arranged by WPC to discuss the report. Present: president of So. Calif. Psyciatric Society; L.A. regional office of DMH; head of L.A. Neuropsychiatric Institute; chairman of CMA Mental Health Committee; highly influential member of CAMH and Los Angeles MHA; counsel for CHA; Dr. Jack Lomas;[b] middle-echelon administrator in L.A. Short–Doyle; and others (L.A.)	Both	E, F, A
13. Dr. Duval, retired Assembly consultant, highly respected by Lanterman (Santa		

Communication With*	By	Primary Purpose(s)
Barbara)	Both	A, E
14. Prominent psychiatrist and hospital administrator, formerly in high DMH post (Sac.)	Bolton	A, E, F
15. CAMH Public Affairs Committee (Sac.)	Both	E
16. Key member of CSAC staff (Sac.)	Bolton	F, E, A
17. Former chairman of Governor's Advisory Commission on Mental Health, prominent judge, pres. of San Francisco MHA (S.F.)	Vieg	E, ?
18. Administrators from Alameda and San Francisco Short–Doyle, both respected and liked in Short–Doyle circles, presumed supporters of reform (S.F.)	Both	E, A, F
19. DMH regional director (place?)	Bolton	?
20. DMH program analyst (Sac.)	Bolton	?
21. CSAC Mental Health Advisory Committee, i.e., key Short–Doyle leaders (Sac.)	Both	E, F, A
22. ACLU lobbyist (Sac.)	Vieg	A
23. DMH Office of Program Review (Sac.)	Bolton	A
24. DMH official counsel (Sac.)	Vieg	A
25. ACLU lobbyist (Sac.)	Bolton	A
26. ACLU lobbyist (Sac.)	Vieg	A
27. Regional DMH administrator (?)	Bolton	A
28. Gordon Duffy, chairman of Assembly Public Health Committee (Sac.)	Both	F
29. California Nurses Association (place?)	Bolton	E
30. DMH legal counsel, and deputy director in charge of hospitals (Sac.)	Vieg	A, F
31. Chief, Bureau of Social Work (Sac.)	Vieg	A
32. ACLU lobbyist (Sac.)	Vieg	A
33. CSAC Mental Health Advisory Committee (Sac.)	Both, plus Roberts	E, F
34. CSAC Mental Health Committee (Sac.)	Both, plus Roberts	E, F
35. CAMH Board of Directors (Sac.)	Both, plus Roberts	E
36. Two-day Mental Health and Retardation Conference. Present: all Short–Doyle admin-		

Communication With [a]	By	Primary Purpose(s)
istrators; state hospital superintendents; DMH top echelon; leaders of CAMH and CCRC; and others (Sac.)	Both, plus Roberts	E, F, A

[a] Abbreviations of place names are: Sac. for Sacramento, L.A. for Los Angeles, and S.F. for San Francisco.

[b] Lomas was a key figure in many important circles in the mental health public: L.A. Welfare Planning Council (he had family ties to influential full-time staff); L.A. Short–Doyle (member of the advisory board); DMH (Medical Advisory Committee); organized psychiatry (delegate from Southern California Psychiatric Society to the California Inter-District Branch Committee); and CMA (long-time member of the Mental Health Committee). He also ran a private psychiatric hospital in the Los Angeles area.

he, Frank Lanterman, had been fighting since 1954 for the civil liberties of mental patients, first on behalf of the geriatrics and nonpsychotic seniles who were inappropriately committed or languished in atrociously maintained nursing homes and now on behalf of all the mentally ill! Lanterman's sponsorship would swing the Republicans and the conservatives behind the bill in the Assembly. Speaker Unruh, who favored the bill even though he would not put it high on his list of priorities, would bring the Democrats into the fold. The lower house would be a cinch for the bill if Lanterman agreed to manage it.

The only obstacle was pressure on Lanterman's time. As vice-chairman of Ways and Means, to him would fall the job of putting a Republican governor's controversial budget through a Democrat controlled Assembly. Of course, his role as administration spokesman made him all the more desirable as the bill's sponsor. The governor would surely owe Lanterman some reciprocity for his exertions on his behalf. What better reciprocity than the governor's public support for the commitment reform bill? In early February, Lanterman, probably spurred somewhat by a personal appeal from Waldie, agreed to introduce and manage the bill.

Pressure on the staff's time was also great. Intensive work on the drafting did not begin until mid-February, when Bolton and Vieg eased up on their circuit riding. By the end of the month Vieg had prepared a rough draft, which they mailed to some fifty blue-ribbon individuals in the attentive public requesting comments and criticism. The motives for this highly unusual move were again a mixture of advice seeking, support gathering, and intelligence collecting. Of these, the first was the most important. Circulating the draft bill was a means of getting answers to technical problems that it would have been too time-consuming for them to solve themselves. Implicitly they made use of the fact that expertise and political interest often go together. The interested would be eager to track down and report on the weaknesses in the draft bill. The subcommittee staff would then be in the position of the judge whose decision-making problems are simplified for him by the adversary character of Anglo–American courtroom procedure. Collating the replies and redrafting the bill all took time, though. The deadline for introducing bills was April 11. The Office of the Legislative Counsel would need at least a week to prepare the bill. A ten-day Easter recess would intervene from about March 22 onward. The draft would have to be submitted to the counsel's office before the recess, for in the week-long interval between reconvening and the deadline the counsel's office would be too busy to complete work on the subcommittee's bulky draft. This gave the staff at most three to four weeks to collate the replies of their blue-ribbon panel and decide on appropriate revisions. The revisions were considerable, it turned out. Details had been neglected in the original bill which to the draftsmen in Sacramento appeared trivial but which, say, to the admitting resident on the night shift at the county hospital psyciatric ward, were extremely important. Would he, for instance, be obliged to give voluntary admissions the same minor personal rights, like ready access to telephones, that the draft bill prescribed for involuntary admissions? The draft was ambiguous on such a point. To buy more time for clarification of the details, Lanterman introduced a "spot bill," numbered AB 1220 ("Coauthor: Senator Petris"), containing only its title, "The California Mental Health Act of 1967." The full text, inserted as "author's amendments," did not appear in print until April 28.

Lanterman more than once sat up with his staff assistants until the early morning hours scrutinizing his bill for the smallest political, practical, and editorial flaws. Petris was only slightly less diligent than Lanterman. Lanterman's first complete reading of the draft of what later became the April 28 "amendments" caused him to raise in earnest an issue that had received almost no serious discussion until that time. It was the obvious issue, in a sense, the issue Bolton and Waldie had long ago imagined might cause the reform effort to fail. In amazement Lanterman asked if Bolton and Vieg *really* meant to turn loose all those

123

potentially assaultive and homicidal patients? The Dilemma Report, which Lanterman had apparently not taken as seriously as he should have, had argued that persons who it was believed *might* commit a crime but had actually performed no criminal act should without exception be released from ESU units after being detained for the maximum of seventeeen days. To send them to state hospitals for an indefinite stay, which could easily mean a lifetime, the report said, amounted to preventive jailing. This was "a dangerous technique in a free society." Perhaps it would be acceptable if psychological diagnostic tools were sharp enough to discriminate the truly dangerous from the rest of the population, but all the professionals agreed that such tools were not then available.[23] Except for one or two hospital administrators and a few doubters at the December 14 NCPS meeting, Lanterman was the first to question the strict libertarianism of the report as applied to this category of patients. (Psychiatrists had previously argued for greater latitude to define a person as "gravely disabled.") The result of Lanterman's intervention at this point was a redrafting of the certification provision to permit detention for an additional ninety days for patients who had "threatened, attempted, or actually inflicted physical harm upon the person of another *after having been taken into custody for evaluation and treatment*" (emphasis added).

We count in Table 11 four entries mentioning the County Supervisors Association of California (CSAC). The subcommittee staff for many weeks cultivated their support and made enough (minor) concessions to the Short–Doyle leaders who sat on the Mental Health Advisory Committee to discourage them from trying to block the staff's efforts to gain CSAC's endorsement. The payoff came on April 6, when the Health and Welfare Committee, following one of Vieg's and Roberts' most compelling performances, voted to endorse AB 1220 "in principle." They also received formal endorsement from the CAMH (entry 35). A large number of other endorsements came into Lanterman's office by mail, from groups like CSPA, social work professional groups, and parent-teacher associations.

By the middle of April the controversy over the budget for fiscal 1968 was well under way. This was one of those contingencies Machiavelli called "Fortuna," and the Assembly group seized upon it to good advantage. The governor had certainly not anticipated the stormy reaction

---

23 Dilemma Report, pp. 143–145.

to his announced staff cuts. Although his popularity with the voters remained high, those with whom he was out of favor mentioned as their primary objection to him his cuts in the mental hospitals more often than any other reason.[24] His own party in the legislature was infuriated that neither he nor his aides had consulted with them or even bothered to inform them of what was coming. Lanterman, too, was angry; for he, Frank Lanterman, long-time friend of the mentally ill, beloved of the CAMH and CCRC, would have to defend the cuts in public. Not only were they indecent in his view; they were also unrealistic. Though an ardent and genuine admirer of the governor, Lanterman was not necessarily so devoted to his assistants. By haranguing the governor's deputies, the word got back to the governor that Lanterman expected the administration (including the DMH, of course!) to support AB 1220. Lanterman's sense for drama, and his natural fluency at thumping and blustering, brought results. In the end, the governor declared his support for the bill "in principle." It was not a strong endorsement, but it was better than nothing.

The first round of hearings began in the Assembly Public Health Committee on May 9. From beginning to end, the May 9 hearing was a masterpiece of legislative showmanship. Lanterman, Petris, and the staff arranged for the most impressive (and reliable) witnesses to come to Sacramento from all over the state. Petris: "This bill is the result of one of the most extensive studies ever conducted by a state legislature." Spencer Williams, director of the Health and Welfare Agency, speaking for Reagan: "I am here to announce the Governor's support in principle. . . . He himself made the announcement this morning." Lanterman: "The Mental Health Act of 1967 . . . is based on factual studies and the fullest participation of hundreds of people with different views. The final product represents a consensus and is generally regarded by all who have participated in its formulation as a major necessary step forward." Bolton gave a crisp summary of the general principles behind the bill. He was followed by Roberts, who came equipped to explain the com-

---

24 The California Field Poll reported, on May 11, that 38 percent of its sample had rated Reagan as doing a good job, and another 28 percent had credited him with a fair job. This rating surpassed any that Brown had received in the Field surveys in the period 1961–1965. However, 27 percent mentioned the proposed mental health cuts as a mark against him. More people mentioned this than any other issue. The next most unpopular item was his proposal to charge tuition at state universities and colleges for California residents; 15 percent mentioned this as a criticism. (San Francisco Chronicle, May 11, 1967.)

plex features of public finance in the bill with large pie charts, a flannel
board, and colorful cutouts. The Short–Doyle director from Alameda
County (Oakland and environs) told of the success of his program in
reducing the rate of commitments, and suggested that AB 1220 would
help them eliminate commitments entirely. No longer would they have
to expend tremendous energies to "*circumvent* the law and the courts."
Judge Karesh gave his usual stirring oration. Maurice Rodgers, spokesman for the California State Psychological Association (CSPA), called
it "the Magna Carta of the mentally ill." Even the DMH, loyal to the
governor, came forward to support AB 1220 in principle. The house or-
gan of the County Supervisors Association described the hearing as the
most impressive their reporter had ever seen in Sacramento.

Only one sign of trouble turned up at the hearing. Dr. John Stroud,
who claimed to be representing all of organized medicine and psychiatry
in California, declared, "Our reaction is quite favorable; we want to
help it work." But he appended, "There are still parts of it . . . which
might impede good patient care."

In the two weeks intervening between May 9 and May 23, the date set
for the second round of hearings in the Assembly Public Health Committee, medical opposition increased. Stroud appeared at the May 23
hearing to say that in the interim he had been in touch with Drs. Harry
Brickman and Richard Levy (of Los Angeles and San Mateo Short–
Doyle, respectively) who wanted to make sure that the bill did not "ab-
rogate medical responsibility." This appeared to have two meanings.
First, the evaluation unit staff should have more power to detain patients involuntarily if the staff believed it was in the patient's best
interest. Again, the definition of gravely disabled was challenged. Stroud
wanted it broadened to "unable to manage his personal affairs." Lanterman and Bolton courteously and circumlocutiously rejected the change.
Secondly, it meant that the law should specify that a physician or psychiatrist had to be the chief administrator of the whole system at the
county level. Lanterman dodged that request. Finally, Stroud raised
objections to the provisions for punitive damages that a patient illegally
detained might recover from the staff. The likely practical effect of this
provision was not so important to organized medicine as the symbolic
effect. Its implication, they felt, was that physicians might not always act
in the true interests of the patient or with proper concern for his liberties or dignity. Lanterman, Bolton, and Vieg agreed to circumscribe the
liability of the physician to malpractice suits for such actions, and made

a few other changes which they hoped would restore calm to organized medicine and keep their support behind the bill. It was the misfortune of the CMA, and the good fortune of the Assembly group, that Stroud had come to the hearing relatively unprepared and had apparently alienated most of the members of the committee.

The Short–Doyle director from Contra Costa County, Dr. George Degnan, then took the stand, commended Lanterman, and stated the opposition of the Conference of Local Mental Health Directors to the bill. Chairman Gordon Duffy, an astute liberal Republican who privately favored the bill (he had clearly been impressed by the May 9 hearing), evidently sensed a bluff. He forced Degnan to admit that he spoke only for the legislative committee of the conference, which had met and come to its resolution only that morning. Duffy pressed further. Just who were these members of the legislative committee? Degnan withdrew in favor of Dr. Harold Chope, the director of the San Mateo Short–Doyle program. Why did Short–Doyle object? asked Duffy of Chope. Chope made a weak reply about the bill's neglecting the problem of aftercare. Quickly sensing that aftercare was of slight concern to the committee, Chope came to the real point: AB 1220 appeared to limit the freedom for the local evaluation and treatment units to initiate expansion without hindrance from the state.[25]

Why should Chope have felt this way? First, let us observe that Short–Doyle no longer feared that it would be replaced or driven out of business by a competitive system. In March, AB 1220 had been redrafted so as to make it difficult for the county supervisors of any county to bypass Short–Doyle (if it existed in the county) or to appoint anyone other than the Short–Doyle director to "prepare and administer the county plan" for evaluation and treatment services that would effectively replace the commitment court-plus-hospital system.[26] This development

[25] "ESU" had by this time disappeared from the text of the bill. Some of Bolton's Short–Doyle allies convinced him that, among mental health professionals, "emergency service" had a very specific meaning, and ESUs were intended to serve a much broader function than their name implied. Moreover, they had become a symbol that evoked much anger in the opponents of the bill.

[26] Section 5050 of the bill read: "The board of supervisors . . . shall appoint a single administrator to prepare and supervise the county plan. The county administrator appointed shall be the county administrator of mental health services under the Short–Doyle Act, or other competent county administrator." In itself, this provision did not necessarily protect Short–Doyle. Sections 5052 and 5053, however, gave Short–Doyle some potential allies at the local level that would very likely have prevented the appointment from going to anyone other than the Short–Doyle director or program

was not without drawbacks, however, from Short–Doyle's viewpoint. If the Short–Doyle 3–1 matching formula continued in use, the counties would be net financial losers, having to pick up a financial burden that had hitherto been the state's. If the state paid 100 percent of the costs for the involuntary admissions, while the counties continued to fund services for the voluntary admissions according to the 3–1 formula, a complicated accounting problem might develop. The DMH strongly feared the latter problem; the CSAC, the former. The solution proposed by Bolton and Roberts—and contained in the version of AB 1220 under consideration at the May 23 hearing—was to fund *all* local mental health treatment and evaluation programs 100 percent with state monies. The matching system of Short–Doyle financing would be replaced by a fixed contribution to be made by each county (based on expenditures in fiscal 1968 plus annual increments automatically determined as a function of the county's population growth) and variable contributions made annually by the state. But here was a prospect truly anathema to Short–Doyle: state control. If the counties lost their right to initiate budget increases and therefore program expansion, the state would end up making decisions about the rate and the direction of growth of local programs. The state would also decide which counties' programs would grow and which would be forced to move slowly. San Mateo and Contra Costa, as represented by Chope and Degnan, respectively, evidently believed that relative to other counties their own Short–Doyle program packages were quite bulky (even if, in terms of "need," "too small"). The DMH would surely not pour more funds into San Mateo, Contra Costa, or the other relatively large programs until it had evened out the quality and scope of Short–Doyle programs for all counties in the state.

Dr. Richard Gerlach, director of Alameda Short–Doyle, directly followed Chope to the stand (at Lanterman's behest). He denied that the full conference had taken a position yet and questioned the legitimacy of the legislative committee's attempting to speak for the conference. He pointed out that San Mateo was a rich county and that the constric-

---

chief. Each county plan was to be subject to the authority of an advisory board. This board would "have authority to advise the county administrator and approve the county plan." Moreover, in a county where Short–Doyle was already operating, seven of the thirteen positions on the new board were to be given to members of the existing Short–Doyle advisory board. (Needless to say, in those few counties in which the advisory board disliked the Short–Doyle administrators, these potential allies were potential enemies.)

tions on local initiative Chope had mentioned would probably be felt more by San Mateo than by other counties. The lobbyist for the County Supervisors Association then stated CSAC's support in principle, recommended several changes that would give the counties slightly more money and more power over the new system, and repudiated the idea that Chope and Degnan might in any way be speaking for the CSAC.

Other witnesses at the hearing were a representative of the state Attorney General's Office, which claimed to be "delighted" with the bill; an ACLU lobbyist who reaffirmed the support of both the northern and southern California branches of his group; and a CSPA representative who reminded the committee of the value of the bill's "interdisciplinary features." This was implicitly, of course, a counterattack against the CMA's warnings that "medical responsibility might be abrogated."

The testimony at the hearing, important as it was for defining the strategic problem emerging for the sponsors of the bill, did not influence the outcome of the vote. The chairman, though he favored the bill, wanted to hold it over for two more weeks, so that his committee could report "a clean bill." He was joined in the motion against reporting it by Assemblyman Don Mulford, a conservative Republican. It was presumed Mulford was acting on behalf of the administration, which was growing more skeptical of the cost estimate attached to funding the new program. The two Democrats present had very probably been alerted by the Speaker that a successful do pass motion was needed that day. The swing vote—do pass—was cast by a freshman Republican who, recognizing himself trapped between hard stares from Lanterman and Mulford, could not but cringe at the irony of the chairman's politely inquiring "his pleasure."

Since early May, the same Dr. Levy mentioned in Stroud's testimony had attempted to organize professional and citizen groups in his county, and indeed in the whole San Francisco Bay Area, to oppose AB 1220. Although it is plausible that Levy was stimulated to action by the same institutional issues that concerned Chope, his administrative superior, it is more likely that ideological issues were even more salient to him. He considered himself a liberal, humane, and dedicated psychiatrist, possessed of an expertise that definitely enabled him to make more intelligent choices for patients than they could make for themselves. He viewed the proposed new law as a senseless, destructive change in fundamentally wise social arrangements. He had been assured by Miss Lois Scampini, an assistant county district attorney for San Mateo with seven years' experience in commitment work, that the present law was perfectly workable, and that AB 1220 was definitely unworkable. Chope brought both Levy and Scampini to the CSAC Health and Welfare Committee meeting of June 2. The three of them spoke against the bill.

That same day, the Conference of Local Mental Health Directors authorized its Legislative Committee to represent it with regard to future political action on AB 1220. Brickman, moreover, was empowered to speak for the Legislative Committee.[27] Since the CSAC and the Short–Doyle Conference were, by coincidence, holding meetings concurrently, both in Sacramento, it was simple enough for Brickman to join Chope, Levy, and Scampini at the afternoon session of the CSAC Health and Welfare Committee. The committee in effect rescinded the CSAC's previous endorsement in principle. It listed eleven recommendations for improvement which would constitute a stand-by policy for the CSAC in case the bill should pass out of the Assembly and start to move in the Senate. Most of the objections dealt with administrative and fiscal matters involving Short–Doyle and the powers of the local boards of supervisors; but one incorporated Levy's recommendation for a broader definition of gravely disabled: "a condition in which a person has a pronounced disturbance in judgment, thinking, or conduct as a result of mental disorder or impairment by chronic alcoholism."

Five days later Levy and Vaughan reported to the quarterly meeting of the NCPS leadership what had recently taken place in the legislature, in the Short–Doyle Conference, and at the CSAC meetings. Levy reported that ever since Bolton and Vieg had visited San Mateo in early January (see Table 11, entry 5), he had noticed their inclination to discount the advice of competent professionals, that is, medicine and psychiatry. He hastened to add that they had indeed accepted a lot of psychiatrically inspired amendments that certainly improved the bill— but not nearly enough. He regretted that he had been forced to bring Miss Scampini to the meeting of the CSAC; it had perhaps been slightly unprofessional on his part to involve a lawyer in medical matters. But the urgency of the matter was great. The bill had to be stopped or there would be no end of problems, administrative, legal, and medical. From the reactions on the faces of his audience, it was clear that they concurred with his judgment. This shows up in our NCPS sample as a 10

---

[27] Just why the conference agreed to this proposal is not clear. It is conceivable that some voting members did not understand that this would imply Short–Doyle's eventually going on record as opposing AB 1220.

percent decline in support for AB 1220 when "the issue was resolved" (Appendix A, item 48). Almost six months earlier Bolton and Vieg had papered over their differences with organized psychiatry while seated in the very same restaurant, but it was inevitable that the ideological rift between psychiatry and the subcommittee would one day reappear.

In recounting his problems dealing with Bolton and Vieg, Levy clearly illustrated how important was the monopoly on up-to-date information enjoyed by the legislative group. Only the Assembly group knew at any given moment what bargains had been struck with whom over what provisions of the bill. It was extremely difficult for persons outside of Sacramento (and even fairly difficult for anyone not in the inner circle of Lanterman, Petris, Bolton, Vieg, and Roberts) to know what the bill said yesterday that it no longer said today. Stroud's testimony at the May 23 hearing suffered at least in part because he had failed to obtain the amended version printed four days earlier. On the eve of the first Public Health Committee hearing, Levy, Brickman, Chope, Degnan, and the three key members of the legislative staff met to discuss the bill. Only Levy, of all the professionals there, had read the bill at all. It had been in print for only three days. Between April 28, when it was first printed in full, and July 11, when it was heard for the last time in committee, it was amended four times. And each set of amendments was quite substantial. The four sets contained altogether over 300 amendments.

The practically continuous flow of amendments would not have been so difficult to cope with if there had been more time between the date the bill finally got into print and the end of the session; or alternatively, if there had been fewer hearings and other procedures to which the bill had to be subjected before it would be finally passed or killed. Levy and the other opponents of the bill had no reason to appreciate the fact, but the shortage of time worked against the Assembly group in much the same way as it worked against the Short-Doyle leaders and the psychiatrists who opposed it.

Up to this point I have indicated the nature of organized support and opposition to the subcommittee's report and its complex, but sweeping, proposals for change. Formal organizational positions, however, do not necessarily reflect the distribution of attitudes of the individuals who are affiliated with them. In Table 12 we may see the distributions of opinion among several subgroups of the sample of individuals in the attentive public. We may observe, first, that 77 percent of the total sample

TABLE 12

INITIAL OPINIONS TOWARD THE COMMITMENT ISSUE,
BY SELECTED SUBSAMPLE AND TOTAL SAMPLE

(in percent)

	Short–Doyle	Bureau of Social Work	State Hospital Physi-cians	NCPS	CSPA	CAMH	Total Sample
Supporting AB 1220[a]	64	71	41	79	96	89	77
Opposing AB 1220	29	13	32	19	0	4	13
Neutral	7	16	27	2	4	8	10
Total Percent	100	100	100	100	100	101	100
Total Number[b]	14	101	22	48	24	27	527

[a] Based on item 47, Appendix A.

[b] Omits nonrespondents.

(excluding those few who had never heard of the issue) supported the subcommittee's proposed legislation and, second, that a clear majority of every subsample favored it except for the state hospital group. Though the number of Short–Doyle respondents is low, the results—two to one in favor—confirm impressions from interviews and field observations. The psychiatrists split four to one in favor.

Though many respondents may have been uneasy about the problems raised by Vaughan in his testimony and would have chosen—had they been given the option in our questionnaire—some response between unqualified support and neutrality, when forced to choose between a risky reform and the unpalatable status quo they chose the former. For the CSPA there was clearly no reason for ambivalence at all. Everything in the report was congenial to them. It was an attack on the medical model in nearly all its dimensions, and they saw in the proposed new system the possibility of increasing the size of the market for private practitioners of clinical psychology: if the evaluation and treatment units would be making referrals to private agencies and private vendors of professional services, then psychologists might easily be on the receiving end of those referrals. The rank and file of the bureau evidently went along with their spokesman, with only a handful of exceptions. The CAMH was solidly supportive. The state hospital group, like the DMH, contained a substantial minority who viewed the report as an unwarranted attack on state hospitals and a naive attempt to change proven and established ways of dealing with mentally ill patients. Table 13 suggests that ideological considerations also played a role in determining positions on the commitments issue. Respondents with a relatively traditionalist orientation were less disposed to support AB 1220 than were those with the opposite orientation. Still, although certain professions and ideological orientations liked the bill more than others, it is clear that it was generally popular throughout the attentive public.

TABLE 13
TRADITIONALISM AND ATTITUDES TOWARD AB 1220
(in percent)

	Traditionalism Index Quintiles				
	1	2	3	4	5
Favor	90	84	81	74	56
Oppose	7	8	10	13	25
Neutral	3	8	9	14	19
Total Percent	100	100	100	101	100
Total Number	113	110	101	95	108

On June 14, AB 1220 was cleared without debate by the Assembly Ways and Means Committee. On June 20, after a half hour of effusive praise all around—for Lanterman for his dedication and energy; for Unruh for his prescience in building such an able staff for the Assembly; for bipartisanship in the name of Progress—the Assembly voted 77 to 1 (with 2 abstentions) to send the bill to the Senate. The only nay vote was cast by the assemblyman from San Mateo. He was at that moment unusually sensitive to the opinions of the political influentials on the county board of supervisors because he was planning to run soon in a special election called to fill a recent vacancy in the U. S. House of Representatives.

In the Senate the bill had a poor prognosis. Petris' credit in the Senate had increased slightly over the past few months, but not by enough to overcome the anticipated resistance in that house. As a body the Senate was ill-disposed to sweeping policy changes, to state spending, to the "intellectuals" on the Assembly staff, and to Speaker Unruh himself. The Assembly proposed, the Senate disposed. In contrast to the "establishment" in the United States Senate, the one in the California Senate had been more reality than myth (in the summer of 1967, at any rate). Its members ran the key committees, they were readily identifiable, and they more often than not acted cohesively. They kept their power largely by means of skillfully juggling factions so as to prevent a majority of their colleagues from organizing to overthrow their regime. Of the five men at the hub of the Senate establishment, the only friend of the bill (Senator Eugene McAteer, of San Francisco) died a month before it reached the upper house. Two were thought to have been neutral or uninformed. There were two sure opponents, Senators Stephen Teale and George Miller, Jr.

Teale had reached the Senate in 1953 and had stayed there ever since. He was known as a moderate liberal on questions of social and economic policy. An osteopath himself, he laid claim to more expertise in the medical field than any of his legislative colleagues and over the years had become the standard by which many of them would choose their own opinions. Although osteopathic credentials were lightly esteemed by most of organized medicine, Teale nevertheless became one of their critical access points to legislative policy making. By an obvious logic, this made Teale the critical point of access for the Assembly group also. Intelligent but taciturn, Teale made it difficult for the managers of AB 1220 to take a reading on his views. His gruff exterior and his preference for monosyllabic utterance made him relatively unapproachable. Emanations from his office, however, suggested that he saw little merit in the bill. His own ideological leanings were more in the direction of the medical model than contrariwise, and probably quite strongly so. He had once worked as a psychiatric technician in a California MI hospital, moreover, and had seen at first-hand both the tragic chronicity of many of the patients and the extraordinary dedication of many of the staff. Teale was not exactly a staunch supporter of large custodial hospitals, but neither could he work up great enthusiasm for abolishing them in a hurry.

To clinch the matter, in his senatorial district were located the two MI hospitals reputed to be the worst in the system, Modesto and De Witt. In 1965 the legislative analyst had recommended closing Modesto and transferring the patients to other facilities in order to reduce DMH overhead expenditures. The analyst's report reiterated this recommendation in two successive years, and in 1967 it added to its proscribed list (without naming it explicitly) the second hospital in Teale's district.[28] Modesto had been saved in the past by pressure from the townspeople and the local California State Employees Association (CSEA). (Teale, in fact, had voluntarily come to their aid even before the legislative re-districting act of 1965 had added Modesto to his district.) During his 1966 campaign for the Democratic nomination for the state Senate, Teale told the *Modesto Bee* that the present hospital site was "prime property" for the DMH in that area, and that "anybody who talks about abandoning it is crazy." [29] The day before the general election Teale ran a three-column, full-length advertisement in the *Bee* which named first in the list of Teale's achievements his role in saving Modesto State Hospital. He lost the new county to his native son Republican opponent and returned to the Senate only by pulling down sizable majorities in his own mountain counties. To my knowledge, the Modesto State Hospital employees group was the only hospital CSEA chapter actively to oppose AB 1220, no doubt anticipating what a reduced population in-take might mean for the fate of their hospital. Teale was the logical audience for their grievances about AB 1220. What impact they had on him may be guessed at but not known positively.

There was perhaps, too, a strictly personal component in Teale's presumed opposition. For most of his fourteen years in the state Senate Teale had enjoyed close to a monopoly on expertise in the health field. But the two major legislative innovations in that field, Medi-Cal and Cal-Med, had both originated in the Assembly and they had been drafted in large part by Assembly staff. Unruh, moreover, seemed to be

[28] The analyst's recommendations actually had little to do with the quality of these two hospitals. It happened, simply, that both these hospitals were underpopulated. De Witt was northeast of Sacramento, near the foothills of the Sierras and relatively remote from major population centers. Modesto was located only thirty miles from Stockton State Hospital on U.S. Highway 99; and commitment court judges in that region generally preferred to send their charges to Stockton when possible. Both these hospitals were "temporary" structures built by the army in World War II and taken over by the DMH immediately after the war to relieve overcrowding. Their construction was in fact much more sturdy than it appeared; but the overall layout—long strings of barracks-like buildings connected occasionally by T-shaped junctions—was depressing. Even without assistance from the legislature, the DMH, prior to 1965, had considered closing Modesto. It is worth pointing out that the analyst's 1966 report also recommended closing Mendocino State Hospital, another small hospital in a rural area. Unlike the others, however, Mendocino was reputed to be the best hospital in the state MI system.

[29] *Modesto Bee*, February 23, 1966. The *Bee* also reported that the Democratic primary had been a "hot" one (June 3, 1966).

picking up the political credit. If Teale had supported the bill on other grounds, these personal considerations would probably not have moved him from his convictions. Given his already negative opinion, though, such feelings, if they existed, could only serve to intensify his resolve to kill AB 1220.

Like Teale, Miller was an old-timer in the Senate. He had first come to the Assembly in 1947 and moved to the upper chamber only two years later. Again, very much like Teale, he was a Democrat with a reputation as a moderate liberal. Although he himself had no strong ideological or professional interests in the health fields, Dr. George Degnan was a close friend, neighbor, and political adviser. The friendship had begun when the two played high school football together and it had remained strong ever since. It was widely believed among both friends and enemies of AB 1220 that Degnan could sway Miller against the bill without much trouble, and that Miller's personal influence with his colleagues, when combined with his formidable powers as chairman of the Senate Finance Committee, which would have to pass on the bill, would be sufficient to kill it.

Assembly and Senate were two different fraternities in California legislative life. Members of one did not ordinarily have much to do with members of the other.[30] Senators typically disdained to use professional staff, relying for advice on the lobbies, the analyst's office, other senators, and their hunches. Thus, Lanterman had no lines of communication with the Senate establishment, and Bolton, Vieg, and Roberts had no more than two or three staff counterparts on the Senate side with whom they could usefully talk.

To the astonishment of the Assembly group and their allies, AB 1220 was first referred to the Senate Social Welfare Committee. This committee was chaired by Clair Burgener, a long-time friend of the CAMH and CCRC and a supporter of the bill. If this was merely an error, however, it was corrected soon enough. AB 1220 was withdrawn from Burgener's committee and sent to the Senate Committee on Governmental Efficiency and Economy (G.E. Committee), an acknowledged graveyard of legislation. Buried there side by side were bills of all ideological persuasions, bills of great and small complexity, bills of Republican and Democratic hue, bills of Senate and House authorship. AB 1220 was as good as dead, and its executioner was alleged to have been Senator

[30] Barriers began to break down slightly in 1967, when, following redistricting, more than ten former assemblymen moved into Senate seats.

Teale, who, it was believed, had successfully urged the move on his establishment colleague, Speaker Pro Tempore Hugh Burns.

On July 11, the G.E. Committee did its customary work. Lanterman, Petris, and the staff had prepared for a committee showdown as though they still believed they had a chance to win. Two weeks earlier they had sent to all persons on their mailing list the latest copy of the amended bill, a summary of its contents, a list of all the important group endorsements thus far accumulated, and, most significantly, a xerox copy of a letter of support from the Attorney General's Office which effectively undermined Miss Scampini's legal interpretations. The cover letter in this package ostensibly solicited opinions about some still controversial provisions in their bill, but the bill's managers would have been able to represent all the responses to their request for criticism and comment as evidence of widespread desire to get some bill like AB 1220 passed that session.[31] They also distributed to all committee members a copy of an opinion from Alan Post, the legislative analyst, implicitly contradicting CSAC's allegation that an extra financial burden would be shifted onto the counties. They arranged for their prize witnesses to be on hand, those with special oratorical skill; however, few of them got to speak. The committee members permitted brief introductory remarks from Lanterman and Petris and then filled most of the rest of the evening with opposition spokesmen (Degnan, Levy, the San Mateo district attorney, CSAC, and another Short–Doyle director opposed to the bill). The members of the committee interrupted frequently to help run out the clock.

As the hearing wore on, Lanterman's frustration mounted. The chairman (Burns) yielded to Lanterman's protests, but warned Lanterman that the hour was drawing late. The hearing could not proceed, so far as he was concerned, past 11 P.M. Still acting as though the committee could be persuaded, Bolton rushed Karesh to the stand. Emotions (mainly anger) were running high in the audience, and Karesh took every advantage of the fact. The committee was evidently impressed— but not very much. Stroud followed Karesh. He might as well have been working for the bill's opponents, for he spent more time indicat-

---

[31] Responses to the opinion survey were also sure to legitimate their own views. Consider, for instance, the definition of one set of alternatives: "Some psychiatrists believe that the definition of gravely disabled should be rewritten to permit the involuntary treatment of *any* person considered to be mentally disordered. Others, such as the Director of the Department of Mental Hygiene, believe that involuntary services should be imposed on a more limited group."

ing what was wrong with the bill than what was right with it. This exchange with Teale was typical: Teale—"Then you would say, would you, Dr. Stroud, that if someone has been committed, there is probably something wrong with him, some illness?" Stroud—"Yes, Senator, if someone is committed there must be something wrong with him."

The committee "took the bill under submission." This meant they could allow the legislative session to end, and the bill's life with it, without having to commit themselves publicly to voting against it.

Within a week following the Senate committee hearing, Lanterman had become chairman of a newly created Ways and Means subcommittee instructed to study four or five Senate-originated bills just then arriving in the lower house for concurrence. All were warmly desired by both the County Supervisors Association and Short–Doyle, for most of them, in one way or another, gave the counties more state money for Short–Doyle. It quickly became clear that these bills would be held hostage in committee pending a more cooperative attitude by the CSAC and Short–Doyle with regard to commitment reform. If the session expired with all sides the losers, the game could be continued into the next session. In Bolton's mind, there was no question who would have to give in first; and if they were acting rationally, they would come to the same conclusion and give in immediately.

The *coup de grace* was dealt by the legislative rider weapon. With the blessings of Speaker Unruh the Assembly group sought to reanimate the lifeless AB 1220 by having it amended in toto into Senate Bill 677, one of those then being held in Lanterman's subcommittee. It provided for across-the-board matching funds for all Short–Doyle programs at the 75-25 rate. This would have been especially advantageous to the counties with large programs, whose expansion had proceeded rapidly before 1963 and whose expenditures for these services were still being reimbursed under the old 50-50 formula. The author of SB 677 was Senator Alan Short (of Short–Doyle). The simplest procedure would have been to have Short graft AB 1220 onto his bill by submitting "author's amendments." Senator Short, however, appeared indifferent, perhaps even unsympathetic, to AB 1220. At the July 11 hearing of the Senate G.E. Committee, Short had filibustered at greater length than any other member of the committee. Would he go along?

Perhaps fearful lest he alienate Lanterman, Unruh, or other powers in the Assembly and have his pet bills defeated for the rest of his legislative career, and perhaps reluctant to risk alienating the CAMH and the rest of the attentive public that backed the Assembly group, Short did go along. The amended SB 677, now titled the Lanterman–Petris–Short bill, cleared the Assembly speedily. It was sent back to the Senate.

Under Senate standing rules a bill originating in that house and subsequently amended by the Assembly might return straight to the Senate floor for a vote on concurrence in the Assembly's amendments. It could thereby outflank the Senate's committee structure. Alternatively, the speaker pro tempore, following a determination by the legislative counsel that the original bill had been amended substantially, could re-refer the amended bill to "the appropriate standing committee of the Senate." For the managers of SB 677, the critical problem was to persuade Senator Burns to permit the bill to come straight to the floor rather than have it sent back to the G.E. Committee. If the Senate refused concurrence, the battle might still be won in the conference committee.

For reasons that are still obscure, Burns did permit SB 677 to reach the Senate floor without being re-referred. Following a vote of nonconcurrence, the bill was sent to conference. Burns was probably confident that the conference committee would kill the bill or else simply allow the bill to expire automatically when the session ended in a few more days. It is possible, too, that Burns or whoever was advising him on the question hoped that the conference committee might delete the forty-page rider and pass out the original one-page version of SB 677.[32] Burns appointed to the conference committee himself, Teale, and Senator Jack Schrade, a conservative Republican from southern California. Since at least two votes from each House's three-man delegation were necessary to report a bill out of conference favorably, Teale and presumably Schrade could stop the bill without additional help.

Burns then acted even more inexplicably than when he had permitted the bill to go to conference. At Petris' request, he allowed Petris to replace himself on the Senate conference delegation. If Burns truly wanted to kill the bill, and if he understood that the Assembly delegation would stand uniformly behind it—both of which assumptions are plausible—he was necessarily counting heavily on Schrade's voting with Teale.

Late Friday afternoon, August 4, Schrade asked to be removed from

---

[32] The only certainties are that Short agreed with Burns before the floor vote that he would move for nonconcurrence and thereby send the bill to conference—he would not try to win a straight fight on the floor—and that the Democratic majority leader of the Assembly, George Zenovich, who like Burns came from Fresno, spent ten minutes in intense conversation with Burns on the Senate floor not long before Burns brought SB 677 to a vote.

the conference delegation. He was replaced by Senator John Schmitz, of Orange County, the only acknowledged member of the John Birch Society in either house. Schmitz now owned the swing vote on the conference committee.

Since the conference committee would meet first on the following day, Saturday, and the legislative session would end no later than Sunday, Bolton, Vieg, and Roberts spent the afternoon and night on the telephone. They were desperately trying to find someone who had enough credit with Schmitz to persuade him to vote with the Assembly delegation.

They did not succeed. However, they did discover in their file of endorsements sent by various groups a letter of support for the Dilemma Report from the public relations director of the Santa Ana Freedom League, a right-wing group from Orange County. This was exactly the right cue for Schmitz. He and the writer, it developed, were old friends. After a lengthy conference committee meeting on Saturday morning, Schmitz indicated he would support the bill if, by the following day, a new version could be drafted that eliminated the funding provisions and other features designed to assist the expansion of local mental health programs. Lanterman and Petris agreed. On Sunday morning the Assembly staff presented Schmitz with an SB 677 revised to meet his requirements. It also met the principal requirements of the Assembly group. Except for the gravely disabled and the visibly dangerous, involuntary detention was limited to a maximum of seventeen days. For the gravely disabled, the guardianship mechanism was retained.[33] Patients were still guaranteed the right to refuse treatment. The multidisciplinary evaluation and treatment features were retained. Schmitz voted with the three assemblymen and with Petris to report SB 677 favorably. Outnumbered five-to-one, Teale also signed the report.[34] Later that afternoon, only a few hours before the end of the legislative session, both houses passed the revised version of SB 677 without dissent. A week later the governor signed it into law.

[33] The technical term employed by the bill was not "guardianship" but "conservatorship." The bill also stipulated that conservatorship was automatically self-terminating after one year, and that the responsibility was on the conservator to have his powers renewed by the court if he wished to do so.

[34] It is probable that Teale's acquiescence was somewhat more complicated than this description suggests. Possibly Teale also wished to avoid alienating Lanterman. Perhaps, too, he felt that on balance the bill should be supported on its merits.

5

The Great Budget Controversy

On March 14, 1967, Governor Ronald Reagan announced that his budget for the coming fiscal year would eliminate funds for some 3,700 positions in the Department of Mental Hygiene. Most of these positions would be deleted from the state hospitals for the mentally ill. The remainder would be taken from the state's day treatment centers in San Francisco, Los Angeles, and San Diego; from preadmission and aftercare clinics in six California cities; and from screening units for the mentally retarded in three cities. All of these would be closed down unless the counties opted to bear a large part of the operating costs. The governor's budget also proposed to withdraw support from the Geriatric Screening Unit in San Francisco and from the Alcoholic Treatment Program at Mendocino State Hospital, both nationally recognized programs.

Following a heated public controversy lasting over three months, the governor backed down from his intention to close most of the community clinics but gained his major point by cutting the funds for over 3,000 positions in the hospitals for the mentally ill. Since the governor of California, unlike the president of the United States, has the constitutional power to veto single items in an appropriations bill, he has the legal means to cut the legislature's budget by as much as he pleases and in any way he chooses. He is constrained only by the right of two-thirds

Note—I wish to acknowledge the assistance of Dr. Alfred Auerback in the preparation of this chapter. This chapter is a modified and expanded version of a paper we delivered at the 123rd Annual Meeting of the American Psychiatric Association, Boston, Massachusetts, May 13–17, 1968, entitled "The Political Vulnerability of State Mental Hospitals." Dr. Auerback bears no responsibility, of course, for the interpretations contained herein.

of the legislature to override his vetoes. Although the legislature restored most of the DMH positions eliminated in the governor's budget, Reagan blue-penciled most of them. Nearly all the cuts fell on the hospitals for the mentally ill. The budget for these institutions declined from $122 million in fiscal 1967 to $112 million in fiscal 1968. Hospitals for the mentally retarded, on the other hand, received a slight increase in funds, as did the two prestigious neuropsychiatric institutes. The total state budget actually increased over the previous year's. Why, then, did the hospitals for the mentally ill fare so poorly? What were the special features of these institutions that made them peculiarly vulnerable to attack? To answer these questions we may begin by describing the nature of the attack and the means of defense that were used.

ADMINISTRATION ATTITUDES

Six weeks prior to the administration's March 14 announcement, the California Commission on Staffing Standards had published the conclusions of its eighteen-month study of California hospitals for the mentally ill and mentally retarded. The commission had employed systems analysts from Aerojet General Corporation to develop a procedure for evaluating the needs of newly admitted and resident patients and for determining the staffing requirements to meet this work load. The commission's report concluded that patient care in hospitals for the mentally ill was 32 percent below an acceptable level. The hospitals for the mentally retarded were 38 percent below the acceptable minimum. The commission recommended a substantial increase in staff levels. Its clear implication was that more funds were badly needed.

The findings of the commission, however, ran counter to the governor's personal beliefs and political pledges. His conservative Republican principles prescribed drastic curtailment of state spending. The state treasury, he claimed, had been "looted" by eight years of Democratic rule; state government was overexpanded and inefficient. When the cuts were announced, though, the administration at the same time claimed that there would be no reduction in the current level of patient care. It alleged that this could be accomplished by reducing the resident patient population in tandem with the staff layoffs, which would be spaced over a fifteen-month period. Since the average daily population in hospitals for the mentally ill had declined from 35,743 in 1962 to 26,567 in 1966, the continuation of this rate would by itself reduce the patient population by more than enough to maintain the current staff-patient ratio. Because staffing patterns had not been changed during that period, the administration claimed that the level of patient care was, quite automatically, being continually "enriched." It said it did not intend to reverse the trend toward improved care, but only to "hold the line" for a year while the state's financial situation improved.

Although many of Reagan's backers and supporters leaned rather far toward the political Right,[1] where opposition to the mental health movement was often strong, there was no evidence of a connection between the ideology of the anti-mental-health movement and Reagan's budgetary decisions. Indeed, there was inferential evidence to the contrary. First, although right-wing groups had opposed Short–Doyle since its inception in 1957, they had not since then paid much attention to the state hospitals. Secondly, Reagan had publicly pronounced himself a friend of mental health, pointing to the fact that he supported a $4.7 million dollar increase in fiscal 1968 for Short–Doyle.[2] Finally, Reagan once characterized state hospitals as "in a sense, hotel operations," i.e., a place where the slothful went for a rest.[3] Whereas the extreme right wing would have seen in the hospitals political prisons, it is the traditional conservative that thinks first of waste and indolence.

THE OPPOSITION

Many groups and individuals, including both professionals and laymen, immediately and vehemently protested the governor's decision. This opposition movement included: (1) a large number of state legislators, who for partisan, ideological, political, or personal reasons opposed the cuts; (2) businessmen, civic leaders, and public officials in communities that counted heavily on hospital payrolls to sustain the local economy; (3) the large and politically significant California State Employees Association (CSEA), in which the largest membership bloc was made up of DMH employees; (4) state and local chapters of mental health professional organizations; and (5) two large citizen groups, the California

[1] H. Sutton, "Politics in the Palm Islands," *Saturday Review*, September 23, 1967, p. 22.

[2] In fact, this money barely covered Short–Doyle's higher expenditures attributable to generally increased costs in medical and related services and to recently established programs for which the state had already pledged reimbursement to the counties. Reagan was making a virtue out of necessity.

[3] *San Francisco Chronicle*, June 1, 1966.

Association for Mental Health (CAMH) and the California Council for Retarded Children (CCRC). In our sample of the attentive mental health public, 77 percent opposed the cuts at the outset and 6 percent supported them. Another 7 percent favored effecting staff cuts by closing certain hospitals, and 3 percent were neutral. Very little shift in attitudes occurred by the time the issue was resolved.

Since the governor's legal powers to cut the budget were so great, the opposition was forced to find some means of changing Reagan's mind about using them. Direct approaches were made to the governor himself, to his high-level aides, and to legislators of both political parties. They used the mass media to stir opposition in the general public. They mobilized organizational support of all kinds. They set up a statewide committee to coordinate a publicity offensive. To give authority and substance to their arguments, the opposition drew on the report of the California Commission on Staffing Standards. Lacking the resources to bargain with the governor, the opposition fell back on a strategy of persuading him that their cause was reasonable and just. To this end, the support of public opinion would be useful; and to gain it, they were able to employ resources they did have, namely effective ideological arguments, high energy, and numerical strength.

The newspapers were generally sympathetic to the opposition. A survey taken in mid-April by the CAMH showed thirty-two papers disagreeing editorially with the governor's position and eighteen in some degree of sympathy. The *Los Angeles Times* ultimately called it "false economy."[4] The *Bee* chain, which dominated circulation in the Central Valley, said "callous regression."[5] More important even than editorial support was sympathetic news coverage, which the opposition received in abundance. Newspaper reporters visited the state mental hospitals and wrote vividly of their poor conditions and of the sharp decline in staff morale. Many television and radio stations supported the opposition. Television cameras took viewers into hospital wards. Stations aired debates between administration and opposition spokesmen. The projected cuts were the subject of numerous call-in radio and TV shows. This sympathetic treatment by the media helped the opposition in two important ways. First, the media influenced public opinion at the mass level. A statewide survey in June, conducted by the respected California Field Poll, showed 58 percent of the statewide sample opposed to the

[4] *Los Angeles Times*, April 11, 1967.
[5] *Sacramento Bee*, April 6, 1967.

cuts and 23 percent who endorsed them. Secondly, they stimulated many legislators and other political elites to press for a modification, if not a complete reversal, of the governor's stand. Even Republican legislators urged him to reconsider the cuts.

During the entire controversy, spokesmen for the Reagan administration constantly stressed the governor's intention to maintain the existing level of care. The more heated the controversy became, the harder these spokesmen tried to make this promise credible. Lowry began to tell his professional colleagues that he had "a letter in his pocket" from the governor that confirmed this intention. To all appearances, the governor's promise had no effect. I spoke to no one who took it seriously. It was not so much that the opposition doubted the sincerity or honesty of Governor Reagan as a person, but that they treated the promise as merely political, worthy only of being ignored.

In mid-April an ad hoc group sprang up called the Citizen Committee for Improved Treatment in Our State Hospitals. It brought under one umbrella many key groups opposing the cuts. The Citizen Committee put out a weekly newsletter, which circulated basic information about the hospitals relevant to making a case against the cuts and up-to-date news on tactical developments. They raised over $40,000 to hire a public relations firm and to sponsor radio and TV commercials in five populous areas of the state.

The professional associations lent authority and the image of disinterestedness to the opposition's activities. The California district branches of the American Psychiatric Association, organized psychology, social work, and nursing—all went on record in opposition to the cuts. Psychiatrists tended to assume the role of spokesmen for all the mental health professions, since all more or less acknowledged the relatively greater visibility and prestige of psychiatry to the general public. Psychiatrists were the most prominent witnesses at legislative hearings and were the only professionals included in a delegation of opposition leaders that met with the governor. An illustrative measure of their prominence as spokesmen is the fact that Reagan singled them out for insult by publicly labeling them "headshrinkers."

POLITICAL VULNERABILITY OF THE HOSPITALS

As much support as the opposition did collect, it was evidently not quite enough. One reason is that they began with a critical deficiency: the state MI hopitals lacked a weighty clientele.[6] Except perhaps for felons in penal institutions, one can scarcely imagine a group more lacking in influence than individuals treated by the state hospitals for the mentally ill. Patients committed involuntarily, who until the mid-1960s probably comprised the majority of first admissions, lost the right to vote while in the hospital and for at least six months after discharge. Collective action was made difficult by the reluctance of former patients to be identified as such. Many were socially and economically deprived persons who had neither the time nor the money to become involved in effective political action. Finally, former patients often felt that their stay in the hospital was an abuse, not a benefit, and therefore had no incentive to act as hospital advocates or supporters.

Of course, a clientele group may have others to look out for its interests. Because the clientele of the community-based clinics, like the day treatment centers, were geographically concentrated, their families and their community leaders had a more concrete sense of the relevance of these facilities to the well-being of their particular communities. The city of San Francisco, in particular, led by its elected officials, successfully raised a storm of protest. Short–Doyle was buttressed politically by the weighty County Supervisors Association; the hospitals for the retarded by many middle class—and highly motivated—families with retarded children; and the neuropsychiatric institutes by the universities, organized medicine, and nearly everyone concerned with the state's progressive image.

The defenders of the state MI hospitals, however, were not quite so weighty. In contrast to the San Francisco protest, for instance, the local opposition aroused by the prospect of payroll losses did not act with a great sense of emergency. After all, no one was threatening to close any hospitals entirely. Moreover, the localities within which the hospitals were located were far less populous, even though more numerous, than the communities threatened by the closure of the outpatient clinics. Or-

---

[6] The influential Farm Bureau Federation, for example, provides weighty clientele support to the United States Department of Agriculture. Richard Fenno, *The Power of the Purse* (Boston: Little, Brown, 1967), pp. 366–371. A thorough study of four national agencies and their budgetary strategies revealed a perfect correlation between the degree of public support an agency could muster at appropriations hearings and its assertiveness, as measured by indicators such as the size of budget increases sought annually and the willingness to seek restorations in cuts by budget officers at higher administrative levels or in the Bureau of the Budget itself. Ira Sharkansky, "Four Agencies and an Appropriations Subcommittee: A Comparative Study of Budget Strategies," *Midwest Journal of Political Science* 9 (August 1965): 254–281.

ganized psychiatry and medicine had a much greater emotional and practical stake in the neuropsychiatric institutes than they had in the MI hospitals. Although officers of the Psychiatric Association district branches and many individual members expended considerable energy in defending the interests of the hospital clientele (and potential clientele), not all of them did so. Like most other groups, psychiatrists are not all of one mind. There was but a weak connection between psychiatry as it was practiced in state hospitals and psychiatry as it was practiced in the private sector. Many psychiatrists in private practice had had little or no experience with public mental institutions. As one CAMH leader put it, "In my county, which is full of psychiatrists, 95 percent of them have never visited [the nearby mental hospital]. What can they possibly know about their problems?" Four hundred members of the Northern California Psychiatric Society and 695 members of the comparable southern group did sign a petition stating opposition to the administration's proposed cuts. This amounted to two-thirds of the membership in both societies. Though from one point of view this was a strong showing, it should also be noted that one-third did not sign. Most of the top psychiatric and medical administrators of the Short–Doyle programs also kept silent, evidently not wishing to jeopardize the political standing of their own programs. Finally, most psychiatrists were Democrats and liberals, and hence, did not have the political credentials to gain favors or concessions from a conservative Republican governor.

By refusing to take a stand on the projected cuts, the California Medical Association in effect acquiesced in them. Many psychiatrists tried to influence the CMA to oppose the cuts, but they were distinctly a minority voice within the association. The CMA Council, moreover, had other medical issues before the legislature—for example, a legalized-abortion bill and a proposal for increasing fees under Medi-Cal—and did not wish to antagonize either legislators or the governor. The psychiatrists' efforts to circumvent the council and bring the issue before the CMA House of Delegates meeting in mid-April were undone by an unusual contretemps. The DMH director assured the CMA Council on the eve of the delegates meeting that all was under control and that there would be no reduction in the level of care. A summary of his testimony subsequently circulated among CMA delegates stated that "no reductions were proposed for patient care personnel in hospitals for the *mentally ill.*" This was an error. Lowry had been talking about hospitals

THE SKILL FACTOR IN POLITICS

for the mentally retarded. There was not enough time for the psychiatrists at the CMA meeting to correct the impression left by this statement, however, and it effectively terminated their efforts to force the issue to the floor of the meeting.[7]

LOWRY IN A BIND

Lowry's public support of the governor's position was a serious blow to the opposition. It is likely that he was taken by surprise by the March 14 announcement. He was caught suddenly in the classic bind of being forced to violate either professional norms dictating preeminent concern for patient well-being or administrative norms prescribing loyalty and obedience to superiors. When he chose the latter, he immediately forfeited his high standing among many legislators, mental health professionals, and large sectors of the public. These persons thenceforth discounted his statements; but many others, especially if predisposed to support the governor anyway, interpreted Lowry's support as demonstrating the professional soundness of the cuts. The governor and his staff repeatedly stated that the cuts had been proposed by Lowry himself. They observed that Lowry's professional reputation was so illustrious that the very persons who then denied him had once urged Reagan, successfully, to keep him on at the DMH even though he was originally appointed by Reagan's Democratic predecessor. In this, the administration misrepresented Lowry's actual role, since Lowry had in fact opposed the cuts themselves even while proposing a minimally disruptive way of making them. Not until April 20, however, at a legislative hearing, did Lowry indicate publicly that in his professional judgment the cuts "could not be recommended."

In my view, Lowry was playing a more subtle game—though not a more successful one—than the opposition gave him credit for. Caught by surprise by the March 14 announcement and not a little dismayed and angered by it, he nevertheless decided to stick by his job and try to

7 William Schwartzman, "The California Mental Health Controversy" (unpublished paper, 1967). Schwartzman was a psychiatrist at Napa State Hospital at the time of the budget controversy. His interpretation of the events at Los Angeles, which he witnessed first-hand, has been disputed by Lowry in minor ways. Neither Schwartzman nor any other observer, so far as I know, is prepared to regard the significant misquotation of Lowry's remarks as intentional.

salvage what he could from the wreckage.[8] The game he decided to play from then on was the one he had learned during his almost twenty years with the United States Public Health Service, much of that time spent in Washington. The informal rules of that game give an administrator the opportunity to appeal to the Congress, on professional or any other grounds, for appropriations in excess of the amount formally approved by his superiors. The informal Washington norms prescribe that (1) administrators must speak officially on behalf of their nominal superior, the president; (2) they must, in their official capacities, defend his recommendations and policies; (3) they must volunteer no information that might be used to attack his policies or recommendations; (4) their private disagreements may be legitimately expressed in public only if they clearly establish that they are voicing personal rather than official sentiments; (5) giving voice to their private sentiments must await their being elicited by some outside agent, like a congressman or a reporter, who puts very direct questions to them on the matter. In early February, while a hiring freeze ordered by the governor was in effect but before the budget cut had been announced, at a meeting of hospital trustees and superintendents Lowry off-handedly remarked that, in the unlikely event of a severe budget cut for the DMH, he would follow this ritual. He urged his worried audience to follow a course of restraint until his own negotiations with the Department of Finance had been concluded. He tentatively expressed his faith that these negotiations would be successful, that the Department of Finance representatives would recognize the imprudence of drastic staff cuts in the MI hospitals.

That Lowry actually did follow this ritual is suggested by the correspondence between his own testimony before the Assembly Ways and Means Subcommittee reviewing the governor's Mental Hygiene budget

[8] I must emphasize that this interpretation of Lowry's actions immediately following the March 14 announcement is based on inference only, but it is at least consistent with the accounts of persons who spoke with him during that period. Shrewd pragmatist that he is, Lowry must have reckoned that resigning in a huff would have only hurt in the long run. Reagan would have filled his position with someone less competent, less dedicated, and less inclined to press the department's views in budgetary matters in future years. The interpretation of Lowry's motives is strictly irrelevant to my own argument, but since there were many in the attentive public who strongly criticized what they conceived to be his motives, I feel obliged to make my own reasoning explicit. I never discussed the question with Lowry directly, however, nor to my knowledge has anyone else. Lowry was known as a man who "keeps his cards close to his vest."

requests and the remarks of an unidentified Washington agency chief recorded by Richard Fenno in his monumental work on federal appropriations politics. Fenno's Washington official said, "If they [the members of the House appropriations subcommittee reviewing the budget for the official's agency] ask me directly what my professional judgment is as to whether we can use any more money, I will tell them honestly. They may ask me what I was planning to do with the money cut out by the Budget Bureau. If they ask me a direct question, I will answer them. I will give them my professional judgment, though I will say that as to a fiscal judgment I cannot say. After all, I am a member of the executive family."[9]

Lowry told the Assembly subcommittee, "The July 1966 level of patient care in the hospitals for the mentally ill and the mentally retarded does not meet the California standards of 1952. Therefore, the continuance of that level of care could not be recommended from a professional standpoint; unfortunately, the Governor and the Legislature have to consider many factors in making decisions about the State budget. Fiscal necessity may dictate undesired economies. Such decisions are painful to those who make them and to those who are affected."[10]

At least in the beginning, Lowry might have expected the opposition to grab onto the fact of his professional disengagement from Reagan's policy and put it to good rhetorical use. As the controversy intensified, however, Lowry found himself increasingly on the defensive. Instead of the opposition helping him to disengage from the governor and his chief personal aides, they drove him more tightly into their embrace. The governor himself became increasingly angry at the intensity of the campaign waged by the opposition. Indeed, by the middle of June, he was accusing them of "blackmail"; and his appointed director of the Health and Welfare Agency publicly speculated that certain hospital employees were deliberately attempting to "sabotage" patient care in order to build a case against the administration.

Lowry too, it seems, came to share their anger. In an interview that took place after the budget had been passed and signed into law by the governor, he remarked disconsolately that there was no code of proper conduct among state employees of the sort that he had known among federal employees. There was no reluctance to violate the proper secrecy that should surround the budget before the governor formally presented

9 Fenno, p. 392.
10 Lowry to author, private communication, September 8, 1967.

it to the legislature. There was no understanding of the proprieties involved in limiting the kind of advocacy that an official might undertake. In Washington there was "a more orderly progression"; political transactions were more businesslike. Politics in California seemed to him much more vituperative and personalized. Lowry was correct. His erstwhile allies had not understood how to give him his needed cues; indeed they seemed to provide only the ones that necessarily drove him more deeply into league with his superiors. Not understanding the differences between the culture of Sacramento and the culture of Washington, Lowry, so far as I can determine, did little or nothing to instruct them how to help *him* help *them*. Consequently, he was obliged to wait until April 20 to deliver his half-hearted lines, a moment altogether too belated to do the opposition any good.[11]

11 If Lowry was borrowing inappropriate principles from the textbook of Washington politics, he had at least a chance to learn them at the right agency. During the period from 1947 to 1962, appropriations for the U.S. Public Health Service grew at an average annual rate of 15.3 percent, the fourth highest growth rate of the thirty-six agencies studied by Fenno (p. 392).

6

The Psychology Licensing
Act of 1967

Politicians, judges, and lawyers, being prudent men, generally ignore their frequent opportunities to intervene in the professional rivalries among the mental health practitioners. Sometimes, however, these opportunities come in the form of responsibilities, and as such, they cannot easily be ignored. When an agency of state government requests counsel from the Office of the California State Attorney General, the latter is under most circumstances obliged to render some sort of opinion. On June 14, 1966, the Office of the Attorney General issued an advisory opinion to the state Board of Medical Examiners that interpreted the Psychology Certification Act so as to exclude from the "practice of psychology" the use of psychotherapy and the treatment of mental illness.[1] The opinion also indicated that these practices when performed by unlicensed persons amounted to misdemeanors under the Medical Practices Act.[2] It did not take long for word of the attorney general's opinion to reach leaders of the California State Psychological Association. They initially undertook a defensive action and subsequently launched a counteroffensive of their own. The result of this counteroffensive was the Psychology Licensing Act, passed in August 1967.

Opinions of the Attorney General's Office were in no sense binding on state agencies or on the courts, yet they did carry a certain weight in the minds of judges, who relied on them for interpretations of the law. Al-

[1] 47 Ops. Cal. Atty. Gen. 204 (1966). Originally numbered 66/130 in the mimeographed release series.
[2] Business and Professions Code, Section 2141.

though leaders of the CSPA and their lawyers believed that the opinion would be overridden if a case ever came to court, they did not wish to become involved in lengthy legal disputes that would sap the financial resources of the organization and would perhaps jeopardize the public image of their profession. More immediate and concrete problems were posed by the availability of the opinion to persons in public or private granting agencies, and to group insurance underwriters who might be led by the opinion to disqualify psychologists as vendors of reimbursable treatment services. In any case, the mere existence of the attorney general's opinion sufficed to make CSPA leaders uneasy; for, given the history of conflict and suspicion between psychology and psychiatry, they could not help imagining that someone, somehow, would find a way to use the opinion to their detriment. The CSPA leadership considered four possible responses: bringing a test case before the courts; persuading the Attorney General's Office to revise the opinion; seeking a clarifying amendment to the Psychology Certification Act; and pushing for an appropriately worded licensing act to replace the existing Certification Act. None of these possible responses precluded any other. However, the CSPA leadership hoped to avoid making their embarrassment any more public than would be necessary to bring an end to it. Hence, the first option was discounted as anything but a last resort. In pursuing the other options, the CSPA leadership determined not to involve or even to inform the organization's membership until they felt that there had been a sufficient buildup to make wider publicity, and perhaps greater pressure, worthwhile.

Critical comment on the opinion poured into the Attorney General's Office from sources other than the CSPA. The opinion had dealt with the practice of psychology only incidentally to its main analysis, which addressed the question of whether or not a person licensed for marital, family, and child counseling might "apply psychotherapeutic measures in his counseling work." The negative conclusion to this question provoked a large volume of angry correspondence from this professional group, which included a large number of social workers. Members of the California Association for Mental Health also registered objections. Earl Warren, Jr., then the president of the National Association for Mental Health and practicing law in Sacramento, wrote that he was "shocked" by the opinion. Many of the letters asked how they could get the opinion tested and presumably overridden in court. Most pointed out "the realities" of professional practice in the mental health field, to wit, that everyone practiced some version of psychotherapy and that this was the generic term used to refer to any sort of personal counseling intended to alleviate emotional stress. The initial response of the deputy attorney general responsible for the opinion, Clarence Brown, to all these criticisms was a terse defense of his reasoning on legal grounds. He was informally supported by the Board of Medical Examiners, with whom Brown had previously developed good working relations.

Brown's position was based on three considerations. First, he felt that the law should be interpreted so as to minimize the possibilities for quacks to exploit the public's confidence in legitimate mental health professionals. At the time he wrote the opinion, he said, he was aware of a case that had been brought against a woman "who was practicing medicine illegally and making a fortune" but who had been acquitted by "a soft-hearted jury." Secondly, he took the view that public policy should permit psychiatrists alone to practice psychotherapy and to represent themselves as psychotherapists. Finally, he genuinely believed that a literal interpretation of the statutes required his conclusion. To escape it, he said, he "would have had to play word games." Although Brown was prepared to stand by his opinion, his superior, Attorney General Thomas Lynch, being politically more visible and therefore more vulnerable, ordered a reconsideration. Lynch had not been involved in the writing of the original opinion. His office was in San Francisco, whereas the staff of seventy-five deputies were all in Sacramento. It was unusual for him to overrule one of his deputies, but in this instance his subordinate's action had generated, in Brown's words, "an unusual amount of static."

Several months later Brown resigned his post with the Attorney General's Office to become director of the Sacramento County Legal Aid Society, and another deputy, Wilbur Thayer, took charge of the issue. On May 23, 1967, nearly a year after the original opinion had appeared, the Attorney General's Office released Thayer's opinion, which explicitly overruled the preceding one. It observed that the previous opinion had relied on a limited and out-of-date sample of dictionary definitions of psychotherapy. Brown had relied on two sources alone for his definitions, the 1961 edition of the *Webster's New Collegiate Dictionary*, and the 1956 edition of *Blakiston's New Gould Medical Dictionary*. Both endorsed a rather medically oriented interpretation of the term, stressing the connotations of treatment of disease "by suggestion." Thayer disavowed Brown's contention that psychotherapy had "a settled and well understood meaning." "The former opinion," wrote Thayer, "does not recognize other areas of mental or emotional maladjustment nor does it recognize the existence of trained personnel in these other areas." He then cited *in extenso* three full pages of a pamphlet entiled "The Psychologist and Voluntary Health Insurance," published and distributed by the American Psychological Association, which aggressively stated the case for the competence of psychologists to "provide psychotherapeutic services" based on their specialized training "in psychological processes and measurement." A footnote indicated that the 1965 edition of *Webster's* defined psychotherapy as "treatment of mental or emotional disorder or of related bodily ills by psychological means." The same footnote indicated that two other medical dictionaries approved definitions that also departed from the medical connotations of psychotherapy.

Comforting though the attorney general's volte-face might have been to the psychologists, the success of their legislative strategy had made the opinion nugatory. At the behest of the CSPA, Senator Anthony Beilenson introduced, in the 1967 session of the legislature, SB 1157 and SB 1158, the former amending the troublesome sections of the current certification act and the latter entirely substituting a new licensing law for the certification act. SB 1157 was intended as a fallback in case SB 1158 should fail. When in mid-July 1967 it became apparent that the licensing bill would pass, the certification amendment was allowed to drop. The principal effect of the new law was merely to enhance the status of psychology by putting it on a semantic parity with psychiatry. The practitioners of both professions would henceforth be licensed.

The licensing bill passed with very little trouble. Yet, the CSPA leadership did have to contend with four minor political problems: neutralizing potential psychiatric opposition; preventing their own membership from becoming excessively or prematurely activated and thereby stimulating a backlash; avoiding entanglement on other issues that might alienate the support of key political figures; designing the necessary concessions to enable several individuals with established practices, but with only marginal competence (or so the CSPA leaders believed), to be brought under the mantle of licensure. There was also a complex technical problem, writing the law so as to exclude from its jurisdiction persons like opinion pollsters and amateur hypnotists whom no one really intended should seek licenses under the law. At certain points, this technical problem came close to becoming a political problem. Beilenson's aides were approached by more alarmed hypnotists, faith healers, astrologers, and pollsters than they had anticipated or cared to deal with. There was always the danger, too, that certain legislators would scuttle the bill entirely if they had reason to believe its technical faults would unduly inconvenience them or would discredit their reputations for draftsmanship. Although annoying, these technical problems were solved —in six waves of amendments—without ever becoming serious political obstacles.

Psychiatric opposition never materialized. In fact, organized psychiatry looked favorably on the bill, although it did not formally endorse it. Only 19 percent of the psychiatrists in our sample were opposed to allowing psychologists to practice psychotherapy (the issue raised by SB 1158).[3] Representatives of the Northern California Psychiatric Society met on April 13 with the president-elect and other executive officers of the CSPA and were favorably impressed by the potential for collaboration with psychology on problems of interest to both professions, for example, clarifying the definition of psychotherapy in the statutes, reworking the laws of confidentiality to protect more stringently the patient and the therapist alike, defending the public mental health budget against the cuts then threatened by the governor, and maintaining interprofessional lines of communication so as to forestall or dampen unnecessary rivalries. There was even discussion about the possibility of sharing the costs already being incurred by the psychologists for supporting a part-time legislative consultant (who functioned in some ways like a lobbyist, though the CSPA preferred to avoid that term). The psychologists had come prepared to show them a draft of SB 1158 and to solicit the cooperation, or at least the acquiescence, of psychiatry. The bill was generally unobjectionable to the psychiatrists. Through their good offices, the California Medical Association also acquiesced in the bill. The psychologists eventually agreed to only one relatively minor change in the bill, allowing psychiatrists, in addition to psychologists, to employ a limited number of unlicensed "psychological assistants," that is, persons with at least a year of graduate training in psychology who "perform limited psychological functions." The substantive character of this amendment was for the most part subordinate to its symbolic char-

[3] Within the NCPS sample, only 15 percent were opposed. On this issue, NCPS members considered themselves slightly more liberal than their southern California colleagues; and our data may suggest that their impressions were correct.

acter. It was a token of mutual professional respect in the drafting of legislation affecting relations between the two professions.

The attorney general's controversial opinion appeared in mid-June, but the CSPA bimonthly newsletter carried no word on the subject until October. The outer face of the October newsletter was stamped with the eye-catching message, "YOU MAY BE ARRESTED." Subsequent issues of the newsletter carried some pointed exchanges between the CSPA leadership and the rank and file regarding both the timing and the rhetoric of the announcement. In these events we may catch a glimpse of the strains within the CSPA and within the psychological profession. The CSPA had at that time roughly 1,500 members. Although there were over 3,300 members of the American Psychological Association (APA) in the state, CSPA, which was independent of APA, managed to enroll fewer than 50 percent of these.[4] Certainly the $25 annual dues—which in the summer of 1967 were about to be raised to $35 or $40—was a deterrent to membership. In my view, however, the major deterrent to expanded membership, and a threat to the existing rolls, was the domination of the CSPA by clinicians in private practice whose interests were not always coincident with the interests of academic psychologists. The executive director of the CSPA estimated that close to two-thirds of the rank and file had some sort of private practice, and that only 10 to 15 percent were academics. Moreover, the practitioners who dominated the executive board and the newsletter editorial staff in 1966–1967 were drawn mainly from "the most militant faction," as one CSPA leader who was sympathetic with their goals described them. Their orientation was not only highly professional but also politically activist. They wanted the CSPA to take positions on social issues and to do battle with the more restrained leaders of the national APA.

The internal solidarity of the CSPA was more shaken than usual during the fall of 1966. The October issue of the *California Psychologist* was the first number edited by Art Kovacs, who clearly intended to set a more militant tone than his predecessors. The lengthy proclamation of his new editorial policy included four parables about love written in a highly evocative and somewhat diffuse style. The next issue contained numerous letters of protest. One Bay Area psychologist in private practice announced his resignation from CSPA and urged Kovacs to resign his editorship. A retired academic psychologist expressed her dismay

4 I assume that nearly everyone who belonged to the CSPA was also in the APA.

that "in so short a time [since its founding] the C.S.P.A. administration is so dominated by one sector of the membership, namely, the private practice group." M. Brewster Smith, a prominent academic psychologist then at the University of California, Berkeley, said,

> By the evidence, C.S.P.A., itself a minority of California psychologists, is currently led by a narrowly professional subgroup that finds most of the rest of American psychology out of step. Kovacs speaks for this subgroup with an especially strident voice. . . . May I plead: as we face the complex and difficult current problems of professionalism and scientific psychology, neither clinical "love" nor *chutzpah* is enough. We need a spirit of reasonableness for mutual accommodation that is notably lacking in C.S.P.A. as represented in the October *California Psychologist.*

If CSPA leaders thought that love and *chutzpah* were adequate nutriment for relationships with colleagues or with clients, they nevertheless wanted no such relationship with political figures who held life-and-death power over the licensing bill and the certification act amendments. Sensing that they could not count on their own rank and file to avoid inappropriate or impetuous communications with legislators, and also that they would be unable to exhort the membership to remain silent and permit their officers alone to manage affairs in Sacramento, the CSPA leadership refrained initially from publicizing the attorney general's opinion. The leadership would need to go to the rank and file with a program of action for which they could then mobilize support. Otherwise their credibility as spokesmen for the profession would be undercut in Sacramento. The leaders' sensitivity to these considerations explains their attempt to keep the opinion out of sight for several months after it was published as well as their rather dramatic representation of the situation when they did inform the membership.[5]

We have observed that the California Medical Association sidestepped the issue of the budget cuts in the hospitals for the mentally ill, in part because they did not wish to jeopardize support for certain policy changes of higher priority to themselves. The CSPA, on the other hand, spoke out forcefully against the cuts. Their conduct was dictated

---

[5] Probably, their hand was forced in October. News of the opinion was spreading by word of mouth. Had the *California Psychologist* kept silent on the issue any longer, their silence might have proven embarrassing.

principally by their sense of mission to speak out on behalf of a cause they considered just. Secondarily, they could not have avoided speaking out without losing the respect of the other mental health professionals and lay activists. Their approach to the commitment bill, however, was somewhat different. They formally endorsed AB 1220, stirred up support for it privately, and even sent a spokesman to committee hearings to speak in favor of it. Yet they did not charge their legislative consultant with lobbying on its behalf, nor was their spokesman at committee hearings an officer of the organization. With regard to the budget issue, they wrote to the governor personally asking him to set up an advisory commission to investigate the desirability of making any cuts before he proceeded with them, and they sent copies of their resolution opposing the cuts to all members of the legislature. On behalf of AB 1220, they merely asked their leaders at the county level to write to legislators urging their support. Our survey shows that 73 percent of the CSPA leadership subsample (N = 26) scored three or more on our budget activity index, but only 54 percent scored this high on the commitment activity index.[6] Although the difference in approach to these two issues is accounted for by many different factors, from my interviews I am reasonably sure that one important reason was the reluctance to become too heavily involved in an issue that might possibly stir up any political backlash at critical points in the career of SB 1158. Although none was seriously anticipated, it was still deemed prudent to dampen their zeal on behalf of AB 1220—especially in light of the fact that many interests other than psychology were committed to helping AB 1220 along.

SB 1158 moved laboriously through the legislative machinery of both houses, amendments being added at practically every stage. It never encountered any serious opposition, however. Token objections were raised by a number of Los Angeles psychologists who felt threatened by the move toward tighter quality control implicit in the licensing act. A group of some sixteen of them, who had managed only with difficulty (it was said) to become certified under the laws already in force, hired a lawyer whose testimony at one committee hearing forced the committee to defer action for a week until the sixteen were assured they would qualify for licensure under the bill. In June 1966 the psychologists had not even dreamed of a licensing act; in October, they counted on some

6 The index score is the sum of all positive responses to Item 51 in the questionnaire. See Appendix A.

three years intervening before they would win their legislative battle; in August 1967 they had their bill. Did political skill play a role in their success? In my view, their skill was only modest. It is at least arguable that had they been more skilled, they would have had a licensing act a year or two earlier. We shall explore their deficiencies and strengths in Part III where we may compare them to some other actors attempting to effect change in other issue areas.

7
The Mendocino Plan

Of the many threats to the Bureau of Social Work since its formal beginnings in March 1946, the most dangerous in the eyes of the bureau's top administrators had been the proposal to decentralize its authority structure and turn the smaller units over to the state hospital superintendents. During the mid-1950s, two successive Department of Mental Hygiene directors, Drs. Walter Rapaport and Marshall Porter, attempted unsuccessfully to implement such a change. Rapaport had been an outspoken critic of the bureau in the years before he assumed the directorship. (In those years he had been superintendent of Agnews State Hospital.) Despite his adverse opinion of the bureau, he succeeded in effecting no real changes in its structure or functions. His successor, who served for roughly two years as an interim director while a permanent appointee was sought, commissioned two hospital superintendents to review the place of the bureau in the system. They recommended turning the bureau over to the state hospitals. This suggestion was endorsed almost unanimously by the other hospital superintendents, who at that time still represented the major policy audience in the DMH besides the headquarters office. The bureau's workers protested vehemently to Porter and some of the superintendents. Moreover, as one informant put it, "Some political forces were brought to bear on Dr. Porter." As a result, Porter delayed action. He assigned the problem for study to the DMH's new Short–Doyle Committee, which talked the proposal to death. When Lowry took over as DMH director in April 1964, he too thought of "doing something" with the bureau. An opportunity to make an effective opening move was given him by Dr. Ernest Klatte, superintendent of Mendocino State Hospital, whose plans for his own facility converged with Lowry's own larger designs.

Mendocino State Hospital is located in the northwestern part of the state, not far from the city of Ukiah. In 1967 its official service area included all the rural counties lying between the Pacific coast on the west and the Coastal Range on the east, between the Oregon border on the north and the border of Marin County on the south. It also served three counties on the eastern side of the Coastal Range and received a large number of alcoholic patients from San Francisco, a three-hour drive south of the hospital. It was widely regarded as the best of the California state hospitals for the mentally ill. Because it served a relatively small civilian population in its rural catchment area, the resident hospital population was usually small. It did not have the atmosphere of a massive custodial institution. The superintendent was young, imaginative, and readily accessible to other members of the hospital staff. Except in times of crisis, like the period in which layoffs were anticipated following Reagan's budget cuts, staff morale was generally high. Klatte had succeeded in obtaining federal grants to underwrite several experimental programs, the results of which had given the staff further cause for believing that they were part of a progressive and enlightened team.

Like most mental health professionals, the staff at Mendocino had been sensitive to the trends promising to make hospitals like Mendocino functionally obsolete and politically unsupportable. The 1966 and 1967 reports of the legislative analyst recommended closing Mendocino on the grounds that it was uneconomical to pay the overhead costs of the facility for such a small patient population. Its relative distance from large population centers made Mendocino an unlikely candidate for survival if Sacramento ever decided to start phasing out hospitals and transferring patients from one to another. The only qualities it had to recommend itself against such dim prospects were the relatively high morale of the staff and the existence of effective ongoing treatment teams. In the eyes of the people who worked there, these were sufficient to justify its continued existence. In the long run, however, these rather intangible qualities might carry little weight in Sacramento. In the short run, the resources of the facility were not being utilized optimally. In particular, the hospital staff had become too "isolationist," not sufficiently involved in the aftercare of the released patient who had returned to the community. If the hospital staff were to become more engaged in extramural work, both short-term and long-term objectives of the institution might perhaps be served.

Over a period of several months preceding Lowry's arrival, Klatte and his staff had developed a proposal for an initial phase of what they conceived to be a five-year plan for the institution. "In essence," stated the original planning paper, "the basic change in the hospital's role would be from that of a hospital whose responsibilities are primarily for inpatient services to that of a mental health center which has the responsibility for administering the Department of Mental Hygiene's participation in mental health services in our service area." It proposed that the hospital assume several new functions. It would become a training center for personnel already in demand by the communities in the service area. It would conduct research of particular relevance to the types of problems prevalent in the hospital's largely rural service area. It would cooperate with Short–Doyle in promoting the development of programs in community psychiatry and in providing mental health consultation services to judges, teachers, probation officers, and so on. Klatte's plan also called for nurses and psychiatric technicians from the hospital to move into aftercare work and, conversely, to have bureau social workers do more intramural work with the patients. Moreover, all social services workers of these kinds would report to a single, hospital-based supervisor. Reorganization of the intramural and extramural social work functions and personnel in this way quickly became the most controversial aspect of what came to be known as the Mendocino Plan.

Klatte touched base with Lowry even before Lowry's arrival to take up the reins of administration. Klatte had been filling the DMH director's post on an interim basis for several months before Lowry's arrival and had therefore found an opportunity to discuss his ideas with Lowry while the latter was visiting California to be interviewed for the job. Klatte found him sympathetic. The proposal that Klatte had sketched fit in well with Lowry's own theories about how public mental health services should be organized. Central to Lowry's thinking was the concept of the service area, a geographically circumscribed population group that would receive coordinated services from a variety of agencies. This concept was central also to the federal Mental Health Centers Act and to Short–Doyle. Lowry saw the principle applying to regionally based populations crossing city and county boundaries. The principle also entailed the integration of state hospital services with private and other public mental health services in the region.[1] It is not clear whether

1 Lowry, "The Mental Hospital," (paper presented at a meeting of the San Francisco Association for Mental Health, November 21–22, 1964). Although this paper was written after Lowry had assumed his post in California, I believe that these were his views earlier too.

or not Lowry at that point perceived the implications of Klatte's plan for the internal distribution of power within the DMH. Klatte himself was not much interested in the broader political implications. His own purposes were limited to solving the problems confronting Mendocino alone. In any case, Lowry made no particular commitments to Klatte at that time. According to one informant, Lowry professes to have done most of his serious thinking about departmental reorganization on the plane trip en route to California when he was returning to become the permanent director. The results of his reflections became evident at his first meeting with the hospital superintendents. He asked that each of them develop a long-range regional plan for integrating state hospital services and community services in the region of his own hospital.

Klatte submitted his own plan to the DMH on June 1. Twelve days later, at the monthly meeting of the Mendocino After-Care Clinic, Klatte presented his plan for the first time to an audience including bureau staff from the Mendocino service area. The After-Care Clinic was a regular monthly event at the hospital, bringing together the mental health workers in the region responsible for planning and monitoring the posthospitalization adjustment of Mendocino patients. To this meeting Klatte specifically invited representatives of the Bureau of Social Work and two community organization specialists who worked in the area but reported directly to the assistant deputy for community services in Sacramento (a social worker). Klatte informed the group that the Mendocino Plan had been approved in principle by Lowry and by Dr. Elmer Galioni, at that time head of the Division of Hospital Services, and that Lowry had also asked for similar plans from other hospitals. The bureau representatives were indignant that they had not been consulted earlier and that Klatte was implicitly criticizing their performance. They were alarmed at his suggestion that intramural and extramural (bureau) social services be managed by a single authority. As the private notes of one bureau representative quoted him: "It is not a matter of who is boss, but that there be a boss." To the bureau people, this could only mean "boss from the hospital." The acrimonious flavor of the discussion toward the end of the meeting is conveyed in these same notes:

> He [Klatte] did not feel that discussion would bring agreement. For example, he mentioned having talked about this matter with Mr. Wilsnack [the bureau chief, with offices in DMH headquarters] who had told him he basically disagreed. Dr. Klatte believed that a structural change was indicated in order to achieve better services and

continuity of care in the rural areas. He did not believe the matter would be resolved by discussion. He was criticized as not being familiar with what the BSW was doing in the communities and having presented a proposal with minimum adequate information.

In subsequent criticisms of the plan circulated among themselves, bureau personnel from the region suggested, by way of counterattack, that the hospital was not even doing its own job very well. "There is little . . . concern about the quality of in-patient care and any methods needed to insure its improvement. The hospital is not making a proposal with clean hands. The patients go out inadequately prepared, without public assistance assured and with little planning."

In mid-September another meeting was held at the hospital, this one more in the nature of a summit confrontation than the June meeting. The two top bureau men from Sacramento attended, along with several of the top medical administrators from Sacramento. Reports of this meeting suggest that very little had occurred during the summer. Wilsnack asserted that nothing should be done to dissolve the bureau, which had developed over the years into a highly productive agency. For Klatte, however, making the bureau workers part of an integrated social services team was a *sine qua non* of success. By the second day, tensions were high. Klatte asked Wilsnack to "authorize various bureau offices to release certain information regarding their present activities, staff, and methods of handling administrative matters." Wilsnack, according to official minutes of the meeting, "indicated that he preferred that the hospital social service staff not contact the bureau offices and that any information needed be requested from him personally." During this meeting an additional point of friction developed, namely, Klatte's desire to transfer the bureau workers in nearby Ukiah to offices on the hospital grounds. To Wilsnack, this symbolically threatened the core of the bureau's ideological mission, being the department's outpost in the community. The result of the two-day summit conference was, in one sense, a standoff, since no agreements were reached and no decisions imposed. In another sense, though, it was a loss for the bureau, since their failure to move Klatte and the DMH medical hierarchy closer to their own views implied that sooner or later an adverse decision would be imposed on them by administrative fiat. From that point on, the bureau sought to buy time. It tried to forestall any such fiat as long as possible in the hope that a way might somehow be discovered to thwart the Mendocino Plan.

Recognizing the diminishing opportunities to stop Klatte's plan by persuasion or bargaining power, the bureau leadership attempted to throw a competing plan into the decision-making machinery. It is doubtful that they expected it to win out over Klatte's. Yet it would serve a number of useful functions: (1) demonstrate that the bureau was at least as capable of constructive thinking as Klatte and the hospital staff; (2) register their agreement that some sort of changes were in order; (3) present a program package equivalent in scope to Klatte's, from which they could make concessions while holding out for demands they considered vital; (4) attract allies for whom their own package held forth certain lures; (5) stall for time.[2] By my own reading of the proposal, it recommended ways to improve arrangements that already existed and suggested the creation of multidisciplinary, multiagency task groups to help communities and counties in the service area develop their own mental health programs. The bureau proposal conceded the desirability of bureau service area lines being redrawn so as to coincide with the hospital's service area. This would have worked some hardship on the bureau, since their own service area lines were drawn (more realistically) to take account of the natural geographical division created by the Coastal Range.[3] It proposed that each task group be allowed to select its own leader. Once the service program for each county had been developed, it was to be coordinated not by any single individual but by means of an "interfacility working agreement which specifies the amount and type of services each facility attempts to provide, and the manner in which these services are obtained." And yet another paragraph implied that the bureau would have the leverage eventually to dominate these services: "One of the participating agencies assumes basic *case planning* responsibilities for each patient. This agency is privileged to draw on the identified services for its patient and is free to *refer patients and their families* for these services in accordance with the plan" (emphasis added). Since the bureau was best equipped to perform these functions for the great majority of patients, the bureau would most probably be the agency with dominant operating responsibility. As a result, its representative would become the

<hr>

[2] I do not know how self-consciously the bureau leaders matched their tactic to these aims. This catalogue of the strategic values of their move is the product of only my own interpretation.

[3] At the same time, the document also proposed that the hospital service area lines be redrawn so as to turn over to DeWitt State Hospital in the Sierra foothills the three counties east of the Coastal Range.

natural leader in the planning group as well. The bureau's plan was not merely a plan to expand services but to control the programs that provided the new services.

Whatever might have been Lowry's theories about the organization of services to clients which underlay his original tentative support for Klatte's proposal, he was not long in the directorship when he began to conceive of the Mendocino Plan as a first step in the dismantling of the Bureau of Social Work as a centralized agency. He saw the bureau as a cumbersome relic of the past, progressive in its youth but by then a force protecting the wrong aspects of the *status quo*. The bureau leadership in Sacramento had been around the department for many years and, in his view, had subverted the processes of orderly medical administration. During the Blain and Lieberman era the bureau had been the dominant influence in the department. The top medical administrators had relaxed their grip on the department's day-to-day affairs and had permitted Philip Sirotkin, a layman with close ideological and personal ties to the bureau leadership, to become, through his office as executive assistant to the director, the effective final authority. Lowry intended to set things straight. Indeed, it was understood by many, and perhaps even by Lowry, that the governor (Brown) and concerned legislators desired him "to be a hatchet man," as one Lowry supporter phrased it. Lowry's reputation in Washington in the Public Health Service was exactly that of a man who "played his cards close to his vest" and who was a tough in-fighter.

The Mendocino Plan was only one of many changes Lowry implemented to streamline the DMH and reassert medical control. By the end of his first fifteen months in office, Lowry had reduced from twenty-eight to six the number of persons routinely reporting to the director. He had removed from the jurisdiction of the bureau-dominated Community Services Division all the community-based aftercare clinics and day treatment centers administered by the DMH. These were transferred to the jurisdiction of the headquarters hospital administration group, which Lowry reorganized as the Division of State Services. The Office of Planning, another ally in the Sirotkin-bureau-Community Services entente, had been stripped of its functions. Most of these were given to one of Lowry's own creations, the Office of Program Review, headed by a psychiatrist. From the bureau's point of view, the most disastrous change of all was its transfer from Community Services to the new State Services Division.

Lowry also shuffled personnel and their jurisdictions. Dr. Edward Rudin resigned as director of the Community Services Division to take a high post in private hospital administration, ostensibly for personal reasons. Although Nathan Sloate had relinquished direct control of the bureau a few years before Lowry's arrival, he had still kept a guiding hand on its operations in his capacity as assistant deputy in the Community Services Division. The transfer of the bureau to the Division of State Services thereby reduced his role at headquarters considerably. It was reduced still further when Lowry removed from his jurisdiction the cadre of nine community organization specialists that he had personally created to do promotional work in the community, on behalf of community mental health programs. Sloate's residual powers were eventually given to a psychiatrist appointed to fill a new assistant deputy director slot in the division—the name of which had by this time been changed, suggestively, from Community Services to Local Programs.

All of these shifts were progressing during the many months of negotiation among the bureau leadership, Klatte, and the other figures in the DMH hierarchy (including Lowry) over the Mendocino Plan.

From the bureau's viewpoint, these negotiations came to very little. The bureau urged that it be "a demonstration program." Lowry insisted that it be seen as a commitment by the department to reorganize other hospital service areas along the same lines as Mendocino. The bureau submitted its own Mendocino plan on October 22, 1964; but Lowry moved to curtail circulation of the bureau plan outside the department while encouraging the attentive public to define Klatte's as the only plan being considered seriously. Lowry took a personal interest in polishing the details of the Mendocino Plan, carefully rewriting and editing each of the long series of drafts that he and his assistants turned out through the winter months. The bureau leadership and its allies opposed each one, but without success.

During the course of the negotiations, Short-Doyle administrators began to be concerned about the Mendocino Plan. They initially feared that the hospital would compete for power and funds with the Short-Doyle programs in its vicinity. The conference went so far as to send its executive committee to visit Mendocino for a day. The committee returned convinced that the plan, at least in the Mendocino area, would not represent a serious threat to the development of Short-Doyle. They reported their conclusions to the semiannual meeting of the conference in May 1965.[4] Lowry had already approached the Mental Health Committee of the CMA and received their support for the Mendocino Plan. Lowry's decision to implement the Klatte plan was announced on June 2, 1965. It went into effect on July 1. The only concession made to the bureau involved questions about how to make the transition from the old to the new mode of organization.

[4] One informant contends that Dr. Harry Brickman, of Los Angeles Short–Doyle, who led the expedition up to Mendocino, was persuaded by Lowry to support the Mendocino Plan in exchange for Lowry's promise to support Brickman in his battle with the NIMH. Brickman was attempting at that point to persuade the NIMH to relax the provisions of the 1963 Mental Health Centers Act limiting the scope of center catchment areas to a maximum of 75,000. There is no evidence to confirm or refute this contention. Brickman and others in Los Angeles Short–Doyle claimed that small catchment areas were inefficient to administer and probably impossible to staff in a city the size and density of Los Angeles. As of August 1967, they had been receiving little sympathy from federal officials.

8
The Bureau of Social Work Transfer

On July 1, 1965, the bureau's fortunes had fallen to their lowest point in its quarter-century existence. With the medical hierarchy firmly in control of DMH headquarters and the hospital superintendents on the verge of acquiring regional leadership powers and responsibilities, it seemed only a matter of time—perhaps a matter of mere months—before the bureau would be wholly decapitated and dismembered. There seemed little the bureau leadership could do to reverse or retard the trend. A somewhat fortuitous combination of circumstances, however, did on their behalf what they could not do themselves. On July 1, 1966, the bureau was removed from the Department of Mental Hygiene and placed under the jurisdiction of the Department of Social Welfare (DSW).

The idea for the transfer originated independently in two different sources. Despite the DMH view that these two sources were linked in an artful conspiracy, I have found no evidence to support this view and inferential evidence to support only the contrary. The first mention of the idea occurred in a memorandum from Mrs. Eunice Evans, a high administrator in the state Department of Social Welfare, to Paul Ward, Governor Brown's director of the Health and Welfare Agency (a loose federation, under a single overseer, of the departments of Social Welfare, Mental Hygiene, Corrections, and Rehabilitation). Her memorandum, dated July 7, 1965, cited the conclusion of an April 1965 DMH planning grant study that case services being provided by the DMH might be eligible for 75 percent federal reimbursement if they were provided by the DSW through the county welfare departments. It also noted, according to one interviewee, that such a transfer would (1) help move DSW in the direction of being a service agency rather than merely a watchdog over financial aid programs, (2) eliminate the appearance of having two state agencies duplicating each other's functions, and (3) counter the threat of having the bureau returned to the hospitals.[1] Ward immediately referred the memorandum to the DMH for comment. Emanuel Newman, Wilsnack's closest associate in the bureau, prepared the first analysis, which was largely favorable. As it passed through other hands in the department, some few negative thoughts were added. Nevertheless, the comments on the Evans memorandum that reached Lowry's desk on November 15, 1965, with the imprimatur of Dr. Elmer Galioni, deputy director in charge of the Division of State Services and Wilsnack's immediate superior, concluded that "the suggestion merits early consideration by our two departments and the Health and Welfare Agency Office." It acknowledged the merits of the argument for transfer as put forth by Mrs. Evans and pointed to "two major disadvantages," the incompatibility of having the DSW strengthening state-administered social services to the mentally ill while DMH was moving toward local planning and administration; and the possible damage to "integrated medical follow-up for out-patients on leave of absence." Despite Galioni's qualifications, the tone of his comments was distinctly favorable. It is probable that Lowry, who later opposed the transfer on the last of these grounds, never forwarded Galioni's or his own comments to Ward.[2]

---

[1] Wilsnack denies that he or his associates consciously stimulated the Evans memorandum, although he concedes that his casually ironic references to the bureau's bleak prospects under DMH administration might have formed the background for the memorandum.

[2] Knowledgeable informants assert that Lowry never sent a report on the matter to Ward. Had Lowry opposed the idea of transferring the bureau—and it is almost certain that he privately opposed the idea in November 1965 as much as he opposed it in public several months later—inaction would have been the most expeditious way to dispose of the Evans proposal. But it is also true that if Lowry had sent a report to Ward and if Ward wanted to scuttle the plan himself, he too would have kept silent. These informants assume that Ward would have reacted to any letter from Lowry on the subject of a transfer and that they would have found out about the reaction. If their assumptions are correct, then their ignorance of Ward's reaction is evidence that Lowry permitted the matter to drop. If their assumptions are wrong, there is no way of inferring whether it was Lowry or Ward (or both of them acting jointly) who tabled the transfer idea.

Nothing was heard of the transfer idea for several months afterward. If the Health and Welfare Agency was still considering the matter, it was silent about its intentions. In light of the agency's reluctance to become involved when the issue heated up again in the spring of 1966, it is likely that it wished to avoid disturbing interdepartmental relations, particularly in an election year. The Department of Social Welfare let the matter drop. The DSW was under enough fire from the public and the legislature for its "too liberal" administration of federal antipoverty funds to risk being publicized as a party to an interagency jurisdictional squabble. It was also uncertain about the actual merits of the proposal and unwilling to risk giving offense to an agency, the DMH, with which it was then attempting to improve mechanisms of coordination.

The idea of a transfer next appeared in a report by the staff consultant to the Assembly Social Welfare Committee, Tom Joe. A leading member of the committee, Eugene Chappie, a Republican, was receiving complaints from the boarding-home operators in his district, who demanded that the state raise the reimbursement rates for leave patients placed in their facilities from the current $130 per patient per month. Chappie asked Joe to look into the matter. Joe started his search for more funds at the door of the federal treasury. He quickly recognized the possibilities inherent in the 1962 Social Security Act amendments, which authorized 3-1 federal-state matching funds for the bureau's work—provided it were administered by the state agency responsible for administering the rest of the state's public social services.[3]

As Joe prepared his report on the original problem he began to conceive of it as a broadly gauged attack on the entire organization of public social services. He had for some time been convinced that administrative agencies should be organized so as to perform distinctive kinds of functions, or services, for undefined population groupings rather than to perform a variety of functions for categorically defined populations. In his view the DMH was a medical facility, and the DSW was a social service agency. Given his preference for functional rather than client-centered organization, as he put it, he believed that ex-mental patients who needed social services should receive them from

[3] Joe's wife was a child welfare consultant in the DSW at the time. Although Joe dismisses the suggestion, it is possible that she was a conduit, though very likely an unwitting one, for the idea of the transfer.

the DSW rather than from the DMH. (In the same report he recommended also that certain programs for the blind be removed from the Department of Rehabilitation and administered, instead, by the DSW.) The members of the Assembly committee—and particularly the chairman, Jack Casey, a Democrat from Bakersfield—responded to the Joe report favorably. They scheduled a hearing for March 2.

Although the official DMH position at the hearing was noncommittal, Dr. Robert Hewitt, Lowry's chief deputy director, emphasized in his testimony only the advantages of the status quo and the disadvantages of change. Witnesses from the Department of Social Welfare were present to answer technical questions concerning the implications of a transfer, as was Wilsnack, but they gave no indication to the committee that they either favored or opposed it. Indeed, at that point, it was not clear even to themselves whether they favored or opposed the transfer. For the DSW, it might cause administrative complications and provoke needless trouble with the DMH. The bureau leadership was not sure that the new working arrangements might not entail some decentralization of the bureau to the jurisdiction of the counties. So uncertain were the bureau's leaders about the possible implications of the transfer that they were nearly prepared to support the status quo themselves, even though the Mendocino Plan was already eight months under way and similar service area plans were in the offing. Not until the third week in March did the bureau leadership begin to view the transfer as the clearly preferred alternative.

FEDERAL MONIES: WHO WANTED THEM AND WHY

Within a week of the hearings, Casey had introduced AB 90, a bill mandating the transfer of the bureau to the DSW. Lowry himself took command of the DMH defense. Together with two close aides, he met with Joe on April 11 (with Wilsnack and Bolton also present) and spelled out his objections to the transfer. Lowry stated his doubts that a nonmedical agency could administer "essentially a medical service" for persons whose "core need is for medical services and who are in the aftercare program primarily for medical reasons." Lowry suggested that Short–Doyle programs assume responsibility for patients on leave. He also argued that the transfer was antagonistic to the department's long-range plan; that there was no assurance that federal funds would be used for

new programs; and that the transfer would prevent him from implementing a new aftercare system which he was then developing.[4] Lowry
failed to convince either Bolton or Joe of his position. Ultimately, however, their opinions would not matter. At a meeting of the hospital
superintendents a week later he referred to AB 90, according to one informant, as "an ill-conception that will miscarry." If not, he said, he was
confident he could induce an abortion.

Bolton, Joe, and some members of the Assembly Social Welfare Committee were anticipating just such a stroke by Lowry. They were preparing such documentation as they could to indicate that aftercare
services to patients would not be harmed by the transfer and might even
be improved. On March 22, the Assembly contracted with Dr. Leonard
Schatzman, a sociologist affiliated with the University of California Medical School in San Francisco, to evaluate the results of a pilot program
then administered by the DSW which paralleled the work of the bureau
in some respects. This program, called Adult Protective Services, drew
upon the pool of federal funds that presumably would become available
to the bureau should it be transferred.[5] Schatzman's study concluded
that "much would be gained in an amalgamation of operations" between APS and the bureau and indirectly countered DMH's previous
objections by stating, "There would be no serious disruption in . . . care
. . . , since there is little enough to be disrupted; and no continuity of
care to be severed, since there is no continuity of any consequence." An
amalgamation in this context could mean only one thing, transferring
the bureau to the DSW. Otherwise the enriched staffing of the APS program which, in Schatzman's view, accounted for the superior performance of APS compared to the bureau, would be unobtainable. Publication of the report on May 2 significantly aided the curious coalition of
interests that had emerged by that time.[6]

---

4 This summary of Lowry's position at the April 11 meeting was reconstructed partly from participants' verbal accounts of the meeting and partly from two separate
memoranda on the meeting prepared by two different participants.

5 The major differences were that the APS had richer staff-to-patient ratios than the
bureau's programs and that the APS dealt only with aged rather than with all classes
of leave patients. The Schatzman report was entitled, "A Comparative Study of Aspects
of the Adult Protective Services of the Department of Social Welfare and Comparable
Services Performed by the Bureau of Social Work of the Department of Mental
Hygiene." It was included in an offset pamphlet published by the Assembly Rules
Committee, and released on May 2, entitled, "Background Information on the Proposed Transfer of Bureau of Social Work Functions from the Department of Mental
Hygiene to the Department of Social Welfare."

6 Schatzman compared the operations of the BSW and the APS in Los Angeles, San

How much money would California actually stand to gain from the proposed transfer? Legislators had to be shown. At Bolton's request, Wilsnack prepared a memorandum stating his own estimates of the dollar benefits to the state if the transfer were approved. Bolton then circulated these to key legislators and their staffs. Wilsnack estimated a minimum of $3,200,000; a maximum of approximately $12,000,000; and a "conservative maximum" of $8,381,000, each figure being contingent on different assumptions about the proportion of the aftercare caseload that would qualify for federal reimbursement to the state.

Although fiscal considerations eventually dominated the legislature's decision about the transfer, they had less to do with gaining monies than with saving those of the state. It was an election year, and legislative leaders of both parties were concerned with making a record of economy mindedness to help them in the campaign. Capturing federal funds would mean that the legislature could safely ignore the governor's request for a $540,000 augmentation to the bureau's current appropriations base. With assistance from Veneman, some other leading Republican assemblymen, and Al Lipson—the chief minority (Republican) consultant—the Republican caucus in the Assembly on May 9 was moved to endorse the transfer. Despite nominal opposition from the Brown administration (Democratic), the Democratic caucus followed suit two

---

Mateo, and San Joaquin counties, three of the eleven in which the APS had its demonstration projects. In these counties, he and his assistants interviewed 24 clients and patients, 12 operators of family care and nursing homes, 6 supervisors, and 12 caseworkers. These were drawn in equal numbers from the personnel and caseloads of the bureau and of the APS. The irony of the Schatzman report was that DMH opponents of the transfer did not use it on their own behalf. Had the issue of federal funding not been so dominant in the Schatzman study, one might have thought it was supporting Lowry's plan to break up the bureau rather than the bureau's move to escape intact from DMH control. Because the APS worker had fewer cases to deal with, he could "be physically present *at all critical points* in processes governing the lives and work of clients, hospital personnel and home operators. This is the hallmark of his operations and quite possibly the principal reason for his apparent success" (emphasis added). The APS worker could be present when leave preparations were being made. "He knows the ward staff and cultivates and maintains a colleague relationship which functions to control the hospital staff's selection *vis-à-vis* his (APS) requirements." This arrangement permitted him to manage the size, rate of input, and quality of his caseload. On the other side of the placement system, he had "built good relationships with selected home operators," which put him in a good position to "make a match." Continuity of care may not have been an issue, but continuity of planning and implementation certainly was. The arrangements projected by the Mendocino Plan would probably have fit the APS model much better than the bureau's ongoing arrangements. These were likely to remain largely unmodified if the bureau slipped out from under DMH control.

days later. The reasons given by leaders of both parties were explicitly fiscal.

A STRATEGIC MANEUVER

It was not AB 90 that either caucus endorsed, however. At some point toward the end of April, those managing the transfer proposal began to consider a major strategic shift. AB 90 was then awaiting a hearing in the Assembly Ways and Means Committee. It began to appear that the bill would not have time to clear all the procedural hurdles in both chambers; and that, even if time were not lacking, the DMH would be waiting at every hurdle to upset it. Casey, Joe, Chappie, John Veneman (the ranking Republican on Casey's committee), and Bolton decided to move the transfer along "the budget route." Since budget bills in California contain numerous pages of specifications about how monies are to be spent, they could insert an amendment into these control sections that would effect the transfer.[7] Success in this move depended mainly on the cooperation of only the party leaders in the Assembly, who had the option to submit author's amendments to the budget bill. The caucus decisions gave them the freedom to do so.[8] Because the appropriations sections were so much more salient to the legislators, especially in an election year, than the control sections, debate over the former would divert attention from the transfer issue.

When word got back to Lowry that AB 90 was being abandoned for the budget route, he was put on notice that miscarriage of the transfer might not occur quite so spontaneously. About the same time, he received the Schatzman report. It must surely have appeared that he was being outmaneuvered in the legislature. On May 5, just three days after the Schatzman report appeared, he wrote a five-page letter to Paul Ward, the contents of which quickly became known to members of the Assembly Social Welfare Committee and to Bolton and Joe. Lowry intimated his indignation at the "precipitous action" being taken on the transfer. He suggested that it would be appropriate for the legislature "to obtain advice and consultation" from the CAMH, the CCRC, the CMA, the three California district branches of the APA, the Governor's Advisory

[7] Control language was usually written for only a relatively small proportion of the budget items.

[8] Some sources believe that Casey was somewhat reluctant to forego the pride of authorship in his own bill, AB 90. Yet he spoke effectively, it is said, on behalf of moving the transfer through the budget route at the Democratic caucus meeting on May 11.

Committee on Mental Health, the CSAC, the Medical Advisory Committee of the DMH, and the Mental Retardation Programs and Standards Advisory Board. He stressed the dangers of placing responsibility for the medical care of leave patients in nonmedical agencies; and he outlined his own new scheme for aftercare services which created six classes of leave patients, according to their need for medical or social services and their placement with state or local agencies. On May 12, Casey and Veneman sent an angry reaction to Ward. Lowry's letter contained, they wrote, "several unsubstantiated and obfuscatory statements." They denied that the transfer was a sudden development, pointing to the two-year history of APS and to the constant publicity since early February of the proposal to shuffle the bureau as well as other agencies among state departments.[9] Whatever merits their other counterarguments may have had, they were merely a prelude to the letter's final rhetorical thrusts. Lowry had predicted dryly that hospital physicians would become exceedingly cautious in their release policies since they would presumably be jeopardizing (in their view) the medical care of leave patients. He had also speculated that turning leave patients over to the Department of Social Welfare "would, in effect, be introducing into the welfare *system* an additional 10,000 or more persons per year. . . . It is not too difficult to believe that many of these 10,000 persons who are unnecessarily interjected [*sic*] into the welfare system might become addicted to this kind of system and continue indefinitely beyond the time when all signs of their mental illness have disappeared." Veneman and Casey called the first statement "most disturbing . . . implying that the Department of Mental Hygiene will not cooperate with a sister agency even though the same psychiatric social workers plus additional staff and medical resources will be available to provide aftercare services." The "addicted" statement they called "shocking." The legislators gave copies of their response to the press. It was the first time in his two years in office, said the *San Francisco Chronicle*, that Lowry had become involved in a public controversy.[10]

By the middle of May, the stakes in the contest were a good deal higher

[9] From the legislative perspective, this may have seemed a long time. From the perspective of the DMH bureaucracy, changes of this magnitude ought properly to have taken, say, two to three years. The APS program, contrary to the Casey–Veneman argument, was never conceived as a pilot program to evaluate the benefits of transferring the bureau; nor was it possible, in Lowry's view, to make any such inferences from a comparison between APS and bureau performance. The latter is a point made in his May 5 letter.

[10] The story appeared, in a prominent position, on p. 6 of the May 14 edition.

than they had been in February or in March. If the proponents of transfer lost, Lowry would surely move to dissolve the bureau before the legislature had a second chance to tinker with his jurisdiction. Lowry had involved his own prestige and the persuasiveness of his office in the struggle. He had been burned—first by the Joe report, next by the Schatzman report, then by the budget route maneuver, and finally by the adverse publicity that followed his exchange of letters with two prominent assemblymen. Lowry's reputation as a tough in-fighter was in the balance. Far more important than his private ego needs, it must be emphasized, was the necessity to maintain intact the image of skillfulness that he had used to advantage in managing the chaotic internal affairs of his department. Lowry could not easily afford, even temporarily, to appear to be a paper tiger. Thus, by May, the gentlemanly feinting of March and April had become an aggressive exchange of thrusts and parries.

The rank and file of the bureau had been aware since early April of the favorable opinion toward the proposed transfer held by the upper echelons of the bureau's leadership. As the issue heated up, the rank and file intensified their efforts to mobilize support and create alliances in the local community. They stimulated family caretakers, whose economic interest in federal funding scarcely made extra stimulation necessary, to write, phone, and visit their assemblymen and senators. One chapter of the National Association of Social Workers endorsed the transfer, and unofficial (and intermittent) assistance came from the California State Employees Association, to which most of the bureau's workers belonged.

Lowry began his drive for support at a considerable disadvantage. It was early May, yet he moved slowly. By his own account, he refrained from approaching the CMA or any of his likely allies in the professions. Lowry did appeal to the Board of Directors of the California Council for Retarded Children (CCRC) at a meeting held in San Francisco on May 20. He had raised the possibility in his May 5 letter that the nursing care of retarded children in private nursing facilities would suffer if the bureau were transferred. Anticipating touble from this quarter, the assembly staff prepared a pamphlet on the subject that was intended to allay such fears.[11] Bolton's own standing with CCRC was at least as great

11 It was issued by the Assembly's Office of the Chief Consultant and was entitled, "Additional Background Information on the Proposed Transfer of Bureau of Social Work Functions from the Department of Mental Hygiene to the Department of Social Welfare." The second sentence of the introduction reads, "Several legislators have been asked about the intent of the transfer as it would affect the mentally retarded,

as Lowry's, owing to his prominent role, one year earlier, as consultant to the Assembly committee that started a program of regional diagnostic and counseling centers for the retarded. At the May 20 meeting, Bolton and Lowry met in something like face-to-face debate. The result was that the CCRC refused to take a position on the issue. Their silence was, in effect, a defeat for Lowry.

Lowry attempted to frustrate the transfer by approaching the Republican leadership through sympathetic legislators and through Lipson. He proposed that the bureau be transferred piecemeal—one patient class at a time—if it was to be transferred at all. Bolton undercut this alternative in short order: in the interim, he observed in a memorandum requested by Lipson, the state would be supporting two bureaus of social work, a condition that was sure to create confusion and irresponsibility; and in any case, because federal monies were to go to patients on a need basis, the fiscal purpose of the transfer would be vitiated. Lowry also attempted, during all this time, to discover how, if at all, federal monies could be captured by tinkering slightly with the status quo. He was unsuccessful. Lowry's only significant coup in the month of May was a unanimous resolution by the Short–Doyle Conference opposing the transfer and proposing, in addition, that the bureau be turned over to their own jurisdiction.

Lowry was more successful with the senators than he was with the assemblymen. He brought the department's case to George Miller, Jr., chairman of the Senate Finance Committee, which would have jurisdiction over the budget bill once it reached the Senate. He also approached Senator Stephen Teale, who, along with Miller, would be on the Senate's three-man delegation to the conference committee to reconcile the differences between the two houses in their budget bills.[12] The budget bill passed by the Assembly and sent to the Senate Finance Committee contained the control language transferring the Bureau of Social Work. But the Finance Committee's version of the same bill omitted this language. On the Senate floor no one challenged the committee's decision on the transfer. Hence the Assembly's and the Senate's control sections would have to be reconciled in free conference. Could Lowry win there as well?

---

and the California Council for Retarded Children has requested the Legislature to provide additional information for review at their Board of Directors' meeting on May 20th."

[12] Miller and Teale, of course, have been described previously as participants in the commitment reform controversy.

Since the subject matter of the conference was the budget, staff members from the Department of Finance were also present. So too were representatives of the Legislative Analyst's Office. Managers of the transfer proposal had previously been able to convince the relevant staff members in the Department of Finance that the transfer would be administratively feasible and financially advantageous. They had won the tentative support, also, of Miller's legislative assistant, to whose judgment Miller deferred quite frequently. I do not know how the six-man committee divided on the transfer issue, since the vote was unrecorded. We can assume that the three assemblymen voted for it. Since the transfer was approved, at least one senator must have concurred with them. Thus, even if Lowry managed to hold fast to the negative votes of Miller and Teale, the two Democrats, he lost the crucial vote of the Finance Committee's ranking Republican, Dolwig, who also sat on the conference committee. It appears that the Republican economy drive in an election year was, ultimately, the decisive force that saved the bureau from dissolution and caused Lowry to suffer his first significant political defeat in his two years in office.

Part III

ENTREPRENEURSHIP
IN PRACTICE

9

The Entrepreneur Designs a Proposal and Seeks Support

At the end of the Introduction, I briefly sketched my own model of the policy-making process and identified the four major political problems with which entrepreneurial skill must contend. To restate the argument briefly, the policy-making process is viewed as analogous to a manufacturing, or production, process. Political resources are combined (as "inputs") to produce what the entrepreneur hopes will be "enough" support (as "output") to win adoption of his proposal; and his four principal problems involve gathering support, mobilizing resources and allies, outmaneuvering opponents, and developing and sustaining effectiveness over time. Each problem has a chapter reserved to it, beginning with this one on gathering support. It should be recalled that support is merely a hypothetical construct, a fiction useful for accounting purposes only. In order to give this construct an empirical referent we need now to introduce the idea of consensus.

BUILDING CONSENSUS AROUND A PROPOSAL—
AND FITTING A PROPOSAL TO A CONSENSUS

Obtaining consensus from a set of sufficiently weighty interests to win a major policy victory is the entrepreneur's basic objective. The interests that endorse a proposal do so for their own reasons, which may not be shared by any other interests. By consensus, therefore, I do not mean anything like "harmony" or "a meeting of the minds." I mean only that there is independent assent to the same proposal. By far the most important obstacle to this objective is the tendency for major policy changes to disrupt a complex ecology of organizational programs and individual practices and, consequently, to displease some interests in the long run and a great many others in the short run, that is, during the transitional period. These consequences cannot be entirely avoided. Indeed, it is impossible to say in general that they ought to be minimized. How the entrepreneur regards these consequences should depend entirely, first, on his evaluations of the benefits and costs of an anticipated pattern of system disturbance and reintegration and, second, on his estimates of the gross level of political support that can be raised for the associated proposal and the gross level of opposition to it. No matter what his choices are in a given situation, however, the entrepreneur surely needs to know how to design the array of alternative policy proposals among which he wishes to choose. In particular, he needs to be able to design features likely to invigorate, rather than disturb, the existing ecology of programs and practices. Designs for disruptive change are relatively easy to conceive, whereas their counterparts require more sophisticated analysis and more disciplined imagination.

Invigorating the existing ecology means improving existing programs and practices in the eyes of at least some who are affected by the improvement and doing so without offending any of them. The concept is analogous, therefore, to the economic concept of a Pareto superior move, a reallocation of economic goods in such a way that at least one party is better off than previously and no one is worse off; and in deference to this established nomenclature, we shall call such policies "Pareto superior." In practice few significant economic reallocations by government (indeed, perhaps none) or policy changes meet these strict criteria. Both constructs serve principally as analytical reference points rather than as descriptions of real events.[1] Probably the closest approximation to a Pareto superior policy proposal described in our five case studies was the Psychology Licensing Act as it was eventually adopted. Even the general public, which is usually ill-served by the licensure of professionals, was made no worse off by the act, simply because it did not restrict market entry for would-be psychotherapists appreciably more than did the existing Certification Act.[2]

[1] Unfortunately, in economic usage Pareto superiority has a much stronger normative than empirical connotation. I am using the term more as an ideal-type construct against which to interpret real policy consequences.

[2] "The general public" is not an analytically acceptable actor in conventional economic analysis, and indeed the notion of Pareto superiority has been a tool that

AB 1220 also incorporated some Pareto superior features along with the controversial ones. The final version of SB 677 adopted by the legislature and signed by the governor provided that a person alleged to be either a danger to himself or others or gravely disabled "as a result of mental disorder or impairment by chronic alcoholism" might be detained for up to seventeen days without a court hearing. A person so detained might request a hearing at any time after the first seventy-two hours, but the burden was on him to request the hearing and to fill out the necessary forms. This changed the current practice of automatically bringing the courts into the process immediately after the first seventy-two hours. This was the point at which commitment proceedings were usually initiated.

Psychiatrists, other mental health professionals, and clinic administrators were pleased with the seventeen-day provision because it enabled them to render such treatment as they thought was necessary or desirable without "having to go through legal red tape," as one psychiatrist put it, after only seventy-two hours. Civil libertarians, on the other hand, endorsed these provisions of the bill because they prohibited involuntary detention for any longer than the seventeen days. The designers of AB 1220 had overturned the hitherto unexamined assumption that the tension between therapeutic responsibilities and legal rights had to begin as soon as a person was detained for treatment.

Conceptualizing the treatment-*versus*-liberty dilemma in the old manner had proven sterile. The proposals of the Midpeninsula Chapter ACLU drawn up in the spring of 1966 sought only to restore due process, by which they contemplated making the detention and commitment procedures more difficult to set in motion and, once in motion, less easy to abuse. The mental health professionals (particularly the psychiatrists) and the clinic and hospital administrators, concerned with fulfilling their sense of responsibility to the patient and the public, sought to avoid due process (or to set up programs that tried to forestall involuntary detention and commitment). The insight incorporated in the design of AB 1220 was that there was a possibility of graduating the tension between due process and professional responsibility.

There are additional illustrations of this graduated tension. The professionals responsible for an individual's evaluation during the first

---

welfare economists have used to exclude the concept. Political scientists have not been comfortable with the idea either. I too am troubled by it, but in the present context, at least, I would be more troubled by omitting it.

seventy-two hours could certify the patient for intensive treatment for another fourteen days under the conditions described above. But in order to do so, they had first to inform the patient of his right to judicial review by habeas corpus; to deliver personally the notice of certification to the individual certified; and to send copies of the notice to the individual's attorney, the district attorney, the public defender, the facility providing intensive treatment, and the DMH. They had to ask the person certified to designate any person whom he wished to have informed regarding his certification. They also had to stipulate in writing which voluntary treatment services they had (unsuccessfully) advised the patient to accept. The written legal affirmation that this procedure had been observed required the signature of two mental health professionals from the agency or facility that had provided the evaluation and referral services. All this amounted to a very complicated administrative procedure, which would deter professionals and administrators from seeking certification casually. On the other hand, it was not as complicated and time-consuming as preparations for a court hearing. Hence, the Assembly proposal injected an intermediate step between total liberty and long-term confinement.

Indeed, there was even a second intermediate step inserted in this process. This was judicial review, which might occur at any time between the certification and the court hearings that were prescribed automatically for the few patients whom the professionals would wish to have confined for some term after the initial seventeen days. Discussions between the professionals and the patient over this matter would presumably force the professionals to be doubly sure of their grounds for recommending certification or postcertification confinement. Thus it appears that the Assembly group's proposal introduced new flexibility into the system by graduating the tension between individual rights and professional responsibilities over a seventeen-day period and by inventing means of expressing the tension other than court procedures. Here was an innovation that could satisfy both legal and professional interests.

Unfortunately, there is no way of reaching a Pareto superior policy alternative when the design elements to be traded back and forth have not even been invented. The staff members who worked out the broad design of AB 1220 as well as its smaller details did not conceive of their efforts as being a search for Pareto superior design features. They used to brainstorm occasionally and role play the supposed reactions of various interests to alternative designs, but it is dubious that these techniques led to an insight about graduating the legal-medical tension in the system. The traditional economic argument is that free market bargaining and trading routinely produces Pareto superior reallocations, but this method does not identify Pareto superior moves reachable only through cooperative behavior. Indeed, even the will to cooperate is insufficient if participants do not see what they can cooperate on—the condition of pluralistic ignorance described in chapter 4. This was exactly the dilemma of those caught in the unproductive treatment-*versus*-liberty definition of the policy problem. The Assembly group staff members seem to have escaped the dilemma through trial and error rather than through any special techniques or insights. Their insight was real and consequential, but unconscious.

For another illustration from the mental commitment controversy, consider the financing formula for the proposed new system which caused so much consternation on the part of the Short–Doyle administrators from San Mateo and Contra Costa counties. Recall that it required 100 percent state reimbursement for all the system's functions, compensated in part by county contributions prorated according to their most recent levels of effort in the Short–Doyle programs. The interests affected by this formula can be described as the large and well-financed Short–Doyle programs like the ones in Contra Costa and San Mateo, the smaller Short–Doyle programs, the economy-minded financiers in the state legislature and the Department of Finance, the County Supervisors Association and its constituencies, and the Department of Mental Hygiene.

The DMH appeared to want more than anything else a formula that would eliminate the necessity for keeping two sets of records, one for the involuntary and another for the voluntary admissions. The Assembly group made this concession almost immediately. This satisfied all the other interests involved also. Yet, as we have seen, finding a single reimbursement formula was not simple. The one that was finally proposed apparently satisfied the smaller Short–Doyle programs but pleased few other interests.

From the point of view of the county supervisors and Short–Doyle, the best formula would have been a no-strings-attached reimbursement formula at the 100 percent rate. It was obvious to everyone, however, that this formula would be unacceptable to the state.

The larger Short–Doyle programs might have been willing to settle for an across-the-board 75–25 matching formula; but since such a formula would have imposed additional costs on the counties, it would not have been acceptable to the CSAC.

The only feasible solution was some formula that would have (1) satisfied the desire for local initiative, (2) made the imposition of new financial burdens on the counties unnecessary and unlikely, (3) permitted the state to have considerable authority to review and evaluate programs and to withhold monies from those that did not meet state standards, and (4) maintained the paper work and red tape at its current level or only slightly higher. Such a formula was proposed tentatively at one point by David Roberts of the subcommittee staff but vetoed by others in the Assembly group as being "too novel" and therefore psychologically unacceptable. Roberts' formula would have required the state to match county expenditures on a 90–10 basis for all treatment given by the new system. In developing this formula, Roberts attempted to estimate the extra financial obligations that the new system would impose on counties as a result of the state's shifting to the counties the obligation to treat persons who formerly would have gone to the state hospitals. He then added this estimate to his estimate of the current average level of state transfer payments to the counties under the provisions of Short–Doyle. By rounding, he ended with the 90–10 formula.

How Roberts hit upon this solution (which, though never discussed in 1967, emerged from the 1968 legislative session as the basic administrative and fiscal framework of the emergent new system) is not clear. He did not seem to have any special method other than trial and error. He was not given to brainstorming or role playing. Perhaps his success hinged solely on his understanding that an equitable distribution of financial obligations for the new system did not necessarily entail a precise accounting to the state of how its dollars were being spent on each patient or service. He understood that estimation and approximation, by reducing the administrative costs involved in precise itemization, could benefit all parties.

In discussing Pareto superior policy changes we have been describing primarily the way a proposal is tailored to fit an existing but latent consensus. Only rarely, and then on minor issues, however, does such a consensus suffice. It produced sufficient support to pass the Psychology Licensing Act, for example, but not enough to pass AB 1220. Characteristically, the bulk of the support behind a proposal is purchased at the cost of having other interests thrown into opposition: interest A dislikes the very features of the proposal that are attractive to interest B. Yet even those interests that favor the proposal may dislike certain features. The entrepreneur's design problem in these cases is to find ways to keep the mix of policy features sufficiently attractive to win and hold the support of interests that are ambivalent in some degree, that is, building a consensus around a proposal rather than fitting a proposal to a consensus. One way to do this is to incorporate special benefits to certain interests which please them greatly but which are not salient to other interests in the emerging consensus or else do not offend them enough to drive them out of it. Although one might imagine that this special-benefit tactic is widely used, only two instances of it appear in the five contests we have described. One was the provision in AB 1220 for a county plan for all mental health evaluation and treatment services, which could have facilitated increased participation by private hospitals and clinics. This appealed to the California Hospital Association. The other instance was the financial benefit to the state that would be realized by transferring the Bureau of Social Work to the Department of Social Welfare, a provision that appealed to both party caucuses in the Assembly.

It is worth noting, moreover, that both instances were unplanned. That is, these features of the two proposals were not incorporated in the original proposal design explicitly to attract the support of these particular interests. This fact suggests another method of employing the special-benefit tactic besides inventing program features to appeal to particular interests: examine the proposal as presently designed and try to think of interests that would find in it a special benefit of some kind. Unfortunately, I can think of no systematic way to accomplish this task efficiently; nor did I observe political actors doing it often. The Assembly group belatedly thought of trying to interest the California Judicial Council in AB 1220, but there is no evidence that it approached other specialized interests or even considered doing so.

Still another problem in forming a consensus around a proposal arises not from the objective incompatibilities among various interests' policy preferences but from presumed incompatibilities. The skillful entrepreneur can resolve this problem somewhat by playing a mediating role. He can establish himself in this role by being respected by all parties more or less equally or by being mistrusted more or less equally. I have tried to speculate on what might have happened had the DMH, the Midpeninsula Chapter of the ACLU, the Northern California Psychiatric Society, or Short–Doyle drafted and sponsored the Lanterman–Petris–Short Act. My hunch is that it would never have proceeded beyond the discussion stage. It was only because the Assembly group was perceived as relatively disengaged from the enduring conflicts between and among these interests that they were all willing to regard AB 1220 as a serious, even if imperfect, proposal. Different members of the Assembly group handled their mediating roles differently. Lanterman mediated between the mental health professionals and the legal libertarians by being respected by both sides. Difficulties that might have arisen between the DMH and Short–Doyle, on the other hand, were neutralized by Bolton, Vieg, and Roberts, who were generally mistrusted by both parties more or less equally.

ATTENTIVENESS TO PARTICULAR CONTROVERSIES

In chapters 1 to 3, I described certain features of the attentive public for California mental health politics. Yet in the five controversies in chapters 4 to 8 I described sets of participants whose boundaries were not at all coterminous with those of the attentive public. The closest correspondence is probably found for the commitments controversy; but the budget issue comprehended the entire routinely attentive public and many others too, the Mendocino Plan engaged only a small subset of this public, and the other two issues combined subsets of this public and

TABLE 14
VARIATIONS OF INVOLVEMENT IN FIVE ISSUES
(in percent)

	Commitment	Budget	Psychology	Mendocino	Bureau
Was aware of issue[a]	92	92	69	36	56
Number	583	583	583	583	583
Followed developments regularly[b]	72	88	34	27	42
Number	549	557	523	509	514
Attempted to gain active support regularly[c]	41	62	19	8	16
Number	524	542	526	523	522

[a] Based on coded response to item 42.
[b] Answered "continuously" or "turning points" to item 45. Base N omits missing data.
[c] Answered "continually" or "on several occasions" to item 49. Base N omits missing data.

actors from outside. Our survey data suggest nothing, of course, about activity outside the routinely attentive public, but they do reflect the variations in involvement within it. In Table 14 we observe, for instance, that while 92 percent of our respondents had heard of the budget and commitments issues, only 36 percent had heard of the Mendocino Plan (before it was brought to their attention by the questionnaire, to be sure). There is almost as great a spread, across the five issues, of the proportions of our sample who regularly followed developments or attempted to gain active support.

In general, the size of the participating public depends on the arena in which final authorization will be given or withheld. At the state level, for instance, a struggle within the legislature probably commands more attention than one over the same proposal that takes place within the governor's office. The governor's office, in turn, is likely to be more visible than the state Supreme Court, which in turn is likely to be more visible than DMH headquarters or the Attorney General's Office. The general visibility of the arena of ultimate controversy, however, is probably not as important a determinant of the size of the attentive public as are its accessibility to various interests and the accessibility of the several arenas leading up to it. By the criterion of accessibility, the legislature, having numerous interfaces with the public, is clearly the arena most conducive to high levels of participation and attention. Leaders of the California State Psychological Association (CSPA) were properly wary of bringing their problems with the attorney general's June 1966 opinion to the legislature as long as they believed that publicity would rouse organized psychiatry and that this latter force would oppose them. Trying initially to settle the question in a bureaucratic arena—the Attorney General's Office—was a rational strategy.

Another and perhaps more important determinant of the size of the attentive public is the extent of impact, or breadth of change, implied by the proposal. This factor determines not only the size of the attentive public but also, to a large degree, its composition: people who think their interests (however broadly construed) will be affected by the proposal pay far more attention than those who do not. Table 15 indicates the involvement in each of the four other issues of those fifty-nine respondents who were most highly involved in the commitments controversy. High involvement in the latter is defined by a rather strict test: the respondents claim to have followed developments continuously and to have solicited support from at least seven of the nine categories of political actors named in item 51, the activity index.[3] This was, then, an unusually energetic group of individuals. Their propensity for involvement is clear also in their responses to the budget controversy. Yet over half were completely inert on the three issues other than the budget issue, and fewer than 15 percent were as active on these as they were in the commitment contest. Fewer than half followed even the turning points of these three contests and fewer still followed these issues continuously.

TABLE 15
INVOLVEMENT IN FOUR OTHER ISSUES OF FIFTY-NINE
RESPONDENTS HIGHLY INVOLVED IN COMMITMENT ISSUE[a]
(in percent)

	Budget	Psychology	Mendocino	Bureau
Activity scores:				
0	5	56	73	61
3, at least	92	32	19	25
7, at least	73	14	10	12
Followed developments:				
Turning points or more	95	44	32	48
Followed continuously	86	17	14	29

[a] High involvement is defined as "following developments continuously" (item 45) plus scoring 7 to 9 on the commitment activity index (item 51).

Of course, an individual can become aware of and follow developments in a particular issue only if the relevant cues reach him. How such cues are transmitted and received within an attentive public such as we have described is a complicated process that social science has yet to illuminate. It is safe to say, though, that the greater a person's readiness to engage in political activity, the greater the likelihood that cues will reach him at all, reach him early, and reach him repeatedly. Table 16 presents data from the commitment issue bearing on these hypotheses. The likelihood of hearing about the issue before the Dilemma Report was published increases slightly with greater organizational involvement (numbers of memberships and holding office), with greater proximity to the mainstream of informal political communication, and with the greater probability of activism. This last factor is measured indirectly, though I believe validly, in Table 16 by actual activity levels

[3] A respondent's activity index score for any of the five issues is simply the sum of affirmative responses to the categories named in this item.

TABLE 16
ATTENTIVENESS TO THE COMMITMENT CONTROVERSY

	Heard Before Report Released[a]		Followed Developments Continuously[b]	
	Percent	Number	Percent	Number
Number of organizational memberships:				
0	32	101	32	127
1	30	107	31	115
2	36	110	39	128
3 or more	47	131	40	151
Held organization office:				
No[e]	31	195	33	195
Yes	36	199	41	197
Proximity to mainstream information:[d]				
Low—on meeting agenda	24	83	26	86
—for "interest" sake	21	57	28	58
High—seeking support	44	52	50	54
—regular informant	54	37	58	38
Commitments activity score:[e]				
0	24	203	13	204
1–2	31	94	33	93
3–4	28	105	37	109
5–9	50	121	73	124

[a] Based on response to item 42. Missing data excluded from base N.
[b] Based on response to item 45. Missing data excluded from base N.
[e] Excludes respondents who belonged to no organizations.
[d] Based on item 44. Includes only respondents who were informed by personal contact and for whom data were known. Omits eight respondents who said it "came up accidentally."
[e] Score is sum of affirmative responses to categories named in item 51. Missing data are scored as "0."

reported after the fact. Relative proximity to the mainstream of informal political communication is reflected in the way a respondent received information from personal informants. If the informant was seeking the respondent's support or else was answering a routine query, I considered the respondent as being closer to the mainstream than if he had heard of the issue merely by having it come up on someone else's meeting agenda or being mentioned as an interesting bit of news. (I shall return to this notion of an informational mainstream when I discuss the entrepreneur's problem of activating potential allies.)

The same factors that facilitate hearing early also facilitate the regular monitoring of developments, a proposition also borne out by data in Table 16. In general, these propositions are supported by similar tests put to data from the four issues other than the mental commitment controversy.

ATTITUDES TOWARD PARTICULAR PROPOSALS

The single best method of predicting an interest's attitude toward a given proposal is to extrapolate from its past attitude toward similar proposals. Hence, it is advantageous to become acquainted with the history of the programs and politics of a given policy domain, as we did in the domain of California mental health in chapters 1 to 3. On this basis it would have been possible to predict the alignment of mental health professional groups, the DMH, the state hospital superintendents, the ACLU, and academic sociology on AB 1220. Alignments on the issue of the Mendocino Plan could also have been predicted in this way, for example the hospital superintendents predicted to favor a decomposition of the Bureau of Social Work and the bureau to oppose it.

Even though it is probably the best single predictive tool, extrapolation from the past is far from being perfectly reliable. It would not have worked very well to predict the bureau's initial vacillation on the transfer proposal, psychiatry's favorable attitude toward the psychology licensing bill, or the widespread reaction to the governor's proposed budget cuts. One reason is that any concrete proposal is bound to overlap only partially with issues that have arisen historically. There is inevitably a special and unique component to any currently contested proposal, and it is sometimes just this component that determines attitudes toward the proposal. Governor Reagan would probably have been right to assume that the attentive public in 1967 would have tolerated a small or even zero increment in the MI hospital budget, just as they had tolerated such in the past. But a decrement was not acceptable —Reagan's argument notwithstanding that it was not a decrement at all when one took into consideration the declining patient population. Opposition spokesmen perceived in the governor's reductions the first step on a road "returning the hospitals to the snakepit era."

Extrapolation from the past is unreliable also because attitudes change. What interests fought for historically may no longer concern them. When the California State Psychological Association was finally propelled into a campaign for a licensing bill, they discovered that their long forbearance had been unnecessary. Organized psychiatry, which had indeed been an obstacle to a psychology certification act years earlier, actually cooperated with the CSPA on the psychology licensing bill. Attitudes change, too, because the conditions that might have made them appropriate in the past may have changed and thereby eroded their logical, moral, or technical foundations. At least some psychiatrists who would have opposed repeal of the involuntary commitment laws in the early 1950s were favorable to such a change in 1967 because they believed that psychotropic drugs, community clinics, and more liberal welfare programs made it possible for patients to receive treatment voluntarily and without round-the-clock hospitalization.

A final danger in simple extrapolation from the past is that even when it leads to a generally correct prediction it tends to conceal the possible existence of minority factions within traditional alliances, within formal organizations, or within less formal social groups and circles. Psychiatric and medical opposition to AB 1220, for instance, was far from homogeneous. In fact the overwhelming majority of our NCPS subsample favored AB 1220 even after all its adverse implications for the medical model had been articulated and publicized. The Assembly group even managed to find a prominent psychiatric spokesman like Werner Mendel who supported the ideological goals of the bill. Even some of the state hospital superintendents privately favored the bill. Others—like Klatte, who favored it with strong reservations—did not exploit their opportunities to oppose it publicly or attempt to attach crippling amendments. Within Short–Doyle, the old guard generally opposed AB 1220, but the young Turks were relatively sympathetic.

Extrapolation from the past does not work for the entrepreneur at all, of course, if he does not know how a particular interest perceives a proposal. This can easily happen when the policy content of the proposal is so novel or its policy implications so uncertain that it engages no prior issue context, ideological or otherwise.[4] Most proposals do fit some prior frame of reference, however, even if obliquely. In such cases, there is a temptation, risky oftentimes, to impute a frame of reference to others. In the contest over AB 1220, its opponents may have failed to understand, at least initially, that the Assembly group actually intended to

4 An effort to describe the variable impact of highly polarized and diffuse issue contexts can be found in Aaron Wildavsky, "The Analysis of Issue-Contexts in the Study of Decision-Making," *Journal of Politics*, 24, no. 4 (November 1962): 717–732. All but the commitment issue were ideologically diffuse, we might mention, in that orientations to this issue alone were related to our traditionalism index.

abolish the commitment system, not merely improve it to make it easier for people to get help. In opposing AB 1220 because they felt the community treatment and evaluation procedures would be insufficient for this purpose, such opponents did not go on to consider how voluntarism might be fit into the existing system of Short–Doyle and state hospitals. They were not able, therefore, to develop an alternative proposal that would have met the bill's libertarian objectives, at least partially, without a major revamping of the system of mental health treatment services. Similarly, neither the proponents nor the opponents of the bureau transfer ever addressed the fiscal considerations of the proposal as perceived by the legislature. (At least, this is my impression drawn from interviews with many participants in the controversy.) To be sure, it was well understood that the administrative status of the bureau was of less concern to the state legislature than saving money. But what money? Not so much the multimillion dollar benefit in federal funds that would eventually be realized by the transfer, but the half-million dollar savings that would be realized in the current year's appropriations bill. To DMH and BSW administrators, it was the absolute size of the agency budget that loomed important. To the legislator running for reelection on an economy plank—or against an economy-minded opponent—it was most important to be able to show how his party had halted superfluous new programs or in other ways "trimmed fat" from the governor's requested appropriations.

It must also be emphasized that interests may find many aspects of a proposal salient and be cross-pressured by conflicting orientations toward each of these aspects. This was quite common in the commitment reform contest. Many Short–Doyle administrators favored AB 1220 ideologically but were put off by its possible implications for their programs. The same was probably true of several state hospital superintendents and some DMH administrators. County supervisors generally favored the prospect of shifting more financial responsibility to the state but feared losing thereby local initiative in mounting new programs. Many psychiatrists believed in the bill's proposed shift to community services but disliked the bill's libertarian features.

When caught in such cross-pressures and unable to resolve the ambivalence, an interest may temporize. Perhaps new information will come to light; perhaps subsequent modifications to the proposal may make present concerns irrelevant; perhaps debate will slowly sift out the objects of lesser concern from those of greater concern. Most important, political developments may themselves change the premises for decision; for what positions other interests are seen to adopt may be of some moment for one's own decision. Developments of this kind we may call compounding effects, of which bandwagon effects are probably the most recognizable though probably not the most common. There are also entrapment effects, which force an interest to support its traditional allies or oppose its traditional enemies, and clearance effects, which permit an interest to act independently of just such long-term considerations. The early public statements of support in principle for AB 1220 from the DMH and organized psychiatry were almost certainly the results of an entrapment effect. This support in turn created a clearance effect, in that it gave Lanterman, Unruh, and other legislators considerably more leeway than they otherwise would have had. Although compounding effects are always important to a certain degree, they are most likely actually to be decisive when more basic values are in conflict or, at the other extreme, when an interest's basic values are not engaged by the proposal at all.

WINNING ENDORSEMENTS FROM NEUTRALS

A neutral may be thought of as any interest that has not yet registered public support or opposition to the proposal. That is, neutrals are in principle still available to any side, though in fact neutrals may be disposed more toward one position than another. This fact makes some neutrals less rewarding targets than others, but for the moment let us consider the entrepreneur's general problem of having to approach at least some neutrals of every disposition at one point or another in the contest. His general problem is simply to find a way of persuading the neutral to register support for or at least acquiescence in his proposal. In one sense this problem is contained in the larger problem of finding means to persuade anyone to do anything—obviously too far-ranging a subject to be treated here. Hence we shall confine ourselves to the uniquely political dimensions of the entrepreneur's problem, namely, presenting the neutral with the politically significant incentives necessary to gain support for the entrepreneur's proposal.

A politically significant incentive exists only in the eye of the beholder, and often the entrepreneur has no reliable way of knowing the mind of his audience. This is inevitable, because in a sense the audience does not know its own mind. If it did, presumably the interest in question would not still be neutral. The reasons, as we suggested above, are either that it suffers ambivalence owing to a conflict within its own value system or that its value system is not engaged by the proposal at all. From the entrepreneur's viewpoint it makes little difference which set of reasons is operative. He proceeds in the same fashion in either case: he attempts to convince the neutral that the proposal implies at least some changes that will promote the neutral's interests or values. To put it another way, the entrepreneur interprets rather than exhorts or instructs. For those who are ambivalent, the interpretive message is translated into a reinforcement of one side of their value system; for those who are indifferent, the message provides a cognitive map that shows the linkages between the proposed policy changes and their values. What is "persuasive" about the entrepreneur's interpretation, rather than merely informative, is that it is partial, one-sided. Like a lawyer's partiality in making a case for his client, the political entrepreneur's one-sidedness it ethically admissible. A neutral interest can easily hear the other side from opponents if it wishes. Moreover, politically experienced actors understand the utility of this nonjudicialized adversary process and value hearing from someone who is an honest advocate in his own cause. And why not, after all? If many such advocates appear on the scene, all trying to interpret for a man how he is best served by their own respective proposals, the chore of thinking through all those particular interpretations is considerably lightened.[5]

Petris, Lanterman, Bolton, Vieg, and Roberts were unusually effective interpreters of their bill to almost all types of audiences. In varying combinations, they explained to psychiatrists that the bill provided for improving early evaluation and treatment procedures; to the CSAC that it would not cost the counties extra money and might even save them some; to the California bar that it mended a tear in the fabric of individual legal rights; to Short–Doyle that it provided for more community-based services; to psychologists and social workers that it took a multidisciplinary approach; to state legislators and the governor's staff that the federal government would pay the lion's share of any additional costs. Their audiences were not always persuaded, to be sure, but these spokesmen had a knack for discovering areas of special concern to their audiences and of clarifying the advantages their bill implied for these

[5] It is hoped that the reader will not construe this as advice not to think for oneself. The point is only that one can and should find ways to help the thinking of others aid one's own thinking.

concerns. By way of contrast, spokesmen for the opposition to the governor's proposed budget cuts only occasionally went beyond their main argument that the hospitals were bad enough without taking steps to make them still worse. Once or twice during legislative hearings, opposition speakers claimed that in the long run staff cuts would cost the state more; but this line of attack was not much imitated, and not because it was implausible or unrealistic. It was just as plausible to predict that staff cuts would lengthen hospital stays and thereby increase the size of the resident patient population as it was to predict that the patient population would continue to decline (Reagan's argument). It would have been quite in order for the opposition to have stated that an increase of X thousand patients would cost the state Y million dollars annually and that a return to the status quo 1967 would take Z years. Neutral legislators and voters might well have responded to this kind of argument, but opposition spokesmen were too preoccupied with their more purely humanitarian arguments to have thought much about the fiscal ones or to have empathized much with the interests for whom these questions were salient.

One significant political incentive that can be offered a neutral interest is the opportunity to do something it believes is right, equitable, meritorious, just, or in the public interest. One need not idealize men of public affairs, be they officeholders or not, to recognize that nearly all do have conceptions like these, even though they do not always articulate them or act in consonance with them. All else equal, political men prefer to act in consonance with them than contrariwise. Moreover, they are prepared to consider reasoned argument on these grounds, provided the arguments themselves are plausible, the source of the arguments is believed to be reliable, and they have not already reached a settled opinion about the merits of the proposal. For instance, it was astonishingly easy to persuade a number of state legislators to support AB 1220 simply "on the merits." Although the sponsorship of Lanterman, Petris, and Unruh no doubt carried the majority of the votes on this issue, there was an evident minority, particularly in the committees that heard the bill, who were impressed by the persuasiveness of the arguments in favor of it. Assemblyman Duffy, who prior to the hearings seems to have had no particular views on the issue, was probably one of these. Even Senator Teale seems ultimately to have been impressed by the arguments on the merits even though he held fast to his original negative position for many weeks because he had been locked in by previous political and

199

ideological considerations. In a sense, too, the support of Waldie, Lanterman, Petris, Schmitz, and Unruh was obtained on these grounds. Tom Joe persuaded assemblymen Casey and Veneman to support the transfer of the Bureau of Social Work, and the CSPA managed to obtain the help of Senator Beilenson, largely by arguing the merits.

Legislators are probably more susceptible to reasoned arguments on the merits of any particular proposal than are most interests in the attentive public, incidentally. This is so not because they are especially reasonable or more high minded, but because they participate in such a great variety of contests that only a minority are of real concern to themselves, to their constituents, or to other politicians to whom they are beholden. For any proposal not in that minority category they are prepared to have their reason and their conscience lead them.[6]

Although it is impossible to prescribe the components of a credible argument for all occasions, it is probably true that statistics and other sorts of hard data are generally useful. The Assembly group made much of the point that they had systematically surveyed a representative sample of commitment court hearings and had discovered the duration of the average hearing to be exactly 4.7 minutes.

In the budget controversy, the governor and DMH spokesmen were able to point to figures showing a secular decline in the resident patient population and then to use a projection of continuing decline to argue that the numerical ratio of staff to patients would not change even after the layoffs. The opposition had their own statistics about the absolute rather than the relative deprivation of patients in MI hospitals; the governor's cuts, they said, would make it possible for bedridden patients to be bathed only once in ten days. This calculation was based on data obtained by the Commission on Staffing Standards.

Dollars-and-cents figures are an especially important class of hard data, even when they are not very reliable. Wilsnack was able to project annual benefits to the state treasury in the range of $3,200,000 to $12,000,000 from transferring the bureau, a matter of great concern at least to those legislators on the Assembly Social Welfare Committee. More often, of course, it is costs rather than benefits that can be measured in monetary units. The Assembly group was weaker on these grounds than on any other; it was hard for them to arrive at a convinc-

6 A similar theme can be found in certain revisionist writings on Congress, a fountainhead of which is Raymond A. Bauer, Ithiel de Sola Pool, and Lewis Anthony Dexter, *American Business and Public Policy* (New York: Atherton, 1964).

ing estimate of how much their bill would cost to implement and what proportions would be borne by the federal, state, and county governments. The rhetoric of the budget controversy, as we observed above, was almost wholly devoid of dollars-and-cents data, despite the fact that it was seemingly a natural context for arguments employing them.

Another important kind of supposedly hard data is the number of individuals who fall or ought to fall into certain categories, for example, 25,000 MI admissions per year, 1,000 involuntary admissions per month, 90 clients per social worker. Often statistics based on such population estimates are proxy measures for the benefits of a proposed policy change. They are often employed, in the absence of more valid measures of benefits, to counter the hard data concerning dollar costs that the opposition can be relied on to marshall.

Another component of credibility is simplicity. An argument that is hard to follow is, as a consequence, hard to believe. More precisely perhaps, it is easier to disbelieve than to believe. The problem of simplifying a complex argument for public presentation was especially relevant to the sponsors of AB 1220. They made use of flannel boards, pie charts, and flow diagrams. The Dilemma Report was itself a paragon of clarity and simplicity. Its organization carried the reader from an account of the basic dilemma in chapter 1, through two chapters on the legal issues and the treatment issues of the commitment process, to a concluding two chapters proposing changes and discussing, in a question-and-answer format, the more complex features of the proposal. The seven-point concluding summary of the proposals (pp. 178–179) is representative of the draftsmanship in the body of the report:

1. The focus of California's concern for its mentally disordered citizens should be shifted from state hospitals to voluntary community services. To accomplish this redirection of emphasis, emergency service units (E.S.U.'s) should be established in each community. These units will offer short-term intervention services including medical, psychological, social and legal evaluations; emergency counseling and suicide prevention; "priority" referrals to appropriate hospitals, clinics, or community agencies; and access to funds for the purchase of services.

2. Citizens who are gravely disabled or who exhibit such destructive behavior that they are an immediate threat to other persons may be certified for voluntary crisis treatment (with legal review procedures) not to exceed 14 days. Beyond that time they must be released to voluntary services or legal guardianship must be established.

3. No legal disability of any kind shall be incurred by citizens using E.S.U. services.

4. A multidisciplinary Program and Standards Board shall formulate policy, adopt standards, and approve contracts for emergency service units. The Department of Mental Hygiene (Division of Local Programs) will contract with various city, county, state, and private agencies to provide comprehensive E.S.U. services in each community and will administer the program.

5. Citizens who previously would have been committed to a state hospital and who are not now eligible for Medi-Cal, will be made eligible for E.S.U. and E.S.U. referral services as "mental health services" recipients. Other citizens' expenses will be met out of prepaid health policies and their own resources (on a sliding scale), Medicare, Medi-Cal, and federal "Community Mental Health Center" funds. Counties will not be expected to participate beyond their present expenditures in the operating costs of E.S.U.-type services.

6. State hospitals will be upgraded and converted to "open hospitals."

7. Mentally disordered criminal offenders shall be processed in the criminal courts which have well-developed procedures for guaranteeing community safety and protecting individual rights through due process. When mentally disordered offenders are confined it must be for treatment not punishment.

To a certain extent, the credibility of an argument is buttressed by the image of reliability conveyed by the source of the argument. The best way for the entrepreneur to convey an image of reliability is actually to be reliable himself, and the next best way is to be known to be in league with others who are, or at least to have access to their expertise. When the Assembly staff team of Bolton, Vieg, and Roberts introduced themselves, Vieg and Roberts were described as the staff team's experts on law and public finance, respectively. Bolton and Vieg were also able to cite with ease the technical works of well-known psychiatrists and lawyers. As another example, immediately prior to the hearing in the Senate Government Efficiency and Economy Committee on July 11, the Assembly Subcommittee on Mental Health Services sent an information packet to over 1,000 persons on its mailing list. Among other things, the packet contained a photocopy of a letter written to Lanterman by A. Alan Post, the legislative analyst and a man with a reputation for sound judgment on fiscal matters. The letter contained a lengthy analysis of the fiscal implications of AB 1220, and concluded, "to the extent possible it appears to us that this bill assures the counties of the intention to protect them against increased future costs and provides the practical means to do so." The packet contained a similar letter from the chief deputy attorney general praising the bill's reformist intent and asserting its constitutionality. The writer was implicitly refuting the arguments of Miss Lois Scampini, of the San Mateo District Attorney's Office, who had vehemently attacked the bill on constitutional grounds and defended the performance of the existing commitment system.

During the budget controversy, the governor constantly reminded audiences of the assurances he claimed to have received from Lowry, a renowned psychiatric administrator, that staff cuts would not reduce the level of patient care.

In this discussion of the arts of political persuasion, I obviously cannot omit to mention rhetoric. In the Golden Age of Rhetoric—whenever that may have been—the great orators were certainly distinguished by their capacity to switch moods, volume, pitch, and so forth. In this Brazen Age of Organization, rhetoric too has become corrupted by principles of the division of labor, so that it is now possible to develop teams of speakers, each member of which has his own distinctive style and all of whom, collectively, compensate for the weaknesses of any single member. The Bolton–Vieg–Roberts team gave many rhetorical performances in a variety of settings. My impression was that Bolton was typically perceived as being shrewd, insightful, intelligent, even—in some eyes—cunning. Vieg tended to be seen as intelligent, bold, proud, even haughty. Between the two of them, they fulfilled Machiavelli's recommendations that the prince, or in the modern case the team, combine the qualities of both the lion and the fox. Roberts typically followed the two of them in their presentations. Elaborating the fiscal aspects of the case for AB 1220, he appeared to be scholarly, gentle, and sincere. This order of presentation seemed to have been unusually effective, suggesting as it did that both the lion and the fox were actually quite tame.

Rhetoric also involves more than speech. Nonverbal communication is perhaps especially important in signifying the intensity of feeling and concern in others whom one claims to represent. The spokesman for the CAMH at the July 11 Senate G.E. Committee hearing, for instance, flew to Sacramento from Los Angeles expressly for the hearing and returned the same evening. Lanterman took pains to point this out to the committee. Also, the flannel board and charts used by Roberts in many of his presentations to legislative and citizen groups impressed audiences mightily. Legislators, in particular, were not used to seeing so many stage props at committee hearings. The Assembly group took pains to distribute careful summaries of AB 1220 and supplementary materials to legislators and others who attended hearings on the bill.

It virtually goes without saying that anyone representing himself as a spokesman for some interest or cause must be careful to avoid giving impressions that would falsify the validity of his credentials as a true representative. During the May 23 hearings on AB 1220, Degnan and Chope clearly suffered a setback when Duffy—later abetted by Gerlach— questioned their title to speak for Short–Doyle as a group.

Our extended concern with the perceptions and cognitions of the entrepreneur's audiences, it is hoped, has not obscured the fact that it is better actually to have an intelligently designed proposal and a competently drafted bill which embodies it than a proposal which only seems intelligent and technically sound. If the realities are sound, this fact will probably become known, as will realities of the opposite kind. This principle holds especially for proposals routed through legislative arenas in the form of bills. A bill is very much like a computer program; it instructs officials and citizens on what to do if certain conditions are present and compiles a whole series of instructions into what is known colloquially, but not accidentally, as a program. Like computer programs, political programs can "blow up" or lead to absurd conclusions if minor details are not ordered properly. As we saw in chapter 6, for example, the licensing bill drafted by CSPA was deficient as a program, and these deficiencies nearly caused the bill to fail. In the initial draft versions of the commitment reform bill, too, the authors had left ambiguous some significant instructions. The bill referred at various points to "evaluation and treatment" as though it were, first, a service rendered a particular individual at a specific point in his career as a recipient of treatment; second, a function each county was to make available to the residents within its jurisdiction; and third, a structural unit organized as part of a community mental health clinic. As a result of these ambiguities, it was possible to see in the draft the implications that both voluntary and nonvoluntary admissions should receive the same kind of evaluation and treatment services, and that the responsibilities of the clinic staff to inform patients of their legal rights were no different for the voluntary than for the nonvoluntary patients. It also seemed to imply that a single clinic or agency would discharge all the evaluation and treatment responsibilities which the counties would be obliged to provide. The Assembly group intended none of these implications, but it took hundreds of man-hours for them to find and remedy the defects in the language that described the new program.

The same relationship between seeming sound and being so holds for the political aspects of the proposal as it does for its programmatic aspects. In particular, although compounding effects can be stimulated by creating illusions about the nature and extent of a proposal's support, it is usually better, because safer, to be able to represent the situation as it really is. Inasmuch as these "realities" are nearly always ambiguous and fluctuating, the entrepreneur does have comparative freedom in this domain. His concern must be not so much with being accurate as with avoiding inaccuracies that would cause would-be supporters to take risks they would otherwise not wish to take. (This seems to be a cardinal principle of ethics among politicians.) It follows, therefore, that the entrepreneur should endeavor to convince neutrals that he is one of the fraternity who lives by this ethical principle and to recognize that, since confidence is inevitably less than perfect, concrete evidence must also be provided. This was at least one function of the highly successful May 9 hearing on AB 1220. Afterward, it was possible to go to Unruh and other members of the legislature and refer to real evidence of widespread support for the bill. One can hardly overestimate the value of the documentation, pulled from the Assembly subcommittee's files, that Senator Schmitz's right-wing associates had endorsed the principal conclusions of the Dilemma Report.

On August 1, 1967, the eve of SB 677 arriving on the Senate floor (with AB 1220 as a rider), the Assembly group distributed to each senator a list of forty-one organizations that had endorsed the bill. The list did not differentiate endorsements "in principle" from those given without any such reservations, which may suggest a slight qualification of the general norms against purveying unreliable risk-inducing information: the confusion is ordinarily so great at the end of the legislative session that legislators have a ready excuse for voting "in error." Thus, misleading them slightly may not, in those low-risk circumstances, be considered unethical. In any case, whether the actual list was precisely correct or not, the Assembly group had probably convinced themselves that it was a true reflection of widespread support and consensus on the principle of commitment reform, no mean achievments in their own eyes. To a certain extent, perhaps, they had convinced themselves by their own rhetoric, much as they had convinced others. Here is an ex-

ample, from speeches by Lanterman and Petris before the Assembly
Public Health Committee on May 9, in which they emphasized that AB
1220 was the product of

> factual studies and the fullest participation of hundreds of people
> with different views. The final product represents a consensus and is
> generally regarded by all who have participated in its formulation as
> a major necessary step forward.... Initially, over 1,500 questionnaires
> were sent to mental health professionals, lawyers, judges, and con-
> cerned laymen.... Following issuance of the [Dilemma Report], two
> additional public hearings were held to secure the reactions of over
> 40 witnesses, and Subcommittee members and staff conducted dis-
> cussions with individuals and organizations from San Diego to Red-
> ding.... In response to the suggestions and criticisms of the Subcom-
> mittee's original proposals, a working draft of a bill was prepared and
> submitted to a panel of 50 health and legal experts.

THE ROLE OF BARGAINING

As an initial approach to neutrals, an entrepreneur usually has little to
lose by trying persuasion and occasionally has much to gain. But the
rate of success is nevertheless likely to be low. At least some neutrals are
inclined toward the opposition and will eventually take a stand against
the proposal. Others will choose to remain neutral or disengage. Still
others will not find in persuasion, whether reasonable or rhetorical, sufficient incentives to come out in support of the proposal. Hence the
entrepreneur must be prepared to resort to a secondary strategy, bargaining, which entails sacrificing something of political value to himself
in exchange for support.[7] Once bargaining is thought to be necessary,
the only remaining questions for the entrepreneur concern what ought
to be sacrificed and how much.

Contrary to much popular and professional opinion on the subject,
not much bargaining takes place in moving any particular legislative or
bureaucratic proposal along. Most significant bargains have been struck
long before the proposal is conceived (that is, alliances exist), and very
few have to be negotiated afresh. Moreover, most interests in the attentive public probably form unshakable opinions on the proposal very
quickly (if they pay any attention to it at all, that is), and of those that
do not a majority will arrive at their own opinions by being persuaded

---

[7] In this respect bargaining differs from the proferring of special benefits, which
cost the entrepreneur nothing.

(even if by the opposition) rather than bargained with. Yet bargaining is indeed much more important in the policy-making process than its low prevalence might suggest. Those few transactions that do have the character of a bargain typically involve interests whose political support is very weighty or whose political resources are very effective. Furthermore, since the entrepreneur can never be entirely sure with whom it may eventually seem profitable or necessary to reach a bargain, he must constantly be thinking of possibilities and nurturing conditions that increase his chances of getting good terms.

When bargains are struck in exchange for political support, in what currency or currencies are payoffs made? We could surely compile a very detailed and variegated catalogue, but it is probably sufficient to think of three broad classes of payoffs: concessions on substantive policy features of the proposal; non-policy-related side payments like patronage, public testimonials, cash, or log-rolling arrangements; and goodwill. The last takes one of two forms: an implied obligation to render a favor of some unspecified kind in the future or a limited release of the other party from existing comparable obligations to oneself.

Looking back over the history of the bureau transfer controversy recorded in chapter 8, we can find no instance of any bargaining at all, at least not in these species of currency. In the case of the Mendocino Plan, there was at most an unverified log-rolling bargain between Lowry and Brickman. In the case of the Psychology Licensing Act, the CMA was content with the one token concession allowing psychiatrists to employ a limited number of unlicensed psychological assistants. One can count perhaps two concessions by Reagan in the budget controversy, the implied promise that layoffs would be slowed down if the rate of decline in the patient population was less than projected and the concession not to close the day treatment centers. (As we noted above, however, the former was not a concession at all in the eyes of those who disbelieved the promise.) In the contest over AB 1220, bargaining played a much larger role than in any of the other four cases: the jurisdiction of the proposed Citizens Advisory Committee was reduced as a concession to the DMH; in deference to organized psychiatry one of the two professionals certifying a patient for postevaluation "involuntary intensive treatment" (for up to fourteen days) was required to be a physician and "if possible a board-qualified psychiatrist"; the primary role in administering the new evaluation and treatment services was conceded to Short–Doyle; scrapping the funding and programming of all projected new mental health services was a concession to Senator Schmitz; Governor Reagan and then Senator Short were permitted to take public credit for sponsoring AB 1220 (and Short likely got, too, a measure of goodwill from Lanterman and Unruh). There may have been bargains struck with Speaker Burns too, but I have no information on the point. It is worth noting that most of the bargains connected with AB 1220 were concessions, and that only one, the concession to Schmitz, actually converted a neutral into a supporter. The other concessions seemed to drain the opposition of its feelings of urgency—a commonly overlooked phenomenon which we shall treat in detail in chapter 11. Whatever may have been the payoffs in side payments and goodwill to Reagan, Short, and Burns and however well they may have fit the traditional bargaining mold, they were political rarities when compared to the larger number of non-bargaining incentives that engaged interests in the commitments contest. Without these payoffs, to be sure, the commitment reform effort would certainly have failed; and this presumption suffices to indicate their importance in the process.

THE RELATIVE WEIGHTINESS OF INTERESTS

I stated at the end of the introductory chapter that interests differed greatly with respect to how much weight their endorsements carried in the eyes of decision-making authorities. For the entrepreneur seeking to align enough interests so that their combined and weighted support is sufficient for victory, there is, therefore, the problem of recognizing which interests count relatively heavily and which do not. Unfortunately, there is presently no articulated and agreed on interpretation of the notion of power or influence, to which weightiness is related, among either politicians or scholars. There is no point in our rehearsing here all the alternatives proposed in the scholarly literature, since our task is limited to interpreting weightiness in such a way that it has operational significance for the political entrepreneur. I would suggest, then, this formulation: An interest is weighty to the extent that its opinions on matters within its presumed competence are seriously heeded by decision makers and to the extent that its views on policy, in the absence of any strong reasons to the contrary, are likely to prevail.

Implicitly, this is a statement only about the past history of an interest's weightiness inferred from a broad range of interactions between the interest and decision makers. Consequently, it provides the entrepre-

TABLE 17
WEIGHTINESS OF INTERESTS IN THE ATTENTIVE PUBLIC[a]
(circa 1966, as seen by state legislature)

Bureaucratic and Economic Interests		Professional and Ideological Interests	
DMH	10	CMA	9
Short–Doyle	8	Organized nursing	3
State hospitals	7	CAMH	7
Bureau of Social Work	6	CCRC	7
CSEA	2	Organized psychiatry	7
State hospital communities	6	CSPA	4
Organized psychiatric		ACLU, etc.	2
technicians	1	Certain judges	3
Family caretakers	1	Organized social work	4
CHA	6		
Short–Doyle contractors	2		

General Overseer Interests	
Assembly group	8
Senate mental health "specialists"	10
Office of Legislative Analyst	7
Academics, etc.	2
Department of Finance	5
Governor	10
Assembly leadership	10
Senate leadership	10
General Public	3
Mass media	4
Community welfare groups	7
CSAC	10

[a] Excludes anti-mental-health interests in radical Right.

neur only imperfect guidance on how weighty an interest will prove currently, in a contest over a specific proposal and with a specific subset of decision makers. The technical difficulties involved in making reliable and valid inferences from the historical record, which is complex and ambiguous, are great. Nevertheless, the entrepreneur may find that a rough picture of the relative weightiness of various interests is more useful than none at all. In Table 17 I have drawn my own picture of relative weights in the attentive public to California mental health politics circa 1966. Since weightiness is measured only with respect to a set of decision makers, I have used, for purposes of illustration, the state legislature as the yardstick. The weights would be quite different, of course, were the relevant decision makers considered to be the director of DMH, the governor, some legislative subcommittee, or any other set.[8]

Often the entrepreneur has no control over which set of decision makers will ultimately pass on his proposal, but when alternatives are indeed available he will naturally prefer arenas in which the interests aligned with him carry the maximum weight. Whether or not he actually moves to have his preferred alternative realized depends to a large extent on what the resource costs are. In the contests over the Mendocino Plan and the fiscal 1968 budget for the MI hospitals, the ultimate authorities were clearly identified—the DMH director and the governor, respectively—and there was little apparent room for maneuver. In its struggle to cancel the attorney general's opinion, on the other hand, the CSPA had at least three prominent options: the Attorney General's Office, the legislature (with the governor's concurrence), and the courts. CSPA's views would carry least weight in the first arena, it might have appeared, and the most weight in the last of these three. Yet the courts were avoided in favor of the legislature on the grounds that the costs of going that route were too high. And the strategy directed at the Attorney General's Office was pursued simultaneously with the strategy directed at the legislature, precisely because it cost so little. The CSPA was in the enviable political position of having many options, none of which absolutely precluded the other.

The preference for decision-making arenas that accord maximum weight to the interest's or one's own side is generalizable from the ultimate arenas we have described so far to all arenas through which the proposal passes prior to reaching the terminal one. Considerations of resource cost are relevant in these circumstances too. The sponsors of AB 1220 would have preferred for the Assembly-passed bill to have been heard in the Senate Social Welfare Committee, rather than in the Government Efficiency and Economy Committee; but even if Senator Burns had been persuadable at all, it would probably have cost too much in goodwill (Burns's and other senators') to have made the preferred arena worth bargaining for. This calculation worked out the other way when Burns was persuaded to substitute Senator Petris for himself on the

---

[8] Since our definition of weightiness permits a probabilistic interpretation ("views on policy . . . are likely to prevail"), Table 17 rates interests' weightiness on an equal-interval scale similar to the scale .00 to 1.00 used to describe probabilities. For convenience, I have simply scaled the probability measure up by a factor of 10.

conference committee. This personnel switch in effect rerouted SB 677 from an arena where its supporters carried little weight to an arena where they had a fighting chance.[9]

What are the sources of political weightiness? To put the question more precisely, why do decision makers heed the opinions of some interests more seriously than those of others?[10] Although even a moderately detailed answer would be extremely lengthy, it does not do reality too much violence to reduce the great variety of details to five principal categories. In a democracy, numbers count; and the more widely an interest is shared, the more weighty it is.[11] Secondly, in almost any political system, intensity of feeling counts; and the more intensely an interest cares about something, the more seriously it is heeded. A third source of weightiness is special competence, including scientific or technical expertise and personal experience which is believed to qualify an individual or group with unusual insight or sensitivity about a problem. Relatively high functional indispensability is yet another source of weightiness. Employees, for example, can go on strike; and administrators can hint that they will not (or "cannot") readily comply with a proposed policy change. These implied threats are in some circumstances taken quite seriously. Finally, there is what may be called prerogative, the legal or customary right to be consulted on certain policy matters. This right often originates in claims to special competence or to functional indispensability, but the right may survive long after the claim has ceased to be warranted on these grounds.

Any proposal that is opposed by interests whose weight comes from either prerogative rights or high functional indispensability needs counterbalancing support from interests of a similar kind. The counterweight need not be completely offsetting, of course, but almost inevitably some counterbalancing is required. If they had had the active support of only Doctors Werner Mendel and Richard Gerlach and no other medical or psychiatric administrators at all, the sponsors of AB

[9] There are certain exceptions to this principle arising from the necessity to route the proposal through a sequence of arenas. The entrepreneur might wish to route a proposal through a relatively less favorable arena if support acquired there had the potential to generate significant compounding effects that would assist the proposal in moving through subsequent arenas.

[10] Let us be clear. The questions is about the weight accorded interests' opinions, not their wishes, desires, or demands, though often opinions do fuse indistinguishably with the latter.

[11] This is true whether one counts numbers of interests, groups, or individuals within groups or interests.

1220 would still have maintained a semieffective shield against criticisms emanating from organized psychiatry and from Short–Doyle. Without even two such spokesmen, however, the bill would have been doomed at the outset.[12] Similarly, Dr. Lowry was the only prominent professional spokesman publicly supporting Reagan's budget proposal. Had he merely remained silent, Reagan's budget request would surely have met even stronger political opposition than it did. Lowry's statements were obviously a great comfort to editorialists who sympathized with the governor's economy drive but did not wish to be accused by mental health professionals of a readiness to endanger the well-being of patients in mental hospitals.

There are a number of distortions that commonly affect people's estimations of their own side's weightiness and that of the opposition. The would-be entrepreneur is hereby cautioned against them. The most serious, because it paralyzes action even before it has been attempted, is to focus on the "absolute" weight of opposition interests rather than on the differential separating the opposition from one's own side. Some partisans of commitment reform, for instance, balked at the thought of fighting the medical-psychiatric-DMH alliance and simply forgot to take account of the very considerable support their own side could muster. In other cases, they committed the fallacy of imputing titanic strength to this alliance out of an undue regard for the weight that originates in prerogative and high functional indispensability. Their own side measured its weight in numbers and to a certain extent in special (even though nonmedical) competence, and in this case there was no reason to derogate these sources of weightiness relative to those of the opposition. Interestingly, this fallacy was committed by the Short–Doyle leadership also, which overestimated the weightiness of their own prerogative and indispensability attributes and thereby underestimated the weight of their opponents.

Another fallacy is to assume that weightiness in general is identical with weightiness in a particular case. If the basis of weightiness has been prerogative, for instance, or claims to special competence, changing times or changed circumstances may have eroded these. A few prominent activists from organized psychiatry, for instance, remembering the

[12] If at least some counterbalancing of this kind cannot be found, the proposal probably deserves to lose, especially because a little bit—like testimony from one professional who happens to disagree with dominant opinion in his profession—goes a long way.

weighty role of organized medicine in the Short–Doyle battles of the mid-1950s, still, in 1966–67, believed that the CMA and organized psychiatry were in a position to act with similarly great effect. They were shocked and angered at how little—in their view—medical opinion was heeded in the contest over certain provisions of AB 1220 (the imposition of strong penalties for breaches of confidentiality, the restricted definition of "gravely disabled"). Some were even shocked (or claimed to be) at how little the governor seemed—in their view, again—to care for the opinion of private psychiatry concerning the advisability of the budget cuts.

The last fallacy in estimating weightiness that I shall mention here is the tendency to extrapolate from successes scored with persons and groups of little authority to officeholders with great authority. Many participants in the broad coalition opposed to the governor's projected cuts, for example, richly impressed with the success of their own campaign within the attentive public and the mass public (as evidenced by the public opinion polls and by the media's faithful reproduction of their spokesmen's rhetoric and arguments), began to think they could actually force the governor into retreating from his position. Some even spoke of mobilizing two-thirds of the legislature to override the governor's vetoes of appropriations for the MI hospitals. This was scarcely plausible, given the fact that the Republicans held nearly half the seats in each house.

HOW MUCH IS ENOUGH?

One never knows how much support is "enough." Even after the contest is over, the entrepreneur knows only whether the existing consensus yielded more or less than enough. Nevertheless, the entrepreneur must play some hunch, and in doing so he runs one of two risks: wrongly believing "enough" is unattainable or wrongly believing "enough" will be easy to attain. Only by assessing the consequences of each type of error can the entrepreneur decide whether to proceed or not. This need not be done blindly. A certain amount of testing is possible, for example, sending up trial balloons. The Assembly group, in effect, was continually testing its market from December 1965 until the spring of 1967 when it was too heavily invested to withdraw easily. Without the benefit of such judicious testing, the CSPA remained needlessly quiescent until the attorney general's decision forced them to act.

Still, some degree of uncertainty and risk taking is irreducible. The conventional wisdom holds that entrepreneurship fails more often than it succeeds. If it is valid, one might conclude that the more common error is overconfidence rather than pessimism. In my view this conclusion is correct but too narrow. One must also add that the consequences of wrongful pessimism are probably more unfortunate than are the consequences of the opposite error. This is so because failure—not attaining enough support in one go-around—usually increases the likelihood of success in the next one, particularly if the weightiness of one's supporters depends on numbers and intensity of feeling.[13] The opposition to the governor's budget cuts failed in 1967, but Reagan has not repeated his attacks on the hospital budget since then. Had the commitment reform movement failed in 1967, it would have been harder to thwart it in 1969, say, just as Short–Doyle succeeded in 1957 precisely because it had failed in 1955. A vigorous social movement cannot be denied repeatedly. This book focuses on the single contest, the short run as it were. It is therefore worth emphasizing here that in the long run enough support is sometimes built out of a lengthy sequence of unsuccessful proposals. In a larger perspective, the costs of wrongful overconfidence may turn out to be assets in disguise.[14]

[13] We must immediately qualify this proposition by saying that failure decreases this likelihood if failure demoralizes and discourages one's allies.

[14] See Albert O. Hirschman, "The Principle of the Hiding Hand," *Public Interest*, no. 6, winter 1967.

10

The Entrepreneur Builds a Coalition

POLITICAL RESOURCES

I have already referred to currency resources—goodwill, concessions, and side payments—that are sometimes employed to purchase support. These resources are relatively exhaustible, as are resources like personal energy and time. When these resources are used they can literally be used up. But there is another type of political resource, used for "production" rather than for direct purchase of support, which is relatively inexhaustible and even more essential to success than currency resources. We can identify three major classes of production resources: analytical, marketing, and managerial. These are political analogues, we might say, of those famous "factors of production," land, labor, and capital, in manufacturing. Analytical resources are the means whereby the entrepreneur produces competent and insightful studies of a policy problem and recommendations that can be transformed into a political proposal. These include generally data (statistics, information about program management and client satisfaction, and so forth), in-house experts and analysts, and outside consultants and advisers. Marketing resources are the means whereby the entrepreneur propagandizes his proposal among others in the attentive public and beyond. These include such things as money, experienced public speakers among his allies, a communication apparatus (leased long-distance telephone lines, a mimeograph machine), personal access to large numbers of groups and individuals. Finally, whatever helps an entrepreneur make more rational decisions about how to acquire and utilize currency, analytical, and marketing resources I shall call managerial resources. These might be political intelligence from sympathetic informants, office space to work in and full-time secretaries to receive phone calls, knowledge of legislative procedure and personalities, and so forth.

Production resources are political instruments that exist independently of the particular individuals or groups that wield them or, in certain cases, actually constitute them. A network of informants spread throughout all the MI hospitals, for instance, fed valuable data to the various organizers of the opposition to the governor's budget cuts, including the CSEA leadership, the citizen committee, and the ad hoc group at Napa State Hospital. This network was certainly an important political resource, yet the particular individuals who constituted it were constantly changing, as were the organizations and individuals who consumed the data that it transmitted. The vocabulary of production resources, therefore, permits us to think in terms of political activities and functions per se without being forced immediately to think about precisely who performs them. The entrepreneur must deal with this latter question eventually, but it helps to have some conception beforehand of the general functions to be performed.

ANALYTICAL, MARKETING, AND MANAGERIAL FUNCTIONS

A full discussion of any one of these functions or even a few of their aspects would necessarily be quite lengthy. Therefore, I shall highlight only the entrepreneur's two or three most important problems in executing each of these functions.

The analytical function may be divided into three somewhat interrelated activities: analyzing existing programs and policies and designing a proposed policy change (basic analysis); modifying the initial proposal to take account of criticisms (corrective analysis); and salvaging the effectiveness and efficiency of the proposal once concessions have been made that jeopardize the internal coherence of the policy design (reintegrative analysis). Basic analysis should take account of four main constraints which bear on the objective of designing a policy that will work as intended: technical feasibility, political viability (whether the favorable consensus will yield enough support), economic and financial possibility, and administrative operability. Basic analysis cannot avoid all errors, however, nor should it attempt to do so. Many of its errors can be picked up by corrective analysis, which characteristically involves a different set of people from the ones who made the basic analysis. Often the corrective analysis is undertaken by persons who are opposed to its basic intent, for example, by administrators who will be charged with implementing the new policy should it be authorized but who were not consulted initially out of fear that they would have sabotaged it then. The responsibility for reintegrative analysis falls again on many of the same persons who made the basic analysis. The entrepreneur must be alert to the possibility, however, that some of this original group may no longer be willing to work on the proposal in its altered form and that replacements will therefore be necessary.

High quality basic analysis increases its value as a political resource in direct proportion to the scope and complexity of the proposed policy change. Proponents of the status quo and of minor or incremental changes do not, in general, benefit from high quality policy analysis quite as much, except when they utilize it to combat an opposing coalition seeking to promote a broad and complex policy change. These, at least, are hypotheses supported by our own case studies. In the case of the commitments controversy, for example, the proponents of reform needed continual inputs of high quality policy analysis, their proposal being both broad and complex. Their opponents did not need to match them in analytical capability, however, since they could simply pick out the weak spots in the other side's analysis. The issues in the other four controversies were relatively narrow and uncomplicated, and policy analysis was therefore employed—or not employed—about equally by opposing sides.

Our case studies provide us with only two examples of corrective analysis. The numerous technical deficiencies in the CSPA's initial version of a licensing bill and in the Assembly group's first circulated draft bill provoked criticism from many quarters of the attentive public. In both cases, critics came forward with ideas for constructive revision. In the latter case many of the ideas came from individuals who were fundamentally opposed to AB 1220 but who did not wish to risk the bill's becoming law without the particular deficiencies being corrected. This suggests that the skillful entrepreneur can utilize the analytical capabilities of his opponents to his own advantage. There are two problems in doing this—first, that the opposition will be able to pillory the proposal entirely through its weaknesses and, second, that the opposition will simply ignore the proposal, will refuse to take it seriously. The first type of risk occurs when the proposal has so much momentum that its opponents feel the time has come to fight to the bitter end. Then they drop the pose of being constructive, even if skeptical, critics. The strategy of refusing to take the proposal seriously, on the other hand, makes sense when the momentum is so slight that any attention at all might give it an unwanted boost. The entrepreneur's problem, then, is to provoke opponents to break their silence without at the same time driving them into all-out opposition. The Assembly group backing AB 1220 calibrated just such a stimulus in their draft legislation which they circulated to persons given to understand that they were numbered among some fifty other blue-ribbon panelists. Among these were included both presumptive friends and presumptive foes, but nearly all responded to the solicitation.[1]

The critical resources needed for marketing a proposal are those that facilitate rapid and efficient communication with individuals and groups both inside and outside the attentive public. Communication may be thought of as being transmitted either by broadcast to an undifferentiated audience or by channels to a relatively specific and identifiable audience. The medium of communication—whether printed, electronic, or personal—is probably of only secondary importance to the mode of transmission (broadcast or channeled), although the two are to an extent related: broadcast communications typically involve mass-media transmission, whereas channeled communications typically involve persons.

The typical role of electronic and especially printed media in broadcast transmission sometimes makes it advantageous for the entrepreneur to stage events that put his proposal in a favorable light and that journalists (and their employers) will consider newsworthy. In the budget controversy, the nascent opposition coalition made sure to pack with their own members the hearing held by Senator Short on March 28 to ventilate grievances against the governor's proposal. It is quite likely that Short staged the hearing with the object of creating such a newsworthy performance. He also took the unusual symbolic step of sending a subpoena to administration officials commanding their attendance. In the commitments controversy, the Assembly subcommittee staff tried to prepare each legislative committee hearing in such a way as to create newsworthy events not only for the mass media but also, and probably more to the point, for the editors of in-house newsletters. The success of the May 9 hearing was in fact reported as such in the CSAC newsletter.

[1] The logic of our exposition calls at this point for a discussion of reintegrative analysis. Unfortunately, there is not much to discuss, since our case studies contain only one instance of it, the frenzied redrafting of SB 677 in order to meet Senator Schmitz's requirements, which sheds no real light on reintegrative analysis in general.

The NCPS newsletter carried a column on the Los Angeles hearing of December 12, 1966.

The significance of interpersonal contact in most channeled transmission implies that the entrepreneur should, over the long run, establish many such contacts and from time to time refresh them so as to keep channels open. The Assembly Subcommittee on Mental Health Services used periodic mailings to over 1,000 persons and groups to keep channels open. The DMH used its monthly publication *Mental Health Progress*. The DMH also compiled a mailing list of persons to whom it sent occasional reports on pending legislation of interest to the department. At least in Lowry's administration, the DMH director had regular monthly meetings with representatives of the CMA and organized psychiatry. An annual CCRC–CAMH awards banquet functioned as a means of keeping channels open among characteristically insulated circles within the attentive public. Since important legislators and executive branch officials (including the governor occasionally) also attended, the banquet helped to keep channels open to important participants in what might be called an intermittently attentive public.

During the progress of the contest itself, it might be useful to keep channels open to certain key allies. For instance, the assembly subcommittee staff kept the house leadership, principally Unruh or his staff, informed about the progress of the commitment reform project. This flow of information had the effect of reminding the Speaker's office that the project was ongoing and that at some unspecified future time it might be necessary for the sponsors of the project to call on the Speaker for help. (It also had the effect, of course, of permitting Unruh to monitor the political implications of developments and, if they appeared adverse, to urge a change in direction.)

Of the many varieties of resources that one could imagine as helpful for performing managerial functions, legitimacy in the role of broker between one's own emerging coalition and outsiders—neutrals, opponents, or relevant authorities—is probably most important. This resource will be discussed in chapter 12, when contest dynamics are treated. Here, only feedback, a hardly less significant managerial resource, will be discussed. The feedback of greatest relevance, of course, concerns the attitudes and actions of opponents and, secondly, of interests who are still neutral. There are two major subfunctions in feedback gathering, data collection and data delivery.

Data delivery depends to a large extent on purposive organization, particularly on having a telephone number or known mailing address where feedback can be directed, recorded, and stored. Secretaries and filing cabinets help too. During the latter part of the struggle over AB 1220, its opponents were constantly frustrated by the succession of amendments and promised amendments to the bill. Only in Sacramento, and indeed only in the capitol building itself, was it possible to keep abreast of the changing provisions of AB 1220 and of the shifting coalitions and sides in the controversy over the bill. The Assembly group had access to such feedback mainly because they held formal jurisdiction over the contents of the bill itself. They also had a full-time staff of secretaries and clerks who could gather, record, and store the feedback coming from within and without the capitol.

Feedback can be created as well as merely gathered. Public and semipublic hearings are an excellent means of generating feedback not only to oneself but to fellow members of one's coalition who might otherwise have a hard time obtaining it.[2] Bolton and Vieg profited greatly from the semipublic meeting arranged by the Los Angeles Welfare Planning Council on January 11, 1967. They learned who some of the key figures were in the Los Angeles area's attentive mental health public and what their initial dispositions were. (It is doubtful, of course, that the WPC staff members who arranged this gathering had this end in mind.) There is also some evidence that CAMH and ACLU activists who attended the December 5 and the December 12 hearings made use of the information generated by these events in planning further moves in their own localities. Following these hearings it was easier for them to identify the issues of concern to many of the psychiatric and medical professionals and to identify which groups and individuals were potential supporters and opponents. Following the May 23 Public Health hearings, a few mental health professionals and lay activists who lived in San Mateo County took note of Chope's opposition to AB 1220 and began to organize a local countercampaign.

[2] The function served by public committee hearings in distributing important political information among interest groups about each other, which they may use to consolidate or shift alliances, has been almost completely ignored in the literature on the legislative process. David Truman's trenchant discussion of the use of public hearings, for instance, gets no closer than describing the use of a hearing "as a propaganda channel through which a public may be extended and its segments partially consolidated or reinforced." (*The Governmental Process* [New York: Alfred A. Knopf, 1951], p. 372.) The problem with such public means, however, is that the feedback is monitored not only by one's allies but by one's opponents as well.

MOBILIZING ALLIES

As we argued above, political resources exist, in an analytic sense at least, independently of the particular persons or groups who control them or compete for them. Concretely, however, it is people who use resources, or have access to them; and therefore it is particular individuals or groups whom the entrepreneur must try to activate as fellow-workers or allies. All the problems entailed in simply winning endorsements are entailed also in mobilizing allies, since the latter have to be persuaded not only to take a stand but also to exert themselves to win the support of still others. Inducing individuals and groups to undertake such exertions presents, therefore, all the foregoing problems plus a few fresh ones.

One problem, at least potentially, is the fact that a winning proposal in many cases benefits those who exerted themselves on its behalf no more than those who put forth but little effort. A winning proposal is in a sense a public good, in the economist's technical sense, like clean air or a naval fleet.

Strictly speaking, it is almost always rational for anyone who stands to benefit from a public good to allow others to produce it and for him to do nothing, provided his efforts do not at the same time create some by-product which he values independently of the public good.[3] Why, then, should any interest exert itself at all? One reason is that this particular kind of public good is produced only by winning a gamble—that enough support can be accumulated in time—and if one believes that the outcome will be close, then it is not irrational to believe that one's own efforts might produce the margin of victory. Another reason is that exertions are rewarded by other activists with a certain measure of goodwill which is useful for a variety of unknown future purposes. Finally, there is in fact a noncollective good produced as a by-product of one's exertions, an augmented claim to be consulted on which concessions or side payments ought to be made in the later course of the contest. In any event, whether the disincentive to action posed by the irrationality of contributing to the production of a public good is ever an important political obstacle for an entrepreneur to overcome, it was not apparent in any of the five controversies I studied.

Probably the most important disincentive was involvement in other

---

[3] Mancur Olson, Jr., *The Logic of Collective Action* (Cambridge, Mass.: Harvard University Press, 1965).

struggles which, for a particular interest at a particular time, had greater priority than one for which the entrepreneur was seeking to mobilize activists. Thus, the DMH was too preoccupied with the budget controversy in early 1967 to commit itself to the battle waged by organized psychiatry and Short–Doyle to modify or kill AB 1220. The CSPA permitted others to fight on behalf of AB 1220 while it concentrated on its own licensing bill and on the budget battle. In the latter contest, the CMA stayed aloof in part because of its concerns with Medi-Cal fees and the abortion reform bill. The vast coalition of opponents of the budget cuts got little assistance either from Short–Doyle, which had to protect its own budget, or from the legislative cadre pushing commitment reform that session.[4]

All this suggests one simple procedure the entrepreneur can follow in planning his campaign for mobilizing additional activists. Take an inventory of those interests who are likely to be favorable to the proposal. Then narrow the field further by considering which are also likely to be relatively free to commit political currency and production resources to the struggle. If the list is too long, trim it further by eliminating interests to whom it is hard to obtain access, that is, with whom there are no existing communication channels whether formal or informal. (It is almost always possible to open such channels, of course, but usually at some cost to the entrepreneur's own time, energy, and perhaps to his stock of goodwill.) This method is later repeated, as the nature of the political situation comes into clearer focus.

This procedure is not only simple but intuitively plausible, so much so, in fact, that relative novices in politics follow it quite spontaneously. I was visiting one of the MI hospitals the morning the governor made public his proposed budget cuts, and I observed a hastily convoked gathering of the fifteen or so top administrators and informal leaders in the hospital. After an hour's discussion, they concluded that it would be advantageous and appropriate for them to help organize a campaign against the governor's proposal. Then, using a roll-away blackboard, the group brainstormed for "places to start" and recorded about thirty groups and organizations, local, statewide, and even national, that they presumed would be opposed to the cuts. Most of these were mental health professional associations and local civic groups (who would be concerned about unemployment and the local economy), including the

---

[4] An even more important reason for the Assembly group's relative quietude was of course Lanterman's obligation and desire not to embarrass a Republican governor.

hospital's own board of trustees. A few were political party committees or clubs. As they went along, they occasionally erased those they realized would be unable or unwilling to give much help, the Republican party committees for instance. Finally, they allocated the task of contacting these interests to individuals who had especially good access to them. Potential allies to whom they had no access were noted, and decision about them temporarily deferred.

An auxiliary procedure to this is to take an inventory of existing lines of access and to follow them wherever they lead. This adds possibilities that are likely to be overlooked in scanning what in effect is only the attentive public and its periphery. The hospital group followed this procedure also, and by doing so turned up primarily the names of individuals who it was believed had access to other political resources or to the governor and legislators themselves, for example, men in the upper levels of the CMA and some persons who were active Republican fund raisers.

Other things equal, it is better to mobilize allies who are more rather than less effective, those who control or have access to relatively effective resources. These are not necessarily the weightiest groups or individuals. Bolton's effectiveness, for instance, was often underestimated by tacticians in the Short–Doyle leadership and in the DMH. They assumed that because he had little weight (apparently only expertise) he would have little effect. He had many resources, however, including widespread personal contacts within the attentive public, high standing with the state legislators whom he served, access to feedback, detailed knowledge of legislative scheduling and procedure, and not inconsiderable rhetorical talents. Moreover, when encouraged and directed to do so by his legislative employers, he used all these resources with a great deal of skill. To take another example, although the CAMH carried little weight compared with other interests, its organizational network, spread throughout the state, made it possible for CAMH to mobilize the weight of others behind any proposal it chose to back. It was constrained, of course, to choose its contests very selectively. Because its resources were highly exhaustible (volunteer time and energy, and goodwill with certain legislators and in the upper echelon of the DMH), it could not afford to expend them on more than a very few proposals in a short period of time.

Although the DMH was relatively weighty in the context of both legislative and executive branch politics, its resources for mobilizing the support of other interests in the mental health public were not commensurate with its weightiness. That is, it was less effective than it was weighty. As we observed in chapter 3, the DMH was principally a holding company. It was in the position of having to take much of the public's blame when things went awry, but received little praise when affairs were handled competently. The department made few efforts to gain allies in its attempt to scuttle, or at least to amend heavily, AB 1220. There is no indication that Lowry made much of an attempt to win allies in his effort to stop the bureau transfer, and the one approach he seems to have made to extra-legislative interests (CCRC) failed.

The entrepreneur should also take care to distinguish between routine, or across-the-board, effectiveness and effectiveness with respect to specific purposes or targets. The California Medical Association had the capacity for working behind the scenes very effectively whenever it chose to do so. Through its lobbying arm, the Public Health League, and the league's very effective lobbyist, Ben Read, the CMA could gain easy access to legislators and administrators. One study of California legislative politics rated the CMA near the top of its list of powerful lobbies in state politics, slightly ahead of the County Supervisors Association.[5] This sort of routine effectiveness was clearly beyond the reach of groups like the CAMH and CCRC. Yet these two citizen groups could mobilize considerable support behind specific proposals under certain circumstances. The CAMH did so with regard to the commitment reform proposal and the budget-cut issue. The CCRC very likely could have done so with regard to the proposal to transfer the Bureau of Social Work. Much of the support amassed behind AB 1220 was mobilized by groups like the CAMH, CCRC, CSPA, and some local chapters of the National Association of Social Workers. Lay activists were responsible for creating much of the support that brought success for the Short–Doyle bill in 1957. As I observed above, the exhaustibility of the resources available to groups such as these makes it necessary, in the short run, for them to concentrate their resources on only a few proposals.

There are many species of resources, and the entrepreneur should keep in mind the possibility that interests or individuals well endowed with one species of resource might be relatively impoverished with respect to other species of resources. The CAMH was relatively well equipped to mobilize support within the routinely attentive public,

[5] John C. Wahlke, Heinz Eulau, William Buchanan, and LeRoy C. Ferguson, *The Legislative System* (New York: John Wiley, 1962), p. 318.

especially among lay activists and among certain professional groups in certain locales; but it was not as well equipped to mobilize support within the legislature. Its resources were those of organization, manpower, and apparent disinterestedness. It had very little currency in side payments to offer legislators. The same was true of the CCRC. To the extent that these groups could offer side payments to legislators they could offer them only in the form of public praise for legislators' efforts. Not all legislators, however, found such praise especially relevant to their own political needs and ambitions. The CSPA had resources of manpower and weak but enduring alliances with other professional groups. These made it possible for them to seek their goals through legislative politics and through political pressure directed at the Attorney General's Office. On the other hand, they lacked the financial resources and the solid base of public esteem that might have enabled them to sponsor a test case in court. Whereas organized psychiatry could utilize the profession's high popular standing as a resource in its public campaign against the proposed staff cuts, it was relatively poorly endowed with manpower resources. The California State Employees Association, by contrast, lacked the appearance of impartiality and professional concern but had access to lots of manpower.

The effectiveness of a resource varies according to the context in which it is used. Although some resources, like rhetorical ability and jurisdiction over one's own time and workplace, are useful in a great variety of contexts, the utility of most other resources is likely to be much more confined. DMH spokesmen, for example, who attempted to persuade legislators that the bureau transfer would jeopardize the continuity of care found their reputation as spokesmen for sound medical practice temporarily canceled by the suspicion that their opinions were dictated primarily by considerations of administrative power. Although the Bureau of Social Work had important allies in the legislature, it was unable to make use of them to help stop the Mendocino Plan. The plan was essentially an intradepartmental matter for which it was difficult to develop relevant support outside.

Our adjuration that resource effectiveness is purpose specific and context specific suggests that possible allies should be located by relatively instrumentalist criteria rather than by the methods suggested above, which stress the attitudes and availability of interests. Under certain unusual conditions this is so. The Assembly group, for example, through its own staff gained access to the Assembly Public Health Committee members through the committee staff, and to legislative analyst A. Alan Post through several members of Post's staff. Assemblyman Zenovich was mobilized as an ally (or so it appears) to approach Senator Burns on behalf of SB 677 as the bill was being considered for re-referral to committee (around August 1, 1967). A similar process was involved in the growth of the Assembly group itself. Lanterman was the last to commit himself fully to the reform project. His support was critical to the effort, however, since he was known to have resources that would be extremely effective in winning the support of the governor and the legislators. Lanterman could not reasonably be asked to engage himself fully, however, until the Dilemma Report was in circulation and the signs of a favorable tide had become visible. It was also necessary for him to receive assurances on the legal and administrative soundness of the basic reform plan from an old personal friend, Dr. Duval (entry 13 in Table 11, p. 120), whose advice he relied on frequently. Hence, Bolton and Vieg journeyed to Santa Barbara to see Dr. Duval, who was persuaded and who then gave the go-ahead to Lanterman.

The obvious advantages of choosing allies in this manner are the clear focus on goals and the economy of effort in reaching them. The disadvantages, however, are also serious. The most important is its restricted scope, in that the political situation must be relatively well crystallized for the entrepreneur's political targets to be so clearly defined. Second, the costs of error or failure are considerable, in that the work which has gone into cultivating allies effective in such specific contexts is all wasted if the entrepreneur proves to have miscontrued the actual or the relevant contextual features. Third, it is often necessary to approach such specific potiential allies via a lengthy sequence of moves; and the time and energy that goes into planning and implementing the sequences of moves can be considerable. These costs, moreover, greatly increase when there is uncertainty over goals, probability of error or failure, and deficiency of information about which resources might be relevant to do what to whom.[6]

---

[6] In a sense, there is an analogy between this method and what Lindblom has called the rational-comprehensive method for designing solutions to complex problems, and which he has severely criticized. Conversely, there is an analogy between the ally-choosing method described first and Lindblom's method of "successive limited comparisons," which he views more favorably. "The Science of Muddling Through," *Public Administration Review* 19 (spring 1959): 79–88. Obviously my own conclusions tend to accord with Lindblom's, although I am perhaps more inclined to see at least an occasional role for the generally less satisfactory method.

This conclusion suggests further that if allies must be identified by criteria other than effectiveness, it might pay the entrepreneur to train them, once they are identified, to become effective. Effectiveness in this context would mean the ability to identify other relevant actors in the contest and to persuade them to support the proposal or even activate them to work on its behalf. If Lowry was deficient at all during the great budget controversy (assuming he did not actually want the cuts), his failure lay in his neglect to teach his naive potential allies how to provide him with appropriate and timely cues.

The training is bound to be primarily casual, in the way of exhortations, reminders, warnings, and unspoken intimations. It is sometimes desirable to complement this ephemeral instruction with a more durable sort, say, a pocket-sized anthology of good arguments for all occasions. The Dilemma Report was just such a reference work. So were the information packets distributed by leaders of the opposition to the governor's budget cut proposal. Such packets and occasional informational fliers were produced by the California State Employees Association, an ad hoc group at the Napa State Hospital, and the Citizen Committee for Improved Treatment in our State Hospitals, to mention only the three most prominent sources. CSPA leaders tried to educate the membership on their licensing bill in part through the bimonthly newsletter, the *California State Psychologist.* The quality of this last educational effort varied considerably, however, ranging from a lucid summary of SB 1158 in the June 1967 issue, to the crude emblem "YOU MAY BE ARRESTED" on the cover of the October 1966 issue.

An interesting example of how political education is assimilated into the vocabulary already familiar to the pupils is also provided by the psychologists' newsletter. In the December 1966 issue, the chairman of the Psychology Examining Committee under the existing Certification Act appealed to the membership to seek a remedy for the attorney general's opinion through legislative action:

> Effecting legislative change is not easy . . . perhaps entailing the same kinds of problems that many of us encounter in therapy (both giving and getting) where change in the direction of growth and development is the central issue. I think that growth and development are precisely the issues involved in calling for new legislation at this time, and we can expect some of the resistance that accompany [sic] any change, to occur in this situation as well. However, the time seems ripe. The situation has perhaps inadvertently been brought to a head and, as often occurs in life, we have been thrust into the position of

moving towards growth under some stress where we might not otherwise have done so at this time [p. 13].

A third general strategy for mobilizing allies may be relevant when the entrepreneur believes that publicity and general commotion will, on balance, create more support for his proposal than opposition to it. Leaving aside the mass media, which are relevant to only a small minority of political controversies, the entrepreneur's problem is to activate the channels of interpersonal communication within the attentive pub-

TABLE 18

ACTIVISM ON COMMITMENTS ISSUE IN THE INTERPERSONAL
COMMUNICATIONS NETWORK
(in percent)

| | Commitments Activity Index | | | | |
	0	1–2	3–4	5–9	Total percent	Total number
Number of *organizational memberships:*						
0	56	18	14	11	99	149
1	43	14	22	22	101	130
2	40	19	21	20	100	136
3 or more	33	14	20	33	100	157
Held organization office:						
No	44	19	18	19	100	213
Yes	33	13	23	31	100	208
Heard before report released:						
No	45	18	21	16	100	369
Yes	29	17	17	37	100	167
Proximity to *mainstream information:* [a]						
Low—on meeting agenda	48	19	16	17	100	88
—for "interest" sake	51	22	22	5	100	59
High—seeking support	13	20	24	43	100	54
—regular informant	21	15	23	46	100	39
Followed developments:						
Once only/outcome	80	6	13	0	99	31
Occasionally	74	11	13	3	101	102
Turning points	37	24	25	14	100	208
Continuously	14	16	21	48	99	189

[a] Based on responses to item 44. Includes only respondents who were informed by personal contact and for whom data were known. Omits 8 respondents who said it "came up accidentally."

lic. This entails approaching individuals who are highly involved in relevant organizations and associations and those who are in close proximity with the mainstream of informal (personal) political communications. Table 18 shows that respondents who belonged to three or more organizations were three times as likely to have scored very high (5–9) on the commitments activity index as those who belonged to no organizations. Holding organizational office also had some effect. Our measures of proximity to the information mainstream are necessarily indirect: constancy of attention to developments, and first hearing about the issue from a certain kind of personal contact, and hearing about it early. Yet all show quite striking positive relationships with political activism. Moreover, testing the relationships observed in Table 18 (p. 228) with the four issues other than commitments yielded substantially the same results.

TABLE 19
INFORMANTS' MOTIVES IN TRANSMITTING NEWS
FOR FIVE ISSUES
(in percent)

	Commitment	Budget	Psychology	Mendocino	Bureau
On meeting agenda	35	33	30	38	32
For "interest" sake	24	24	22	28	37
Seeking support	22	27	30	12	12
Regular informant	16	13	12	16	11
Accident	3	3	6	6	8
Total percent	100	100	100	100	100
Total number[a]	248	132	174	177	273

[a] Includes only respondents who received information personally and who checked pre-coded categories, item 44.

The notion of a mainstream of informal political communication, which we introduced in the preceding chapter, warrants further comment. To be in the mainstream is to pick up political signals rapidly—signals that something of political significance is happening or about to happen. Table 19 shows the frequency with which a variety of personal contacts serves to communicate such signals, but only two of these, we have seen (in Table 16, p. 193), do so more rapidly than the others, that is, seeking information regularly and being sought out by others as a potential supporter. Intensive analysis of the survey data shed little light on the differences between persons who were more sought out than seeking or the links between these roles—although further research might succeed in doing so—and served mainly to highlight the similarities. Respondents connected to the informal communications circuitry in these two ways were considerably more involved in organizations (number of memberships and holding office), more active on any single issue, more likely to be involved across a range of issues, more likely to pick up cues earlier and to follow issues regularly. They were also somewhat more likely to be middle aged than either young or old and to have held their current jobs for an extended period. Clearly such individuals make useful allies if only the entrepreneur can find them. Fortunately, this is not too difficult, since one of the reasons they have entered the information mainstream at all is that they have established visibility either as a valuable source of information or as a valuable place to deposit it, and sometimes (probably) as both. Since the entrepreneur's assumption is that publicity and general commotion are net benefits, he need not be overly concerned about whether he accidentally or even deliberately activates foes as well as friends by means of the interpersonal communications network. This was the strategy followed at various times by the Assembly group backing AB 1220 and to good effect.

Finally, there is the general principle of complementarity, which should also guide the entrepreneur in assembling a coalition. Since there are many different kinds of resources, many of which are relevant to accomplishing only one or a few objectives, it is desirable to build a coalition of allies with diverse but complementary resources. The Citizen Committee for Improved Treatment in Our State Hospitals (CCITSH), for instance, attempted to apply this principle of complementarity. From the CSEA, it obtained money and manpower; from organized psychiatry, a reservoir of high-prestige spokesmen and the appearance of professional disinterestedness; from the CAMH and CCRC, access to local notables in fields outside that of mental health and the appearance of civic mindedness; from disparate (but numerous) hospital staff, technical information and anecdotal material about the plight of patients and staff that was generally unfamiliar to outsiders. Once the organization was established it could anoint leaders whom television and newspaper journalists could quote regularly. The CCITSH, therefore, obtained the additional resource of being newsworthy. It could also employ a public relations firm to manage its campaign of television spots, a move that none of the member organizations could have risked (or afforded financially) by themselves.

11

The Entrepreneur Meets an Opposition

The entrepreneur's problems have so far been limited to identifying and exploiting the opportunities inherent in a pluralistic political system: mobilizing enough resources from enough allies to produce sufficiently weighty endorsements from enough interests to constitute, in the aggregate, enough support to win approval from the relevant authorities. This lengthy and cumbersome description of the entrepreneur's central strategic objective reflects the complexity of his decision-making problems. Unfortunately, both for the entrepreneur as actor and for ourselves as analysts, we have now to magnify this complexity by two or more orders of magnitude. In this chapter, we shall introduce a coalition of opponents determined to block the entrepreneur's proposal; and in the next, and concluding, chapter we shall examine the evolving patterns of opportunity, uncertainty, and risk that confront him as the contest develops.

How can an opposition coalition hurt the entrepreneur's proposal? Since the entrepreneur and his adversaries regard each other merely as political opponents, and not as entrepreneur and adversaries, we may begin by considering the larger question of how opponents in a given contest can hurt each other. In general, they can do so by undermining each other's weightiness and resources and by maneuvering to set the arena and scheduling parameters of the contest advantageously for their own side. Beyond this generalization, it is hard to say much that is useful about the nature of political gamesmanship. At this point, therefore,

we shall simply collect the most prominent examples of political gamesmanship that occurred in the five controversies we have been examining.

UNDERMINING OPPONENTS' RESOURCES AND WEIGHTINESS

Probably the most vulnerable components of a coalition's overall weightiness are its perceived breadth and the credibility of its experts. Lowry
attempted in his May 5 letter to Paul Ward to represent the campaign
to transfer the Bureau of Social Work as having been launched "in a
covert fashion" and without "public review" by "those who can represent the mentally ill and retarded to present information on the impact
of the transfer." He then referred to ten groups who he said ought to
be consulted, implying thereby that none of them had yet been consulted. Spokesmen for both the governor and the opposition in the
budget controversy repeatedly attempted to demonstrate the inadequacy
of the statistics, facts, and interpretations presented by experts from the
other side. The opposition was particularly adept at this tactic. Consider the following exchange, which occurred at the Assembly Ways and
Means hearings on the DMH budget on April 20, 1967:

> *Assemblyman Britschgi*: I've gotten letters of complaint from Agnews
> State Hospital that patients *supervise* other patients!
>
> *DMH spokesman*: No, it doesn't happen. . . .
>
> *Assemblyman Hinkley*: Does it have some therapeutic value for pa-
> tients to change bedpans, etc.?
>
> *DMH spokesman*: Yes. The milieu therapy aspects . . . [Interruption].
>
> *DMH spokesman*: Let's compare the situation to 25 years ago, when
> patients sat around, or pushed a block of wood around.
>
> *Assemblyman Ralph*: Are the blocks bigger now? . . .
>
> .   .   .   .
>
> *Assemblyman Meyers*: How is morale? Are we having trouble re-
> cruiting staff now?
>
> *DMH spokesman*: I am not aware of any mass exodus. There may be
> trouble in recruiting nationally, because of the publicity.
>
> *Dr. Robert Spratt* (superintendent of Napa State Hospital): Turnover
> is escalating. We have now nine vacancies in the medical staff, up

from zero. We will certainly not be able to maintain services. . . . It takes years to recruit again the trained people we'll have to lay off . . . [Interruption]. Patients at Napa certainly *do* supervise other patients. . . . For instance, there is now a security staff of only five. . . .

During the Senate Governmental Efficiency and Economy Committee July 11 hearing on AB 1220, Petris presented a comparison of commitment rates to the state MI hospitals prevailing in both Alameda and Contra Costa counties. While Contra Costa showed a per capita expenditure on Short–Doyle twice as high as that of Alameda, it had a higher per capita commitment rate and a higher per capita state hospital admission rate. Petris was supposedly proving the innocuous point that commitment practices varied widely from county to county across the state. He was at the same time, though, implicitly contrasting the professional expertise of Dr. George Degnan, director of Contra Costa Short–Doyle and an opponent of AB 1220, with that of Dr. Richard Gerlach, program chief of Alameda Short–Doyle and a supporter of AB 1220.

One of the resources most vulnerable to attack by opponents is the capacity for communications, and it is sometimes possible to use hierarchical authority to reduce the communications capacity of one's subordinates. The DMH headquarters teletype message to hospital superintendents informing them of the governor's budget cuts contained a directive to make no statements to the press and to redirect all questions to the headquarters office. This directive was heeded only temporarily by most of the superintendents, but long enough to permit Lowry and the governor to issue follow-up statements to the press trying to clarify and justify their decision without dispute or interference from their subordinates. In at least one hospital it seems that opposition activity at the staff level was diminished by the superintendent's strict construction of the DMH directive and by his own personal sympathies with the objectives of the cuts.

It is sometimes possible to create dissension and mutual suspicion within the opposition coalition. Certain opponents of AB 1220 approached Lanterman at one point and implied that the Assembly staff had exceeded its authority and had subverted what they believed were the legislators' true intentions. (I do not know just how well this tactic worked or to what extent those who made these allegations were sincere in their belief.) To be sure, it is often possible to anticipate opposition attempts to undermine the weightiness or resources of one's own side, and so to take precautionary measures. Bolton and Vieg, for instance, tried to deflect charges that they were exceeding their authority by keeping in constant touch with Lanterman and Petris and by insistently reminding audiences that they themselves were only staff members and that "Mr. Lanterman and Mr. Petris make all the decisions." Similarly, Lowry usually handled the charge that he was muzzling subordinates by stating that the controversial DMH directive had actually done nothing but restate official DMH policy, that is, no one speaks for the department except the director. As far as he was concerned, he said, anyone had a right to speak his mind as long as it was made clear that the speaker was not representing the official position of the department.

It would be pointless to say more about the nature of general precautionary measures that are intended to baffle attacks on one's resources or weightiness. Since the forms of attack are so various, so too are the means of self-protection. We may leave the subject, therefore, with the sole observation that one can sometimes cause an adversary's tactics to backfire if they can be represented as grossly unfair, illegitimate, or unjustified. It is at least plausible that Lowry's harsh accusations in his letter to Paul Ward concerning the bureau transfer were effectively turned against him by the Casey–Veneman rebuttal. In the same way, Reagan's disparaging references to "headshrinkers" and his aide's insinuations of deliberate "sabotage" of patient care probably cost the administration some goodwill in the mass public and in the legislature.

MANEUVERING FOR ARENA AND SCHEDULING ADVANTAGES

The maneuvering to gain advantageous arenas and schedules can be quite complicated and can occasionally determine the outcome of a contest. I have already described the maneuvers by various parties to route the psychology licensing bill, AB 1220, and the bureau transfer proposal through preferred arenas or away from arenas that were dispreferred. In the case of AB 1220, these maneuvers included alternative route selection (switching AB 1220 from the Senate Social Welfare Committee to the Senate G.E. Committee); arena creation (constituting a new subcommittee of Assembly Ways and Means to revive AB 1220 as a rider to SB 677 and to hold other bills hostage); and arena composition (replacing Burns with Petris on the conference committee). In the bureau transfer case, the maneuvers involved principally route selection (moving the proposal from the policy committee route to the budget committee route) and arena creation (Lowry attempting unsuccessfully to broaden the scope of public participation). We shall turn now to an analysis of a contest's schedule parameters and a coalition's maneuvers to set them to its own advantage.

By schedule parameters, I mean those events, conditions, or rules that cause strategically relevant action to take place on, before, or after certain dates, for example, the date of a legislative hearing, the termination of the legislative session, or the public announcement of the governor's budget. Typically, these dates are of importance only insofar as they demarcate a deadline past which strategically relevant action becomes inefficacious or impossible, or an "opening date" before which such action is inefficacious or impossible. Further, it is probably safe to say that neither deadlines nor opening dates are intrinsically significant except insofar as they demarcate the later, or farther, bound of a time interval. Time that elapses toward a deadline I shall call lead time. This is a period in which the entrepreneur and his allies characteristically find themselves trying to allocate their time among competing projects and, therefore, experience their situation as harried, pressed for time. Conversely, a calendar interval elapsing toward an opening date is lag time, during which the entrepreneur anxiously hopes that his support or his coalition will remain intact until the opening date finally arrives.

From the entrepreneur's point of view, a contest may have many lead-time (and lag-time) intervals, at least some of which run concurrently and some in sequence. The most important of all of these is the lead time available till the projected conclusion of the contest. It must be emphasized that conclusion dates are often indeterminate ("we fight till we win"), probable ("mid-May, give or take a few weeks"), or contingent ("May 12 if X occurs; June 30 or later if X does not"). The same may be said equally of other lead-time intervals in the contest. Yet it is often necessary for the entrepreneur to make estimates of his various lead times, and especially of the most inclusive lead-time interval, that which runs into the final deadline. Many important planning decisions, for instance, made by the Assembly group from January 1966 on were predicated on an estimate of their final deadline occuring at the close of the 1967 legislative session, that is, in mid-July. Within this framework, they allocated a certain amount of lead time to writing the Dilemma Report and a certain amount to converting the report's proposals into draft legislation. Similarly, once the report was released, in late November 1966, they divided the remaining lead time between largely extramural (public) and largely intramural (legislative) marketing activity.

How are lead-time parameters set? Many, and often the most important, are determined by institutionalized rules and routines, like the budget review cycle in a large government agency or the bill calendar procedures in a legislative body. Still others are determined by the entrepreneur's coalition itself, for example, the Assembly group deciding how long to spend preparing the Dilemma Report and when to make it public. Finally, the opposition coalition too has a hand in setting lead-time parameters: in the commitments contest, the Senate G.E. Committee (chaired by Burns) scheduled its hearing of AB 1220 for as late as July 11 because its leaders wished to leave the other side little time to revive the bill between that date and the end of the legislative session.

In general, the later in the contest opponents begin actively to compete over arena and schedule parameters, the better for the entrepreneur and his coalition. (The major exception to this rule is when the entrepreneur needs a long lead time in order to counterattack successfully.) There is no general tendency for opponents to commence their campaign either early or late in a contest, however; in our five cases there was a great range of strategies, from a quick and immediate countercampaign launched by the opponents of the governor's budget cuts to the watchful waiting of the opponents of the Dilemma Report. Hence, there is latitude for the entrepreneur to attempt to stall the potential opposition for a least a short time, perhaps even for a long time, and occasionally even for the duration of the contest. When stalling continues for the duration, then we may say that the potential opponent has been neutralized, a special case of the more general stalling strategy but worthy of being distinguished by its own label.

The advantages of stalling or neutralizing opponents are so great, yet so rarely extolled, that it is almost impossible to stress them here adequately. The primary reason they are so little noticed is that they do not usually follow upon some overt action. Stalling and neutralization simply do not manifest themselves as such very readily. The general importance of these strategies may be better appreciated, however, if one tries to imagine what difference it would have made to the outcomes of (1) the commitments controversy, had the Assembly group not stalled

DMH, medical, and psychiatric opposition until as late as May 1967; (2) the dispute over the professional practice of psychotherapy, had organized psychiatry not remained neutral; (3) the bureau transfer contest, had Bolton not been able to neutralize the CCRC; (4) the great budget controversy, had Lowry not been able to neutralize the CMA. The outcomes of these contests would not necessarily have been any different, but the activists in the stallers' coalitions would certainly have expended many more resources to obtain the same outcomes. In every instance just cited, stalling and neutralization strategies were undertaken deliberately, and in every case some resource cost was incurred. Yet these strategies were not nearly so visible as the mobilization strategies employed by the participants in these controversies, and on that account it would be easy to undervalue their significance.[1] Even some of those actors who planned and executed these moves may not consciously have realized their full significance.

The most clear-cut stalling tactic involves keeping the proposal secret from its likely enemies. In the initial stages of designing the proposal—collecting data, analyzing alternatives, drafting reports and recommendations—secrecy is nearly always the norm, since it is assumed that a proposal in its incubation period is unusually vulnerable to attack by its presumptive opponents. Preserving secrecy imposes costs on the proposal designers themselves, however, and for that reason secrecy is almost never perfect. It is rarely even tight, furthermore, and certainly not for very long. There are numerous reasons why this should be so, but probably the most important is that there are also costs to presumptive opponents of finding out what is afoot. A reliable spy network permeating all interests in the attentive public is hard to create and to maintain. Where it is not functioning, therefore, is where the most threatening plots are hatched. Once hatched, taking modest precautions against infiltrators is relatively routine, simple, and effective. On the surface, the Assembly group did little to prevent presumptive opponents from learning about the contents of the Dilemma Report; Tom Joe did little to prevent outsiders from learning of his proposal to transfer the bureau; and Klatte interposed no iron curtain between the bureau and his early

---

[1] After examining the history of nearly a dozen legislative contests at the national level during the Eisenhower, Kennedy, and Johnson years, James L. Sundquist concludes that, "at some point in the course of building public support, the opposition became divided—and this was the key to victory" (*Politics and Policy.* [Washington, D.C.: Brookings Institution, 1968], p. 509). Although it is not clear how this conclusion follows from the case studies Sundquist has presented, the point itself is well taken.

ideas for a Mendocino Plan. Yet in every case, the launching of the proposal did take opponents by surprise. Whether the surprise itself helped or hurt in each of these cases may be questioned, but it is almost certain that the preceding periods of secrecy during which the proposals were designed were advantageous.

A more general formulation of the strategy involved in maintaining secrecy and near secrecy is the manipulation of uncertainty: provide presumptive opponents with just enough information to make them believe that their present degree of uncertainty makes the risks of action unacceptably high. The probable success of this type of strategy can be augmented by manipulating the perception that uncertainty will be decreased in the future. Consider, for instance, the tactic generally known as "touching base," which typically occurs early in a contest. In touching base, an entrepreneur might (1) indicate the existence of the proposal; (2) suggest that it is not yet in its final version; (3) avoid too deep a discussion of the features that might be objectionable to the audience; 4) give assurances that future consultations will be frequent and "meaningful"; and (5) intimate only a few of the reasons that the audience might find favor with it, while implicitly promising that more reasons will shortly become apparent. Although there is obviously great potential here for cynical conduct, touching base is a procedure that can be used perfectly candidly. If touching base were not a common and respectable procedure, politicians would scarcely be able to stay in business.

The best example of touching base in our five controversies is provided by the Assembly group's approach to the CMA during the spring of 1966, when the staff was gathering material for the Dilemma Report. It was necessary to defer to the CMA's self-image as the leading non-public trustee of the public mental health system. Therefore, it would have been impolitic to have surprised them completely with the report. On the other hand, it would have been risky to have informed them of the group's provisional conclusion that commitments ought to be entirely abolished. Hence, the CMA was told that a major study was under way on the organization of public mental health services and it was even invited to undertake a complementary study of the Short–Doyle system. The CMA eventually did launch such a study, but not quickly enough to make it relevant to the work of the Assembly group. Meanwhile, the Assembly group, at the same time that it acknowledged its political obligation to keep open the lines of communication, did not have to work under the scrutiny of the medical profession. For its part, the CMA was alerted to the fact that major policy changes were being contemplated, that it would probably have to involve itself at some point in shaping them, and that involvement at the present time would be premature. Thus, touching base is a tactic that serves the interests of the attentive public as well as those of the entrepreneur, even if it does not serve them equally.[2]

Another useful stalling tactic involves entrapment—defining the proposal in such a way that interests whose support is problematic will appear to the attentive public to be inconsistent, unprincipled, or hypocritical if they rise to oppose it. When the Dilemma Report first appeared, for example, it was virtually impossible for the DMH to avoid endorsing the proposals for change contained in the report without seeming to condone the evident inadequacy of the existing commitments-plus-state hospital system. By way of contrast, in the Short–Doyle conference meeting of December 1–2, 1966, the participants could afford to express criticism of all aspects of the report because they were not quite so much in public view as the DMH director. At the Los Angeles hearings on December 12, organized psychiatry was also obliged to voice support for the principles in the report and to subordinate its criticism of the details. All these interests eventually ended up opposing AB 1220; but their open opposition was effectively delayed for several months by the embarrassment they could have suffered from a public statement of their objections.

For maximum effect with regard to stalling an entrapped opponent, the entrepreneur must take care to preserve the potential for his being embarrassed and, therefore, to refrain from actually embarrassing him. Like nuclear weaponry, political embarrassment is useful primarily to deter one's opponent from doing battle and not as a means of fighting once the battle has started. Apart from being good manners, helping a likely opponent out of his political embarrassment is sometimes tactically sound. While the DMH was refraining from criticizing the commitment reform project, for example, spokesmen from the Assembly group constantly praised the cooperation they had received from the depart-

[2] During Lowry's visit to California when he was considering the post with the DMH, Klatte touched base with him regarding the Mendocino Plan. In this case, though, touching base was not part of a stalling strategy.

ment. To alleviate Lowry's embarrassment in responding to reporters who sought his reactions to the Dilemma Report, Petris issued a statement on December 1, 1966, which contained the following:

> What is in the report is in keeping with the objectives of the Department of Mental Hygiene and the Department has cooperated without reservation in providing assistance requested by the committee. In fact, in 1965 the Department asked the Assembly to look into California commitment laws and procedures.
>
> The Department is not the committing agency and it is not responsible for the administration of commitments. Knowing only too well the considerable harm commitment can effect upon a person's future, the Department has urged strongly that voluntary rather than involuntary commitments are necessary. . . .
>
> It will be found in reading the report that after its considerable investigation into commitment laws, procedures, effects, and care and treatment after commitment, the committee is in general agreement with the testimony advanced by Dr. James V. Lowry, the Director of Mental Hygiene, last December.

12

The Essential Entrepreneur

This chapter explores certain strategies for dealing with the dynamic features of a political contest. In general there are two important aspects to the development of a contest over time. First, at any given point in time, the entrepreneur and his allies work with at least some production resources that they have themselves created by prior action, presumably to serve their own strategic ends; and second, at any given point in time, the opportunities, risks, and uncertainties to various interests, including the entrepreneur himself, are (or at least appear to be) changing in certain directions. How can the entrepreneur best exploit these developmental stages?

CREATING PRODUCTION RESOURCES: INTERMEDIATE STEPS

The entrepreneur in a manufacturing concern must bring together a number of resource inputs, subject them to various processes determined in large part by existing production technologies, and arrange the timing of these processes so that the output of some becomes available as the input for others. The scheduling of these production processes is only one part, furthermore, of a larger scheduling program with many interrelated components like the accumulation of finance capital, the development of adequate prototype models, the hiring and training of a sales force, the staging of a marketing and advertising campaign, and so forth. The political entrepreneur faces problems similar to those of his economic counterpart, in that he too must initiate and complete various political activities in a temporal sequence. How effectively he can perform a given activity at a given time depends in part, therefore, on how well he has created the conditions that make the present activity feasible and productive.

What sort of activity sequence is optimal for a political entrepreneur? This question can be answered properly only if we specify the parameters of the political system in which the entrepreneur is trying to operate. Perhaps the crucial parameter is the probability of extensive or sustained coverage of the contest by the mass media. A campaign involving mass publics entails a very different set of activities than a campaign that excludes (or tries to exclude) them. Similarly, very different activities are involved in bringing a court case and in seeking a legislative remedy; in seeking incremental adjustment and in fighting for basic reform; in maneuvering a proposal through a system with favorable or unfavorable arena and schedule parameters. Let us therefore begin to deal with the question of an entrepreneur's optimal activity sequence by focusing on a single concrete case, the facts of which are already known to us, which is sufficiently complex to make for interesting analysis, and which is fought out in a system that does not seem to entail idiosyncratic parameters—the commitment controversy. The system parameters of greatest relevance to that contest appear to have been the following: (1) the legislature and the governor were the ultimate authorities, and this was anticipated by all the contest participants; (2) mass publics were largely uninvolved in the contest; (3) no players were consistently and systematically secretive in their conduct; (4) the time span of the contest was roughly two to three legislative sessions; (5) there were a large number of players, indeed, at least thirty major interests; (6) since all participants were more or less in favor of larger and better public mental health programs (and also opposed to inappropriate, if not involuntary, commitments), their interests were not completely incompatible; and (7) there were basically only two sides to the contest, being for or against the Assembly group's proposal package. In examining the concrete details of this case we shall look first at the certain changes taking place over time that were least controllable by the Assembly group, the exemplary entrepreneur in that contest. We shall rely here, as we have so far, on economic metaphors to serve as the basis for our analytical vocabulary.

If we construe the interests still uncommitted at any given time, but potentially mobilizable, as the market for a proposal, we can posit that over time the market becomes progressively more peripheral, more differentiated, and more elastic. By "peripheral" I mean the opposite of routinely attentive. The interests in the routinely attentive public have rather highly structured attitudes on most matters. Hence, on any given issue they probably establish their positions and drop out of the market quickly. Over time, therefore, the uncommitted public—the market—is made up more and more of interests only intermittently attentive to the issue area and of those whose attention has been aroused more or less accidentally. During the early phases of the contest, the Assembly group was dealing with such routinely attentive and weighty interests as the Department of Mental Hygiene, the CMA, the CAMH, the Los Angeles Community Welfare Council, and so on. By March and April, however, it was casting about for support among such peripheral interests as the California Bar Association, the California Judicial Conference, PTA groups, and community welfare groups in minor counties and cities. By mid-June, it was concentrating on a market consisting of a few key senators and some audiences to which they and other senators were likely to be responsive, for example, the Attorney General's Office and the office of the legislative analyst. At the end, the relevant market had shrunk to Senators Burns (intermittently attentive) and Schmitz (accidentally attentive).

Increasing differentiation of the market occurs as a result of the tendency for interests whose own focal concerns are with the central ideological issues of the proposal to commit themselves to one side or another relatively early in the contest. Ideological issues typically define a more unifying frame of reference than other issues; and if the former are not salient to interests, they are likely to be oriented toward quite disparate features of the proposal. As time passes, then, and as the more ideologically concerned interests leave the market, there is a residue of increasingly varied interests which comprise an increasingly differentiated market.

These residual interests also have a more elastic demand for the proposal, in the sense that they have less intense attitudes toward the proposal than do the more ideologically oriented interests. This implies that the passage of time leaves in its wake the relatively less intense interests, and thus the demand function of the market as a whole tends over time to become more elastic.[1]

[1] A technical definition of the elasticity of demand: "the percentage change in price p divided into the percentage change in the quantity demanded of x" (David S. Huang, *Introduction to the Use of Mathematics in Economic Analysis* [New York: John Wiley and Sons, 1964], p. 70). To elaborate, if demand is relatively elastic (in-

When the Dilemma Report was first released, many interests in the attentive public took up ideologically oriented positions, either publicly or privately, which they did not change for the duration of the contest. The ideological axis around which they grouped themselves was, of course, the medical model. The interests still in the market at the end of the contest were, however, quite different. The CSAC swayed back and forth depending on how their leadership perceived the fiscal and administrative impact on county governments. Senator Teale, who was ambivalent about the medical model, was moved by a complex and highly personal set of perceptions and attitudes—none of them too closely related to the primary concerns of the CSAC. Other interests still mobilizable or detachable during the late phases were similarly differentiated from one another with regard to what they considered salient in the reform package. The governor was concerned about his image as an anti-mental-health politician and oppressor of helpless state hospital patients, an image acquired during the spring's fight over the state hospital budget. He was also concerned about the possible costs of AB 1220 to the state treasury, as was the Department of Finance. Senator Schmitz, of course, acted on premises not even remotely like those of any other major participant in the contest.

With the exception of Senator Schmitz, all these mutually differentiated interests had relatively elastic preference schedules—at least from the point of view of the Assembly group. While the mere fact of elasticity did not permit the Assembly group to capture the support of all these interests, it did give it the opportunity to keep trying, to keep amending its bill and revising the rhetoric of salesmanship, so as to increase its attractiveness to this variety of interests without substantially affecting its own principal policy concerns. Even the amendments that the group made to satisfy Schmitz were from its point of view marginal, since the abolition of involuntary commitment was the group's principal aim, and it was confident that in the subsequent legislative session a proposal similar to its design for a changed mental health treatment system would be approved.

How ought the entrepreneur to cope with these predictable market changes? By acquiring production resources suitable for each market condition. This implies, in general, *increasing the sophistication of his analysis, marketing, and management capabilities.* This tends to occur

_____

elastic), a small change up or down in price will have a proportionately greater (lesser) effect on the quantity demanded.

naturally anyway, but the skillful entrepreneur can promote and exploit such tendencies.

Consider first the increasing sophistication of the Assembly group's analytical capability. The commitment reform project began in the fall of 1965 with two or three assemblymen who had long been concerned about mental health and mental retardation and knew a good deal about the state's current programs in these fields. Associated with them were two or three full-time staff members with similar interests and expertise drawn from a variety of locations within the Assembly staff system. After the public hearings in December 1965 and January 1966 and the decision to do a full-scale subcommittee study of the commitment problem, the staff was expanded to include a man with legal expertise. The ACLU staff in Sacramento also cooperated on the legal analysis. A contract was let, in February 1966, to a social science consulting firm to conduct a survey of commitment court proceedings and to accumulate data on the characteristics of persons moving through the commitment and mental treatment systems. Certain limited assistance was also elicited from the DMH and the CMA. As the drafting of the report took the group more and more into the realm of intergovernmental fiscal relations and the larger problem of financing the reformed mental illness treatment system, the group borrowed an in-house expert on these matters from another legislative project. Once the Dilemma Report appeared, the staff solicited and received recommendations from psychiatrists in private practice, from DMH and Short–Doyle administrators, and from other interested or affected parties. As time went on and the reform movement began to look as though it might succeed in some way, opponents of the movement were obliged to contribute their suggestions in advance of legislative committee hearings rather than try to sandbag the bill at the hearings themselves. Medical practitioners and administrators, in particular, were obliged to defend themselves against what they saw as the excessively punitive provisions in the draft legislation for failures by treatment personnel to protect the legal rights of patients. In order to protect their interests in the unlikely contingency of the bill's passing, they were forced to improve the bill's defects, thereby making the contingency less unlikely. By the time these suggested amendments started drifting in, the Assembly group had already learned enough to be able to distinguish—within its own frame of reference at least—helpful and necessary amendments from hostile or irrelevant ones.

In more abstract, and therefore more general, language, I could perhaps describe the growth of sophistication in analytical capability as
follows: The entrepreneur's earliest analytical capability is, of course,
his own, which permits him to identify and bring together inputs from
in-house staff and outside experts and informants. These inputs may or
may not constitute a face-to-face work group; and if they do so at all,
they may do so intermittently and segmentally, that is, by working in
partially overlapping subgroups. In any case, the entrepreneur can draw
on such persons' capacity to identify additional relevant experts and
informants. As time goes on, therefore, the variety and number of analytic inputs grow, and the entrepreneur finds some way to integrate the
analyses and to coordinate, at least loosely, the work and activities of the
analysts. A parallel development is the inclusion of analytical inputs
from sources ill-disposed toward the entrepreneur's basic policy goals.
Initially, the entrepreneur surrounds himself with men whom he trusts
to emphasize in their analytical work the solution to problems of great
saliency to the entrepreneur. It is virtually inevitable, though, that a
fully developed policy proposal will effect changes that neither the entrepreneur nor his friendly group of analysts is capable of anticipating
or completely understanding. Since failure to take account of these in
the proposal design might severely damage the marketability of the proposal, the entrepreneur must eventually elicit—or spontaneously be
given—corrective analytical inputs from persons who are likely to be
neutral at best and highly antagonistic at worst. The entrepreneur's
analytical capability must also become sophisticated enough, by the
time this occurs, to protect himself against the frequent distortions and
infequent falsehoods virtually certain to be found in analyses received
from such sources.

During the earliest stages, the Assembly group's marketing resources
were limited primarily to those they themselves provided. It was they
who did all the work of sounding out other legislators, interest group
leaders, administrators, and the like. By the time they were ready to
embark on their campaign for broader public support, however, they
had improved their marketing capacity substantially. They had a publicity vehicle in the Dilemma Report, and they had influential allies in
the CAMH, both in the statewide organization and in its larger county
chapters, who were aware of the emerging legislative reform effort and
eager to help it along. They could count on some help from the leadership of the Bureau of Social Work. The Assembly group also had allies

in the leadership of the Northern California Civil Liberties Union and, in effect, in several newspaper reporters who were ready to give the Dilemma Report prominent treatment when it was released. The two legislative hearings that immediately followed the release of the report gave it additional publicity. As a result of these preparations, the Assembly group succeeded in enlarging the activist coalition rather quickly after the report was released. The payoff was the considerable support generated in local communities for commitment reform, through the activities of local community welfare councils, CAMH chapters, ACLU chapters, and so on. The outreach of this coalition extended, eventually, even to certain trade unions, the Barristers Club of San Francisco, the National Council on Alcoholism, and other peripheral organizations of this sort.

As the third stage in the evolution of the Assembly group's marketing capacity, the group had transformed itself into a smoothly operating road company, with its own props, customary script, specialized repertoires for different audiences, alternative repertoires for repeat performances and even an understudy capability. The full show consisted of a low-key introduction by Senator Petris, some pitchman-like oratory by Lanterman, a flannel-board talk on the new system design by Vieg, shrewd fielding of audience questions by Bolton, and a velvet-smooth demonstration by Roberts of how few additional funds would be needed to run the new system. Variations on the basic theme were developed so as to be suitable for presentations to hostile as well as sympathetic audiences, to individuals as well as groups, to private citizens as well as public officials, and to the completely uninformed as well as to veteran observers of California mental health problems and politics.

Now let us attempt to abstract and generalize. The initial stage in the development of a marketing capability typically involves a nuclear group of staff members, public officials, and private elites who are dissatisfied with the status quo and prepared to mobilize support for any viable and satisfactory alternative. There are typically a large number of such nuclear marketing groups searching for such alternatives and a large number of nuclear analytical groups with alternatives to offer them. The convergence of any two such nuclear groups is certainly the result of a complicated process. How this process occurs is beyond the scope of this book; but suffice it to say that once the entrepreneur manages to consolidate one such natural alliance, he confronts the problem of developing its capability to meet subsequent marketing requirements.

Thus, the next stage in this development is the mobilization of a starting team—interests (like ACLU lawyers, CAMH leaders, and the like) who will not only be committed to marketing the proposal but will also be sufficiently sophisticated analytically to persuade others of its programmatic merits. Ideally, the starting team would be able to impart their own analytical sophistication to the allies whom they themselves mobilize, thereby maintaining the average effectiveness of the enlarged coalition. This is highly unlikely, though, and the characteristic trend is for rapid expansion of the activist coalition to be accompanied by a steady decline in its average sophistication. This trend is probably accelerated if the mass media enter the communications network.[2]

The third stage in the development of a marketing capability supplements this extensive but undifferentiated communications apparatus with a custom-designed capability for penetrating an increasingly differentiated and elastic market. The entrepreneur must differentiate his and his allies' approaches to different audiences. The search intensifies for optimal linkages to each audience. If the coalition has no direct access to a desired audience, then access must be created. If the audience is important enough—the governor, say—the development of access linkages may result in a fairly lengthy chain.

The Assembly group from the first was very well equipped to perform managerial tasks. They were able to assign at least one staff person full-time to the commitment reform project. They could utilize the state's leased-line telephone system and they had access to abundant resources for in-state travel. Secretarial services were sufficient if not abundant and of generally high quality. We have, indeed, already discussed other aspects of their feedback generating and monitoring capability in chapter 10. More important, though, the group's being attached to the legislature and located in the state capitol gave it a claim to leadership among its allies and preeminence as their spokesman and negotiating agent vis-à-vis neutrals and opposition leaders. Especially during the earlier phases of the contest, allies from around the state would check in with the group staff by phone to find out what was happening and to solicit suggestions on what useful jobs they might undertake. In late February the group staff circulated a mimeographed copy of the draft bill to some fifty blue-ribbon experts around the state in order to solicit constructive criticism and to take a sounding of the proposal's political viability in

[2] It is conceivable that if they enter late enough they will introduce more sophisticated interpretations than are held by a large segment of the current activist coalition.

that particular form. If there had ever been any doubt about who was the chief negotiating agent in the reform coalition, this procedure dispelled it. During May, June, and July, the Assembly group wrote several hundred amendments to the version of the bill as first introduced and printed at the end of April. The more they amended the bill, the more they established their legitimacy and indispensability as leaders of the reform effort and the more flexibility they had vis-à-vis their own allies. It proved a useful flexibility, too, since the Assembly group was obliged eventually to concede certain provisions to the CMA that displeased their allies in the California State Psychological Association and to make certain concessions to the DMH that displeased certain leaders of the CAMH. These concessions were not of such a nature that the offended interests would have threatened to abandon the coalition had they been informed in advance. Nevertheless, without the cadre-like flexibility that the group had earned itself over the months, the time and goodwill that would have been expended in intracoalition bargaining would almost certainly have damaged the coalition's capacity to bargain effectively with opposition interests.

What may be the more general implications of this pattern? Initially, coordination and management functions are performed by collegial consultations. As collegial groups multiply, however, and transform themselves into something more like a starting team of activist groups and individuals, the entrepreneur assumes informal leadership functions, particularly with regard to allocating various marketing tasks among different team members, both to reduce redundancy and to ensure that important tasks are being accomplished. As time goes on and the coalition expands, it becomes less feasible for the entrepreneur to coordinate the various activities. The expanded coalition makes it feasible, however, for the entrepreneur to enrich the information flow from the environment back to the analytical component of the production system. His principal managerial function is no longer the coordination of marketing activities but the consolidation and interpretation of feedback for analytical purposes. When design changes are made in the proposal—as is likely—he faces still another managerial problem, namely, reducing discontent within the existing activist coalition. It may be necessary to cut loose some former allies and to insulate himself from too frequent interaction with the remaining ones. In effect, the broad, loosely-knit coalition is transformed into a small but well-integrated cadre, whose principal resource is the capacity to maneuver in an in-

TABLE 20

MARKET CHANGES OVER TIME, FOUR ISSUES OTHER THAN COMMITMENTS

	Budget	Psychology	Mendocino	Bureau
Shift to Periphery	Attentive public activated Newspaper coverage activates mass public (March) Citizen committee campaign reaches out to TV viewers via spot announcements, commercials (May)	CSPA leadership CSPA membership Senate Business and Professions Committee (intermittently attentive) Special interests, e.g., hypnotists (accidentally attentive)	Mendocino service area professionals DMH headquarters Bureau workers and social workers outside Mendocino service area Short-Doyle	DMH and legislative committee specialists Legislative nonspecialists[a] CCRC and Short-Doyle[a]
Increasing Differentiation	Single dimension of cleavage: for/against mentally ill and hospitals (April, May) Day treatment centers, Short-Doyle, CMA, show separate interests Opposition coalition splits (June) along partisan lines into Democratic bitter enders and Republican accommodationists	Single frame of reference is issue of professions' rights to practice psychotherapy Special interests, e.g., hypnotists, pollsters, L.A. group, etc., concerned over *terms* of psychology licensing bill	Mendocino–DMH–bureau all have common frame of reference Short-Doyle has separate frame of reference	Frame of reference is organizational: bureau's functions and its departmental location Legislature adds fiscal concerns Services for retarded
Increasing Elasticity	Initial polarization Comparatively small concessions to CSAC and CMA effectively neutralize them Reagan's promises and Lowry's assurances neutralize Republican mental health activists	Initial polarization Comparatively small changes serve to neutralize splinter groups potentially in opposition	Initial polarization Short-Doyle's interest and concern are unclear but probably not intense	Initial polarization over organizational issues Comparatively small benefits to legislators in electioneering material mobilize support for transfer Reassurances to CCRC neutralize it

[a] These entries occur in a sequence that is not compatible with the hypothesis of an increasing shift to the periphery.

creasingly turbulent environment. If the entrepreneur has performed his previous managerial tasks effectively, he will by this time have created: (1) a reliable analytical capability; (2) a reservoir of trust and goodwill among his own allies that permits him to insulate himself and the rest of the cadre from troublesome and perhaps embarrassing scrutiny; and (3) in the eyes of neutrals and opponents, legitimacy as spokesman and negotiator for the alliance. All these are necessary conditions for the sophisticated maneuvering capability that the entrepreneur and his cadre now require.[3]

How well do the patterns inferred from the commitment controversy match events in the other four mental health contests we have been analyzing? The pattern of market changes—becoming progressively more peripheral, differentiated, and elastic—can be seen in virtually every case. The argument on behalf of this proposition is summarized in Table 20. With regard to the corollary pattern of shifts in the entrepreneur's resource pool, the other four cases do not wholly reproduce the pattern of increasing sophistication observed in the commitments case. It is nowhere at all visible in the contest over the Mendocino Plan. It is visible in the controversies over the budget and the bureau transfer only dimly, and there principally as a natural response to market changes rather than as a deliberate entrepreneurial plan to create resources needed for future operations. Only in the case of the Psychology Licensing Act can we see evidence of concern with developmental planning. The optimizing policies seem to have been roughly similar to those pursued by the Assembly group in the commitment contest. The CSPA leadership deliberately evolved an increasingly sophisticated marketing capability: mobilizing first itself; then mobilizing the concern of the association membership (via the newsletter) and other professional groups, who in turn contacted public officials; and finally targeting on key opponents, neutrals, and legislators. Creating more sophisticated analysis and management capabilities does not seem to have been a deliberate strategy of the CSPA leadership. This pattern did in fact emerge, however, as market changes, like the appearance of opposition from many unexpected quarters, forced increasingly sophisticated analytical responses, and ally discontent (among the CSPA membership) forced more sophisticated managerial responses.

[3] On the general question of how organizations adapt to the requirements of managing different sorts of communication and production technologies, see James D. Thompson, *Organizations in Action* (New York: McGraw–Hill, 1967), pp. 12–82.

As in nearly all production processes, the production of political resources is affected by economies and diseconomies of scale. Marketing
resources, to take the simplest example, manifest increasing returns to
scale, at least within a certain range, because they improve their potential for continued growth with every increment in actual growth. Allies
recruit other allies, that is, and the larger the ally pool at any given
time, the larger it is likely to grow in the next time interval. Support
accumulates as a function of the size of the ally pool, and a schematic
representation of its time path under these conditions would look like
the curve *OA* in Figure 2. Because the potential ally pool and the po-

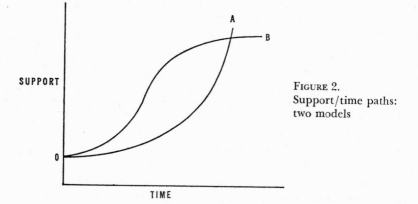

FIGURE 2.
Support/time paths:
two models

tential mobilizable public are both finite, the exponential growth of
total support is gradually inhibited, as eventually is further growth of
any kind. The result is a support/time path over the whole contest that
resembles the logistic curve *OB* rather than *OA*.

Economies of scale also apply to analytical resources, in the sense that
activities like gathering data, reviewing other relevant research and
policy studies, conceptualizing and designing new policies, writing reports, and drafting legislation all benefit from concentrating efforts in
large and relatively uninterrupted blocs of time. At least, this generalization is probably valid for most people and for work on most policy
problems.

If efforts concentrated in time produces certain economies with regard to both marketing and analytical resources, as I have argued, there
is an obvious implication for an entrepreneur's method of scheduling
these two activities. He should alternate periods of concentrated public
relations—marketing activity—with periods of concentrated office work

—catching up on analytical problems temporarily left untended and also planning strategies and schedules for the future. The Assembly group backing commitment reform worked generally in this manner, and quite effectively. The cycle of peaks and troughs in their public activity occurred in approximately the following time pattern:

> September 1965 to December 1965—A relatively low level of marketing activity, while the Assembly subcommittee and staff sounded out potential interest at the Legislative level and prepared questionnaires for distribution to the subcommittee mailing list.
> December 1965 to January 1966—A peak period, with public hearings, around which were concentrated preliminary recruitment and follow-up activities.
> February 1966 to November 1966—Preparation of the Dilemma Report and the gathering of supporting technical data and information. A relative trough in public activity.
> December 1966 to early February 1967—Another high-intensity marketing phase, including two public hearings and trips throughout the state to stimulate allies, gather feedback, and obtain more technical information and specific suggestions about what provisions to incorporate in the projected legislative bill.
> Late February 1967 to early May 1967—A relatively slack phase for public activity, devoted mainly to drafting, introducing, and preparing amendments to AB 1220.
> Early May 1967 to early June 1967—A peak period of public activity, including two committee hearings, gathering feedback, and attempting to neutralize growing opposition from Short–Doyle and the CSAC.
> Early June 1967 to July 11, 1967—Preparation of new amendments to AB 1220 and planning for the Senate G.E. hearing on July 11; a less intense period than the preceding one, but still marked by public activity directed more toward gaining support than gaining new allies.
> July 12, 1967 to August 6, 1967—An extremely high level of activity, both in seeking new allies and in seeking new support at the legislative level, culminating in passage of SB 677.

OPTIMIZING CURRENCY EXPENDITURES OVER TIME

In chapter 10, I distinguished between relatively inexhaustible resources, like most production resources, and those which, upon being used, were in effect used up, like most currency resources. In this chapter I have so far discussed how the entrepreneur might build up his production resources over time through a sequence of planned intermediate stages. We are now in a position to ask how exhaustible currency resources can be expended over the course of the contest according to an equally deliberate policy. Clearly, the first necessity is to map likely changes over time in currency requirements, that is, the opportunity or necessity to use one's currency to advantage.

First let us consider the risks of losing, by which I mean some combination of the costs of losing and the contingent probability of losing.[4] As a contest proceeds, both components of risk increase. The cost of losing rises, because all the political currency invested up to that point is wasted if victory does not ensue and if the losers are unwilling soon to repeat their investment in another go-around. The contingent probability of losing increases over time simply because the number and variety of contingencies mount up which can cause one to lose. The pluralistic structure of most political systems in America permits an entrepreneur's opponents to terminate the contest—on terms favorable to themselves, that is, continuing the status quo—at any number of points. As often as they fail, they can keep trying again; the entrepreneur thus faces a sequence of possible fatal contingencies, and the probability that the sequence will actually prove fatal increases with its length. Its length, in turn, increases as the contest proceeds, thereby causing the probability of losing to increase and hence the entrepreneur's risk.

Since currency resources are often a prophylactic against dangerous contingencies, a consideration of risk alone would lead the rational entrepreneur to hoard his political currency until as late in the contest as possible. But risk is not the only consideration. We have already argued that there are considerable advantages in expending currency resources early in the contest, when expending them is necessary to complete the intermediate steps creating desired production resources. There is also a second reason not to hoard them. If the logistic curve in Figure 2 is an adequate, even though approximate, depiction of how support accumulates over the course of a contest, then it has implications for the timing of compounding effects, particularly bandwagon effects. These latter effects would probably cluster in the middle portion of the contest, that is, when support is visibly accumulating with some rapidity and before saturation effects have set in. The only clearcut instance of a bandwagon

---

[4] By contingent probability I mean the same thing as conditional probability. I use the former phrase principally in order to avoid the technical connotations of the latter.

effect in the commitment contest, Governor Reagan's endorsement early in May 1967, occurred during a phase such as this one. Here is another opportunity to profit from currency expenditures, that is, by inaugurating a special effort to capture the bandwagon market just when the growth in primary support is most accelerated.

Consider also the necessity to expend currency resources to cope with the opposition. If the opposition crystallizes almost simultaneously with the first public airing of the entrepreneur's proposal and continues its own campaign in tandem with the entrepreneur's, then the logistic curve of Figure 2 would still be adequate to describe the general form of the contest's support/time path. On the other hand, suppose the opposition does not surface until much later in the contest, perhaps preferring to wait to see if the proposal might not simply lapse for want of any weighty support at all. When it finally did mobilize, it would face the task of thwarting a proposal that had already built up momentum and possibly even enough support to win if the termination date were to fall in the near future. Under such conditions, the opposition would not wish to rely merely on activating interests favorable to its own views but would seek also to detach certain weighty interests from the entrepreneur's side and to manipulate schedule and arena parameters.

Sudden parameter shifts can disrupt the entrepreneur's plans, blunt his strategies, and forestall his opportunities. The entrepreneur, after all, has been basing his strategies and plans on certain assumptions about the arena and lead-time–lag-time parameters of the contest. If either or both of these parameters suddenly shift, the entrepreneur finds himself in trouble, especially if these shifts are executed near the end of the contest, when the lead time for adapting to the new parameters is short. The support/time path in such a contest would perhaps look something like the curve in Figure 3, with the entrepreneur suffering an initial setback after a peak support level and then alternating with the opposition in phases of temporary ascendancy and decline. It is in just this period of alternating fortunes that parameter manipulation—by both sides—is most likely and, therefore, that currency resources are needed, whether for offensive or defensive purposes. The jagged pattern at the very end of the contest represents a volatile situation in which both sides attempt to outmaneuver each other under conditions of unusually high risk and perhaps uncertainty about when the contest will be terminated and how much support will be enough.[5]

5 Except for the tail end of the curve, Figure 3 describes the characteristic behavior

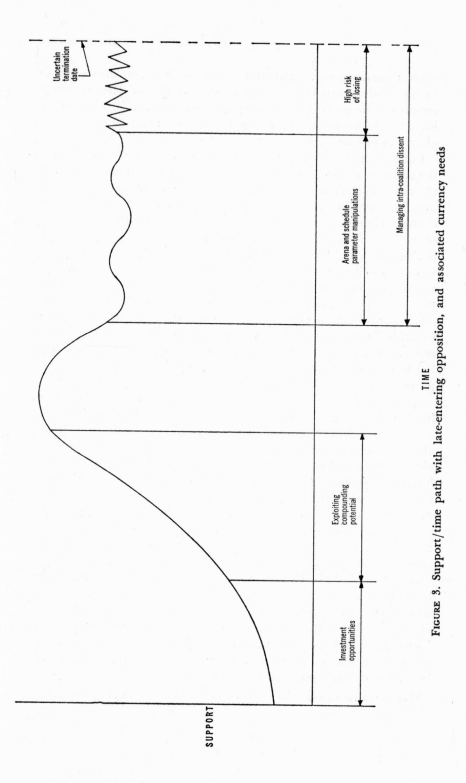

FIGURE 3. Support/time path with late-entering opposition, and associated currency needs

Aggravating the entrepreneur's burdens at such times are his ongoing commitments to allies who have supported the proposal up to that point. Not only are schedule and time parameters likely to be shifted during this conflict-ridden phase, but so are certain substantive elements of the proposal. Concessions and amendments are inevitable—and so is discontent within the coalition. Even if the entrepreneur has performed his previous preparatory projects well, there will probably still be a need to expend currency during this period, either to prevent defections or to bring in new allies as substitutes.

I have thus described five types of conditions which, in a sense, require currency expenditures, and I have linked them to certain developmental stages in the policy contest. In effect we have a map (Figure 3) of the temporal succession of varieties of currency requirements, and the question now becomes how an entrepreneur ought to use it. To be sure, it is a map of limited utility, since it informs us only that certain types of requirements lie in a certain temporal sequence without specifying how large the requirements are and how great are the temporal distances between (and among) them. Such information cannot be had, though, for it would require accurate prediction of the future. The map is not a crystal ball; on the other hand, its utility is not to be despised. It puts the entrepreneur on guard against the equally dangerous tactics of hoarding all resources for dire emergencies, like the final high-risk phase of the contest, and of expending all resources at the outset simply in order to get the proposal launched. It points out, too, the diverse nature of currency requirements. Finally, it suggests the importance of being able to create currency resources for temporary use, and to do so in a timely manner. If the first ingredient of a rational currency management policy is a map of anticipated expenditure requirements, the

---

of a large class of natural systems, to which certain political contests—those with late-entering oppositions—may belong. In the vocabulary of systems analysis, the system couples a positive feedback loop, the growth loop which gives rise to the first half of the curve, and a negative feedback loop, the goal-seeking loop, which produces the oscillations in the second half of the curve. It describes systems of real-world behavior as diverse as rapid growth of an animal population which overtaxes its food supply and then decreases to an equilibrium level and the nuclear activity of an atomic power plant which rises rapidly until it is brought down to operating level by a control system. It also represents the way in which a new product enters a market, oversaturates real demand, and drops back to some acceptable range of sales. The theory of how such a system works, along with the three examples given, comes from an unusually lucid textbook in systems analysis by Jay W. Forrester, a professor of management science at MIT, *Principles of Systems, Text, and Workbook*; second preliminary edition (Cambridge: Wright–Allen Press, 1969), chap. 2.

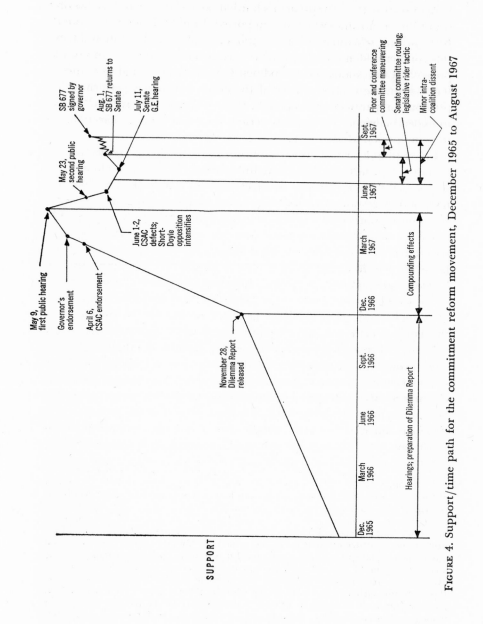

FIGURE 4. Support/time path for the commitment reform movement, December 1965 to August 1967

second such ingredient, then, is a map of anticipated currency receipts.

My hunch is that it is an unusual contest in which currency expenditures do not exceed currency receipts, and that therefore the entrepreneur does well to start the contest with a goodly store of working capital. Even in the typical case, however—if indeed it is typical—there are at least two ways to create currency for later use. One certain means lies in the design of the initial policy proposal, which can incorporate features intended to be bargained away later as "concessions." A second means that the entrepreneur can count on lies in creating goodwill among his allies, tendered him because of his success in managing the initial analytical and marketing problems of the contest. The first method of currency creation is a kind of counterfeiting, whereas the second is a kind of legitimate borrowing. Legitimate borrowing takes other forms, too, and occasionally entails high "interest" obligations, for instance, to a legislator who assists in schedule or arena manipulations behind the scenes and demands (tacitly, of course) public credit for sponsoring the proposal should it eventually pass.

The final ingredient in rational currency management is a sensitivity to the possibilities of gambling in what may be called a free trial. Often it is impossible to know very accurately just how high a price in currency one will have to pay in order to obtain some particular outcome. Yet just as often it is possible to test an individual or a situation to see what price—if any—will be required. If the entrepreneur approaches a presumptive opponent with an offer of all possible concessions he hopes will neutralize him, he may miss the chance of discovering that the presumptive opponent would have settled for a great deal less.[6]

Let us observe how these propositions about the progression of expenditure requirements, and entrepreneurial skill in anticipating them, fit our most complex and interesting case, the commitment contest. In Figure 4, I have plotted approximate support levels for AB 1220 over its nearly two-year history and connected these points with line segments. It seems clear that if these segments were smoothed out into a geometric curve representing a continuous and differentiable function, the curve would look quite like the curve drawn in Figure 3. I have also indicated the nature and succession of currency expenditure requirements during this period, and it seems clear that they generally match the theoretical pattern represented in Figure 3.

6 Sometimes, of course, these trials are anything but free. That is, testing to ascertain a price and trying to escape having to pay the price are activities for which there may also be a price!

The ways in which the Assembly group prepared to meet such requirements also fit our model of skillful entrepreneurship. They started the contest reasonably well supplied with currency resources. Lanterman was one of the most respected Republicans in the Assembly and in addition was the ranking minority member of the powerful Ways and Means Committee, which passed on all bills requiring money appropriations. From the fall of 1965 to June 1966, Assemblyman Jerome Waldie, a Democrat and house majority leader, was also part of the Assembly group. He had high standing among the attentive mental health public for his role in leading a successful movement to renovate the state's system of programs and services for the mentally retarded. Arthur Bolton, the principal staff assistant in the group, had worked closely with Waldie on the mental retardation project. He had ties with Unruh, having originally been a protégé of the Speaker. But he also enjoyed a reputation for honesty and intelligence among all factions in the Assembly, liberal and conservative, Republican and Democrat. Furthermore, the group "counterfeited" additional currency in the form of potential future concessions by advocating a nearly pure civil libertarian and antitraditionalist treatment system in the Dilemma Report and later by holding hostage those several Senate bills besought by Short–Doyle and the CSAC. They engaged too in legitimate borrowing, utilizing Senator Short's right to make author's amendments to SB 677 in return for allowing him to take credit as a cosponsor of the bill once it was enacted.[7]

How well does our theory of currency mangement fit the four cases besides the commitment controversy? We have already established that the temporal map of currency requirements does not indicate how long each interval will last or how great the requirements will be, since these contours are so largely determined by the conduct of opposition forces. Hence, the fact that the contest over the Psychology Licensing Act lacked a noticeable high-risk phase at the end and that the budget contest had no noticeable early investment phase signify nothing certain. The only test to which our other four cases can subject the present theory is a minimal one, namely, that the temporal sequence in which types of expenditure requirements arise, when they arise at all, should not in any way be the reverse of the one we have specified. My own inspection of the other four cases reveals no discomfiting reversals of

[7] As noted in chapter 4, other considerations were probably at work here also.

this kind, but perhaps the reader will wish to conduct his own search for negative evidence.

THE ESSENTIAL ENTREPRENEUR

In Plato's dialogue *Protagoras* the question is raised whether or not virtue can be taught. We may ask the same about entrepreneurial skill. Taking a further cue from Plato, we may answer that, yes, skill can be taught—this whole book has tried to teach it—but how well it can be learned is more problematic. Some people are no doubt better learners than others. Native intelligence is a great asset, as are certain character traits like high ego strength, tolerance of ambiguity, and a kind of readiness for prudent risk taking that I shall call poise. It is this quality of poise that makes it possible for the entrepreneur to face up to decisions about if, when, and how to engineer or avert a sudden parameter shift and how to keep his balance when such a shift occurs unexpectedly. Having the poise to make decisions of this sort distinguishes the skillful political virtuoso from the merely rational entrepreneur, whose rationality may not save him from disaster.[8] As Machiavelli put it in his remarks on "fortune," "if it happens that time and circumstances are favorable to one who acts with caution and prudence he will be successful, but if time and circumstances change he will be ruined, because he does not change his mode of procedure."[9]

By the time a man is old enough to become a professional practitioner of political entrepreneurship, if he does not already possess these valuable personality traits it is probably too late for him to acquire them. Yet there is also a set of politically useful character traits—perhaps "sensitivities" is a better description—which an entrepreneur can cultivate with experience, practice, and self-discipline:

(1) The ability to find in the raw materials of a given situation the means to implement strategies and tactics that the entrepreneur under-

---

[8] Compared with the general population, in America at least, political leaders do in fact score higher on psychological tests designed to measure ego strength and tolerance of ambiguity. These propositions are overwhelmingly supported in the data collected by Professor Herbert McClosky from over 3,000 persons who attended the 1956 major-party presidential nominating conventions and from a cross-sectional sample of the national adult population. These data, to be sure, do not bear directly on my own hypotheses about entrepreneurial skill, but in an inferential manner they are supportive.

[9] *The Prince*, Modern Library Edition (New York: Random House, 1950), pp. 91–92.

stands in the abstract. He must know, for instance, not only that a side payment is necessary to win X's support but also what, concretely, could be used as a side payment.

(2) The ability to think in terms of political functions as well as structures, units, or elements. No matter what vocabulary or imagery an entrepreneur uses, and no matter at what level of consciousness, he must somehow be able to think about exhaustible and inexhaustible resources, currency and production resources, political support and political weightings, arenas of competition, stages in the evolution of risk and opportunity, arena and schedule parameters, parameter shifts, and proposal design. It is not enough to think about these functions only as they are expressed in particular structures, for example, interest group A, legislative committee B, or bureau C.[10]

(3) The capacity to perceive and invent functional substitutes. To the skillful politician one vote is just about as good as another, one interest-group endorsement approximately as good as another, and one marketing resource roughly as good as another. When he perceives one slipping out of his grasp, the skillful politician is quick to search for or invent a functional equivalent.[11] He is committed only to his ends, not his means.

[10] As an academic discipline, political science has been slow to invent a useful functional vocabulary. It is a difficult task. I hope my own efforts in this direction will encourage others to try their hands at it.

[11] Political scientists' descriptions of actors' strategies too frequently obscure this elementary political fact. The results are either too mechanistic, with one thing inexorably leading to another, or too vitalistic, with creativity breaking out all over. In *Congress Makes a Law* (New York: Columbia Press, 1950), for example, Professor Stephen K. Bailey's classic account of the policy-making process in Washington, a tale of political strategy is told which by our lights must be regarded as spicy but nevertheless routine. The issue was the passage of the full employment bill, S. 380, and the problem was how to liberalize the bill in the conference committee. Senator Charles Tobey, a cosponsor, was a relatively liberal Republican from New Hampshire. Representative William Whittington was a conservative Democrat from Mississippi. "A carefully conceived strategy . . . was developed by certain people in the Executive branch. Towards the end of the conference, Tobey was approached by an administration friend of the original bill and given the following sales talk. The original bill, of which Tobey was co-sponsor, was being cut to pieces, not by Republicans but by Southern Democrats. The year 1946 was an election year. If Tobey in conference could press for a liberal version of S. 380, the Republican Party could take the credit for saving the Full Employment Bill. Tobey was impressed, and agreed to present a strong bill to the conference on February 2. The strategist then went to Whittington and informed him that a rumor was abroad to the effect that Tobey was going to put the Democratic Party on the spot, and that unless the Democrats succeeded in bringing out a liberal bill, the Republicans could make a successful campaign issue out of the

(4) The capacity to discern marginal differences in utility between functionally substitutable elements. While it may be true, for instance, that one marketing resource is approximately as good as another, it is not exactly so; nor are endorsements of exactly equal weight. Hence, when trade-offs have to be made at the margin—for example, less support from psychologists exchanged for less opposition from psychiatrists—the ability to discern small differences is useful.

(5) A trained intuition about the complex rhythms of a political contest, which supplies answers to the questions of how long the intervals are—and when they will occur—in which certain currency expenditures are necessary, desirable, or possible.

(6) The psychological balance of these two rival truths about political action: every oppotunity is seized at some cost in alternative opportunities, and almost any single opportunity is within reach if one cares to spend enough on it. The Assembly staff, for example, which fought for commitment reform in 1966–1967 won an arduous victory on that front but postponed until the following year its fight for better manpower programs and air pollution control legislation.

Finally, there is an important moral attitude toward political entrepreneurship, the learning of which is not only intrinsically worthy but also useful for warding off feelings of frustration and despair. Our existing institutions and processes of representative government simply cannot survive the challenges of an increasingly pluralistic and technologic-

---

situation. Whether or not this news impressed Whittington will never be known, for on February 2, the Edwin Pauley affairs broke, Tobey raced off to the new fray, and failed to appear at the conference session on S. 380" (pp. 225–226).

Consider, for a moment, what Bailey may have omitted from this account, and in particular how the decision was reached to make Whittington the target of this complicated maneuver. Since the conference committee was ideologically split, 6–6, the political problem at hand was to create a slim margin of support for a liberalized bill. This could have been accomplished either by converting or by neutralizing one conservative vote. If conversion was the preferred means, this could have been accomplished by switching any of the six conservatives, not necessarily Whittington. Robert Taft, for instance, was potentially the most detachable of the three conservative Senate conferees. He was the most liberal of the three, and he had good reason to seize this chance to mitigate organized labor's hostility toward him before he entered the 1948 presidential sweepstakes. That the practitioners in fact moved on Whittington suggests, of course, that Taft was not as good a target, even if but marginally less good. Yet in Bailey's account it is not the routine and rather simple method of problem solving, of identifying functional substitutes and choosing among them, that stands in relief. It is the concrete and admittedly dramatic detail of how a modified prisoner's dilemma strategy was developed and brought to bear against the party loyalty of Mississippi Democrat William Whittington.

ally complex society without an infusion of political skills such as I have been describing. By supplying more energy and purposive activity to the system of representative government, such skills will improve the variety, the quality, and the scope of political competition and bargaining. Political competition and bargaining as a system of collective decision has many merits and defects, but the balance of these is not at issue here.[12] This system is more or less the one we now have. It is not likely to change much in the foreseeable future; and to the extent that it does change substantially, we are not likely to applaud the results—demagogic dictatorship, barbarous technocracy, terror-filled anarchy, or a grotesque combination of all three. A new breed of skillful political entrepreneurs may not actually save representative government in the long run, but they will perhaps forestall its demise long enough to give us time to scratch about for alternatives.[13] The more pronounced their consciousness that on their skills rests so great a responsibility, the harder they will try, one hopes, to develop them adequately to shoulder the burden.

[12] See, for instance, Charles E. Lindblom, *The Intelligence of Democracy* (New York: Free Press, 1965), for a defense of mutual partisan adjustment. For an alternative view, that is, one more favorable to planning, see Yehezkel Dror, *Public Policy-making Reexamined* (San Francisco: Chandler, 1968).

[13] Liberal reformers, whose goals and resources tend often to lead them into complex and sustained efforts at consensus building and resource gathering, will probably benefit more from improving their general level of entrepreneurial skill than political reactionaries or defenders of the status quo. Since I am more sympathetic to the moral values implicit in liberal reform than I am to the values applauded by these alternative ideologies, I see an additional moral significance to skillful entrepreneurship.

APPENDIXES

Appendix A

Mental Health Survey

Instructions: Please try to answer all the questions as accurately as possible. There are no "right" answers, of course; we wish to know only about your own personal opinions or actions. Please keep in mind that your responses will be kept in *strict confidence*.

PART I: INFORMATION ABOUT YOURSELF

1. Name (for identification purposes only):
2. City in which you now reside:
3. County:
4. Sex: Male___. Female___.
5. Place of birth. Give city and state (and country if not U.S.):
6. (If born out of state) When did you move permanently to Calif?
7. Are you the chief wage earner in your family? Yes___. No___.
8. What is your main occupation or usual line of work?
9. How long have you worked in that job?
10. What job did you hold immediately prior to the one you have now?
11. How long did you work at that job?
12. Into which of the following categories does your average family income fall?
    ___(1) Under $5000   ___(5) Between $15,000–22,500
    ___(2) Between $5000–7500   ___(6) Between $22,500–35,000
    ___(3) Between $7500–10,000   ___(7) Over $35,000
    ___(4) Between $10,000–15,000
13. Age:
    ___(1) Under 25   ___(4) 45–54
    ___(2) 25–34   ___(5) 55–64
    ___(3) 35–44   ___(6) 65 and over
14. What is your religious background?
    ___(1) Protestant   ___(3) Jewish
    ___(2) Catholic   ___(4) Other. Please Specify.

15. Education: Please check the highest level of school completed.
___ (1) Grade school   ___ (4) College graduate
___ (2) High school   ___ (5) Advanced degree(s).
___ (3) Some college   Please specify:

16. Generally speaking, do you identify with the Democratic or Republican party?
___ (1) Democratic   ___ (3) Independent
___ (2) Republican   ___ (4) Other (please specify):
                                               ___ (5) Don't know

17. If Independent, toward which party do you lean?
___ (1) Democratic   ___ (3) Neither party
___ (2) Republican   ___ (4) Don't know

18. When it comes to your views on public policy, would you consider yourself a liberal, a conservative, or a middle-of-the-roader?
___ (1) Liberal   ___ (3) Middle-of-the-roader
___ (2) Conservative   ___ (4) Don't know

19. For whom did you vote for governor of California in the 1966 election?
___ (1) Reagan   ___ (3) Other (please specify):
___ (2) Brown   ___ (4) Did not vote
                                               ___ (5) Don't know

20. Do you belong to any nongovernmental groups or organizations that take an interest in California mental health policy? How many?
___ (1) Belong to none   ___ (3) Belong to two
___ (2) Belong to one   ___ (4) Belong to three or more
                                               ___ (5) Don't know

21. If you do belong to any such organizations, please name them here:

22. Within the past three years, have you held office in any of these organizations?
___ (1) No   ___ (2) Yes (please specify):

PART II: YOUR ATTITUDES

For each of the statements below, please CIRCLE the response that most closely represents your *own opinion* about the statement. Indicate whether you STRONGLY AGREE (SA), AGREE (A), are NEUTRAL (N), DISAGREE (D), or STRONGLY DISAGREE (SD).

23. The most important cause of mental illness is probably heredity .... SA   A   N   D   SD

24. "Mental illness" is nothing but a label we apply to people who happen to deviate from conventional social norms .... SA   A   N   D   SD

25. Someday we will probably be able to trace all mental illness to psychological causes .... SA   A   N   D   SD

26. Most mental illness originates in people's immediate personal environment .... SA   A   N   D   SD

27. More often than not, you cannot really help a mentally ill person without trying to effect some sort of change in his personality structure .... SA A N D SD
28. It would probably cause more harm than good if state hospital patients were to become much more conscious of their legal rights .... SA A N D SD
29. We could go a long way toward solving the mental health manpower shortage if each of the mental health professions would stop insisting on its traditional job assignments .... SA A N D SD
30. All things considered, increased reliance on "nonprofessionals" in therapeutic roles would be a good thing .... SA A N D SD
31. Even the best system of community mental health services will never do away with the need for large state hospitals .... SA A N D SD
32. State hospitals don't get enough credit. They really do help people to overcome their mental illnesses and return to the community .... SA A N D SD
33. Hospitalization for mental illness rarely helps the patient—and often it is downright harmful to him .... SA A N D SD

PART III: OPINIONS ABOUT GROUPS

34–37. When it comes to influencing the development of mental health services in California, which of the following groups, in your opinion, have *too much say?* Which have *too little say?* Check as many as you like in columns I and II below.

38–41. On most important questions about mental health, which of the following groups would you be most likely to *trust and take advice from?* Which would you be least likely to *take advice from?* Check up to four or five in columns III and IV below.

	I Have Too Much Say	II Have Too Little Say	III Most Likely Take Advice	IV Least Likely Take Advice
Psychiatrists	—	—	—	—
Physicians (nonpsychiatric)	—	—	—	—
Psychologists	—	—	—	—
Social Workers	—	—	—	—
Nurses	—	—	—	—
Psychiatric technicians	—	—	—	—
Legislators (state)	—	—	—	—
Legislative staff	—	—	—	—
Judges	—	—	—	—

269

County district attorneys ....   — — — —
County supervisors ....   — — — —
California Medical Association ....   — — — —
California Mental Health Assoc. ....   — — — —
Dept. Mental Hygiene, Sacramento ....   — — — —
"Bureau of Social Work" (Officially, Div. Adult
    Protective Services) ....   — — — —
Hospital superintendents ....   — — — —
Federal Government ....   — — — —
Short–Doyle ....   — — — —
Mental health advisory boards ....   — — — —

PART IV: POLITICAL INVOLVEMENT

All the questions in this final section refer to the five mental health issues described below. Each issue came into focus at some time during the last two or three years. Some of these issues involved large numbers of people; others were limited to a relatively small public. The questions in this section ask for your own *personal* actions and opinions regarding each of these issues. Please remember that your responses will be kept absolutely confidential, and that you may therefore answer freely.

FIVE MENTAL HEALTH ISSUES

A. *The 1967–68 Mental Hygiene Budget.* On March 14, 1967, a member of Governor Reagan's staff announced the administration's intention to eliminate over 3,500 positions in state mental hospitals, and to close state-operated screening, aftercare, and day treatment facilities in several local communities. Mental health professionals and state employee groups raised an immediate protest. The governor, supported by the director of Mental Hygiene, promised that patient care would not be harmed by the cuts. Though reversing his stand with regard to some of the community facilities, the governor, in signing the Budget Act on June 30, 1967, did abolish 1,700 hospital staff positions and promised that the rest would be abolished if the patient population continued to decline during the coming year.

B. *Commitments.* On November 28, 1966, the Assembly Sub-Committee on Mental Health Services published a highly controversial report condemning the present judicial commitment procedures for persons alleged to be mentally ill. It also recommended, as a substitute for hospitalization, a community-based system of emergency service units. After considerable consultation with interested parties, the recommendations of the report were modified and incorporated into AB 1220, introduced by Assemblyman Frank Lanterman and Senator Nicholas Petris in early April. After an easy passage through the Assembly, in early July the Senate Committee on Governmental Efficiency killed the bill. With the help of Senator Alan Short, AB 1220 was revived by being attached, as an amendment, to SB 677, then being heard in the Assembly. A conference committee of three assemblymen and three senators deleted most of the provisions of the bill concerning the proposed new community-based mental health services system. In that form, SB 677 passed without dissent in both houses on the last day of the 1967 legislative session.

C. *Practice of Pychology.* In an "informal opinion" delivered on June 14, 1966, the Office of the California Attorney General held that psychologists could not lawfully practice psychotherapy. Psychologists and numerous others protested this decision vigorously. The State Psychological Association moved to obtain a new licensing act which clarified psychologists' rights to practice psychotherapy (SB 1158). At the same time, the Attorney General's Office, responding to extensive public reaction, undertook a review of its decision. On May 23, 1967, it issued a second opinion on the question, which explicitly reversed the earlier one. SB 1158 passed both houses of the legislature on August 6.

D. *The Mendocino Plan.* Soon after Dr. James Lowry assumed the directorship of Mental Hygiene, in April 1964, he began—at the urging of Dr. Ernest Klatte, superintendent of Mendocino State Hospital—to explore the possibility of transforming Mendocino into something like a community mental health center. The major administrative change would have been to transfer control over the Bureau of Social Work personnel in the Mendocino service area to the jurisdiction of the hospital. The principal occasions on which the plan was aired were two meetings of 20–25 persons each on June 12, 1964 (the aftercare clinic) and September 13–14, 1964 (Department of Mental Hygiene representatives, hospital personnel, bureau administrators, etc.), both held at the hospital. On both occasions the representatives of the bureau strenuously opposed the plan. In October 1964 the bureau developed its own plan for community services in that area and began to advocate that as an alternative to the Mendocino Plan. Controversy continued over the next several months. On May 24, 1965, Dr. Lowry formally sanctioned Klatte's proposed plan.

E. *Transfer of the Bureau of Social Work.* In early July 1965 a top administrator in the state Department of Social Welfare raised the possibility of securing additional federal funds for the bureau's operations by the device of transferring responsibility for the bureau from the Department of Mental Hygiene to the Department of Social Welfare. The whole question largely dropped from sight, however, until February 1966, when the staff consultant to the Assembly Social Welfare Committee, acting without knowledge of the earlier discussions of the matter, advanced a similar proposal. The committee approved, and the proposal soon received the endorsement of both party caucuses in the Assembly. The Department of Mental Hygiene strongly opposed the move, arguing that its own medical responsibilities to the bureau's clients would be impossible to fulfill if the department could not assume jurisdiction over the bureau's workers. Supporters of the transfer in the legislature, at some point in late April, withdrew AB 90, the bill that would have brought about the transfer, in favor of writing language into the budget bill that would have the same effect. Opponents of the transfer failed to eliminate this language from the budget bill, and the bureau moved from Mental Hygiene to Social Welfare on July 1, 1966.

THE SKILL FACTOR IN POLITICS

42. *When*, if ever, did each of the above issues *first* come to your attention? Please give date as precisely as possible.

	Budget Issue	Commit- ments Issue	Psych. Issue	Mendo- cino Plan Issue	Bureau Transfer Issue
Date	—	—	—	—	—
Never	—	—	—	—	—
Don't know	—	—	—	—	—

43. *How* did you first learn of it? Did you learn of it: (1) from another person? (2) at a group meeting? (3) through a written memorandum or organizational newsletter? (4) through the media? Check one, and complete as appropriate.

	Budget Issue	Commit- ments Issue	Psych. Issue	Mendo- cino Plan Issue	Bureau Transfer Issue
(1) Person (whom?)					
(2) Group meeting (which group?)					
(3) Memorandum or newsletter (from whom?)	If you received report in mail, check here___.				
(4) Media (which?)					
(5) Other (specify)					
(6) Never heard of it					
(7) Don't remember					

44. If you heard of the issue from another person, or at a group meeting, which of the following *most closely* describes the reason your informant was passing on the information? Check the appropriate line in each column.

	Budget Issue	Commit- ments Issue	Psych. Issue	Mendo- cino Plan Issue	Bureau Transfer Issue
(1) He thought you would be interested to hear the news ...	—	—	—	—	—
(2) He was attempting to enlist your support	—	—	—	—	—

(3) You make it a point to get information from him regularly about mental health politics   —   —   —   —   —

(4) It just came up accidentally   —   —   —   —   —

(5) It was part of the agenda of the meeting ....   —   —   —   —   —

(6) Don't remember ....   —   —   —   —   —

(7) Other (please specify) .....   —   —   —   —   —

45. Once you had become aware of the issue, how closely did you follow its development? (That is, did you obtain information as to who was on what side, what was the current balance of forces, etc.?) Select the phrase below which *most nearly* describes how closely you followed each of the issues. Check the appropriate line in each column.

	Budget Issue	Commit-ments Issue	Psych. Issue	Mendo-cino Plan Issue	Bureau Transfer Issue
(1) Followed it almost *continuously*	—	—	—	—	—
(2) Did not follow continuously, but was aware of nearly all significant *turning points* ...	—	—	—	—	—
(3) Heard or read about it *occasionally*	—	—	—	—	—
(4) Learned of the *outcome* but not much else	—	—	—	—	—
(5) After first hearing of it, learned *nothing further* about it at all	—	—	—	—	—
(6) Never heard of it	—	—	—	—	—
(7) Don't remember	—	—	—	—	—
(8) Other (please specify)	—	—	—	—	—

46. To *whom*—if anyone—did you most often turn for information about developments. Please give name of informant and position.

	Budget Issue	Commit-ments Issue	Psych. Issue	Mendo-cino Plan Issue	Bureau Transfer Issue
Name and position of informant					
Never sought information					
Don't Remember					

47. What was your *original* stand on the issue? Record your answer by checking the appropriate space in column 47.

48. What was your position at the time the issue was *resolved*? Record your answer by checking the appropriate space in column 48.

47 48

A. Budget
   (1) Opposed cuts .... __ __
   (2) Favored cuts .... __ __
   (3) Favored savings by closing *some* hospitals, e.g., Modesto ... __ __
   (4) Neutral .... __ __
   (5) No opinion .... __ __
B. Commitments
   (1) Favored AB 1220 .... __ __
   (2) Opposed AB 1220 .... __ __
   (3) Neutral .... __ __
   (4) No opinion .... __ __
C. Psychology
   (1) Favored restriction on practice of psychotherapy by
       psychologists .... __ __
   (2) Favored latitude for psychologists to practice psychotherapy __ __
   (3) Neutral .... __ __
   (4) No opinion .... __ __
D. Mendocino Plan
   (1) Favored the plan .... __ __
   (2) Opposed the plan .... __ __
   (3) Favored the bureau's proposal .... __ __
   (4) Neutral .... __ __
   (5) No opinion .... __ __
E. Bureau transfer
   (1) Favored transfer to Social Welfare .... __ __
   (2) Favored retaining bureau in DMH .... __ __
   (3) Favored turning bureau over to counties .... __ __
   (4) Neutral .... __ __
   (5) No opinion .... __ __

49. Did you ever attempt to gain *active support* for your position on the issue? If you did, how frequently did you make such attempts? Please check the appropriate space.

	Budget Issue	Commit- ments Issue	Psych. Issue	Mendo- cino Plan Issue	Bureau Transfer Issue
(1) Continually	__	__	__	__	__
(2) On several occasions	__	__	__	__	__
(3) Just once or twice	__	__	__	__	__
(4) Never at all	__	__	__	__	__
(5) Don't remember	__	__	__	__	__

50. If you did make any attempts to gain active support, *how* did you go about it? Did you do any (or all) of the following:

	Budget Issue	Commit- ments Issue	Psych. Issue	Mendo- cino Plan Issue	Bureau Transfer Issue
(1) Write anything for circula- tion or publication	—	—	—	—	—
(2) Speak to organizations or groups	—	—	—	—	—
(3) Write letters to government officials	—	—	—	—	—
(4) Talk to individuals privately	—	—	—	—	—
(5) Never sought to gain active support	—	—	—	—	—
(6) Don't Remember	—	—	—	—	—
(7) Other (please specify)	—	—	—	—	—

51. If you did make any attempts to gain active support, did you *personally* *speak* to any (or all) of the following:

	Budget Issue	Commit- ments Issue	Psych. Issue	Mendo- cino Plan Issue	Bureau Transfer Issue
(1) Friends	—	—	—	—	—
(2) Co-workers	—	—	—	—	—
(3) Members of organizations to which you belong	—	—	—	—	—
(4) Members of organizations to which you do *not* belong ...	—	—	—	—	—
(5) Officials and staff of organ- izations to which you belong	—	—	—	—	—
(6) Officials and staff of organ- izations to which you do *not* belong	—	—	—	—	—
(7) Elected officials and staff, state level	—	—	—	—	—
(8) Elected officials and staff, local level	—	—	—	—	—
(9) Administrators in public ser- vice, state level	—	—	—	—	—
(X) Administrators in public ser- vice, local level	—	—	—	—	—
(Y) Spoke to no one personally					
(O) Don't Remember	—	—	—	—	—

52. As the issue developed, at what point were you most actively involved in seeking support for your position

	Budget Issue	Commit- ments Issue	Psych. Issue	Mendo- cino Plan Issue	Bureau Transfer Issue
(1) At the beginning	___	___	___	___	___
(2) Near the middle	___	___	___	___	___
(3) Toward the end	___	___	___	___	___
(4) Involvement was fairly con- stant at all times (either low or high)	___	___	___	___	___
(5) Never was involved	___	___	___	___	___
(6) Don't Remember	___	___	___	___	___

53. Who was the most *influential* individual, group, or organization to whom you *spoke personally* while attempting to enlist support? (By "most influential" we mean potentially able to exert the greatest overall impact on shaping the outcome of the issue.) List more than one if you are in doubt as to who was *most* influential.

	Budget Issue	Commit- ments Issue	Psych. Issue	Mendo- cino Plan Issue	Bureau Transfer Issue
Name and position of informant					
Never attempted to enlist support					
Don't remember					

PLEASE BE SURE YOU HAVE ANSWERED ALL QUESTIONS. THANK YOU FOR YOUR COOPERATION.

Appendix B

Sampling Procedure and Rationale

At the end of August 1967, that is, after my fieldwork was completed and after the budget and commitment issues were concluded, a mail-reply questionnaire was sent to a sample of about 1,300 persons. In December 1967 and January 1968 a follow-up questionnaire was sent to most of those in the original sample. A total of 583 usable questionnaires were returned, or 45 percent. The sampling procedure was as follows:

1. Northern California Psychiatric Society. Every tenth name on the 1967 (alphabetized) membership roster, plus thirty-two past or present officials. N=80.
2. All Short–Doyle directors and program chiefs, excluding those who had indicated they would not respond. N=68.
3. All members of the state executive board and all chapter legislative representatives of the California State Psychological Association. N=63.
4. All 1967 members of the state board of directors of the California Association for Mental Health who had been elected at large; all 1967 chapter presidents and chapter executive directors; all 1967 members of the statewide public affairs committee. N=78.
5. All physicians, including psychiatrists, employed at one of California's nine state hospitals for the mentally ill. N=50.[1]
6. Every other person on the mailing list of the Subcommittee on Mental Health Services of the California State Assembly, but excluding from the sample all persons known to be on other mailing lists and those who had already refused to cooperate in the study, and including all those persons on the list known to have been at either the December 5 or December 12 hearings of the subcommittee concerning their report, "The Dilemma of Mental Commitments

---

[1] The questionnaires were left in the physicians' mailboxes at the hospitals with return-addressed envelopes. I left fifty-six questionnaires, but I am sure some of these mailboxes belonged to persons who were not in fact physicians and others who had left the employ of the hospital but whose mailboxes were labeled with their names.

in California." Sampling the list assured geographical representativeness, because the list was previously arranged by zip code. N=725.

7. Every second professional worker in the Bureau of Social Work in each of the district offices of the bureau. N=200.[2]

8. Lobbyists and others who were known to be active in the mental health public but who appeared on none of the other lists, including all superintendents of state MI hospitals. N=35.

Although it has been difficult to ascertain exact response rates for each subsample because respondents frequently omitted their names on the replies and because there is considerable duplication of names from list to list, my estimates of the returns by subsample are:

	Percent of Total Sample	Questionnaires Returned	Sent
1. NCPS	9	55	80
2. Short–Doyle	3	15	68
3. CSPA	5	26	63
4. CAMH	5	29	78
5. State hospital physicians	5	27	50
6. Assembly list	32	189	725
7. Bureau of Social Work	20	115	200
8. Others	5	30	35
9. Unidentified	17	97	—
TOTALS	101*	583	1299

* Not equal to 100 percent because of rounding.

Why these particular groups and individuals? Since the extent and composition of the attentive public are uncertain to begin with, it would be mistaken to say that these subsamples represent it in some statistical sense. Parameters describing the aggregate of individual respondents in the sample, therefore, are discussed only occasionally and then only for very gross purposes. Our principal interest is with the relationships among groups within the public and, more specifically, among ideological, professional, and institutional interests. These are expressed in our sample by individual respondents, however, since "interests" cannot fill out questionnaires. If it makes sense to speak of representativeness at all, these 583 respondents certainly overrepresent the

[2] These questionnaires were distributed through the interoffice mailing system of the bureau, with the cooperation of the bureau's chief, Mr. William Wilsnack. The number of professional workers in the bureau at that time was in the neighborhood of 400, although I do not know the precise figure on the day the mail went out. The bureau subsample is the only one to which I sent no follow-up questionnaire, since this would have imposed too great a burden on the bureau's clerical facilities. Anticipating that no follow-up would be possible in this case, I "over-sampled" this group.

highly engaged, active, and attentive members of the routine mental health public. This is a consequence of the greater disposition of those who are particularly interested, and of those who need to feel they are interested, to fill out and return a questionnaire on the subject of California mental health politics. From my perspective, this response bias is advantageous, since such a bias is likely to magnify slightly the nature of the cleavages and alliances within the public.

A more significant problem is the representativeness of any particular subsample with regard to the interests it embodies. For instance, is the Northern California Psychiatric Society subsample representative of psychiatry or organized psychiatry or California psychiatry or what? Does the CAMH leader subsample represent informed lay activists? These questions would persist even if we had responses from the entire NCPS membership and CAMH leader stratum. Next to this fact, the importance we can attach to the response rates—low or high—of individuals from particular subsamples diminishes considerably.

The Northern California Psychiatric Society subsample accounts for just over half the psychiatrists in the sample. Psychiatrists in California are not representative of psychiatrists nationally; and the northern California group is perhaps slightly unrepresentative of all psychiatrists in California. As an organization, NCPS was probably slightly more liberal, or progressive, in several senses than organized psychiatry in the nation or in the state of California. NCPS members, however, were not so unlike other groups of psychiatrists with regard to the ideological orientations I was concerned to study. The similarity was evident from interviews. It was also evident from comparing NCPS responses to those of several Los Angeles psychiatrists who happened into the sample by other means.

The California State Psychological Association leadership subsample, on the other hand, was not at all representative of "psychology." CSPA, first of all, greatly overrepresented clinical psychologists and underrepresented academic psychologists. Moreover, the CSPA leadership was not altogether representative of the general membership of the association. It was slightly more avant-garde, slightly more sensitive to questions of professional identity, and slightly more aggressive in defending a distinctive professional role for psychology in the practice of psychotherapy than the general membership. My inferences on these matters are drawn from interviews and from an examination of the contents of the CSPA newsletter (*The California State Psychologists*), particularly the letters-to-the-editor sections, for a two-year period. Again, this unrepresentativeness is an advantage from my point of view. The CSPA leadership subsample in effect expresses that which is most distinctive about psychology compared to the other professions—a contrast that we want our survey materials to illuminate.

The Bureau of Social Work subsample is quite useful for suggesting the attitudes of psychiatric social workers in general, but not very useful for describing the attitudes or behavior of the bureau's leadership. Interview and documentary evidence, however, readily supplements the survey data with regard to the bureau's leadership echelons.

There was no motive other than expediency for selecting the particular state hospital for the mentally ill from which was drawn the subsample of state hospital physicians. At the time I wished to distribute the questionnaires, I was in the geographical vicinity of the hospital, and the superintendent was agreeable to my using the hospital's mailboxes as a means of distributing the questionnaires. There is no reason to believe that this subsample is unrepresentative of state hospital physicians in any other such facility.

Although the total sample contains 201 members of the California Association for Mental Health (CAMH), it is usually preferable to examine the CAMH leadership subsample as a way to represent the distinctive qualities of the association.

The response rate from the Short–Doyle group was rather low, only fifteen respondents being coded as having been drawn from the Short–Doyle subsample. The number of actual Short–Doyle respondents is probably considerably higher, perhaps twenty-five; but it was not always possible for the coders to identify the Short–Doyle respondents. The questionnaires were not marked with a subsample code before being sent out, and respondents frequently omitted their names on the returned questionnaires. The fifteen coded Short–Doyle respondents do appear representative of the entire group in many respects; but no attempt was made to make much of their responses, since the N is so small.

To our good fortune, the Subcommittee on Mental Health Services of the California State Assembly had accumulated, between 1965 and 1967, a mailing list of some 1,500 persons to whom the subcommittee sent informational packets from time to time about its work. This mailing list provided a highly operational, although not a highly reliable, definition of at least one sector of the routinely attentive public. (I also added to the initial sample thirty-five names of persons whom I knew to be attentive but who did not appear on this list or any other.) The Assembly subcommittee mailing list returned only 189 out of 725 questionnaires. Even taking into account the number of respondents that the coders could not identify as coming from this subsample and the number of persons who had moved and could not be located, the return rate is low. There are several reasons for this. The most important is the fact that the list contained a large number of individuals who were not in fact interested in or knowledgeable about mental health politics. Many had been added to the subcommittee list because of an interest they had once expressed in mental retardation. Although there is considerable overlap among the attentive public for mental retardation politics and the attentive public for mental health politics, the overlap is far from complete. Secondly, a considerable number of the persons on this list had, at some time in the past, occupied organizational offices or roles that brought them into the attentive public; but more recently they had become uninvolved. In some cases, these persons forwarded their questionnaires to the current role occupants; if the latter returned them, their responses were included in the analysis. Finally, a number of persons on the subcommittee list were actually surrogates for other persons or for institutions, for instance, secretaries or clerks whose names were listed only because they (presumably) transmitted materials from the subcommittee to whoever in their organization they believed was the appropriate recipient. If they followed their usual procedure by passing this questionnaire along to these appropriate recipients and the latter returned the questionnaires, they were included in the analysis.

In short, then, the sampling methods were imprecise but nevertheless adequate for the limited exploratory and descriptive purposes to which I intended to put the data. Given the abundance of data collected by methods other than the survey, moreover, our 583 respondents are rarely required to sustain a proposition without assistance from other sources of evidence.

Index

Accreditation practices, 60

Action for Mental Health, 55, 71

Activity index, defined, 192 and *n*

Adult Protective Services (APS), 174 and *n*, 177 and *n*

Advice seeking, 119 and table, 122

Aftercare, 74*n*, 127, 174, 175, 177

Alameda County Short–Doyle program, 126, 128, 233

Alameda County Welfare Planning Council, 113

Alaska Mental Health Enabling Act, 85

Alcoholic Treatment Program, 141

Allies: channeled communication to, 219; search for effective, 222–226; instrumentalist criteria, 225–226; training, 227

American Civil Liberties Union, 104*n*, 105, 113, 129

American Psychiatric Association and branches, 34–35

American Psychological Association (APA), 157 and *n*

Anti-mental-health movement, 83–85, 85 *n*, 143

Appropriations, politics of, 149–151

Assembly: votes on commitment bill (AB 1220), 129, 133; compared with senate, 136

Assembly group (Assembly Subcommittee on Mental Health Services and staff): support-gathering activities, 105–108, 117–122 and table, 120; approach to CMA, 106; and commitment court survey, 106–107; and Dilemma Report hearings, 111–117; and budget controversy, 124–125; activities on commitment reform bills (AB 1220, SB 677), 125–140; and organized psychiatry, 130, 131; as mediators, 190; persuasion techniques, 198; reliability of image, 202; use of rhetoric, 203; and choosing allies, 226; managerial capabilities, 248–249; political currency resources, 260–261. *See also* Bolton, Arthur; Lanterman, Frank; Petris, Nicholas; Roberts, David; Vieg, Karsten; Waldie, Jerome

Assembly Office of Research, 108, 118

Assembly Social Welfare Committee: and bureau transfer idea, 172–173; and aftercare services, 174–175

Assembly Subcommittee on Mental Health Services: and mental retardation, 101; beginnings of reform efforts, 101; use of interpersonal contact, 219. *See also* Assembly group; Dilemma Report

Associations, professional, 34; and lobbyists, 35. *See also under various names*

Atascadero, 18*n*, 19 table, 20

Attentive mental health public: described, 25; mapping, 25–37; factions, 68; nonideological sources of controversy, 69; interests defined, 94*n*; alliances, 95; enemies, 95; attitudes toward commitment system, 103–104; and commitment reform bill (AB 1220), 122–123, 131–132 and table; attitudes toward budget cuts, 143–144; weightiness of interests, table, 209. *See also* Ideological attitudes; Ideological cleavage; Ideological consensus

Attentiveness of public: variations in particular controversies, 4, 190–191 and table; and political arenas, 191; and information mainstream, 192–193

Attorney General, Office of: and commitment reform bill, 129; effect of opinions, 152–153; opinion on Psychology Certification Act, 152–155

Auerback, Alfred, 141*n*

ment in Our State Hospitals (CCITSH), 145, 230

Clients of mental health system: as tracer in mapping policy, 16; and treatment, 16, 18–25; as attentive public, 25–26; defenders of, 146–147

Coalition building, 8, 10, 221; search problems, 221; complementarity principle, 230. *See also* Allies; Political resources

Coalition of interests: in bureau transfer issue, 174; managing discontent within, 249–251, 257

Commitment controversy: and political processes, 3–4; ideology, 58–59; change, opposition, and support, 59; involvement in, 191–193 and tables; undermining tactics, 233; system parameters, 242; and political resources, 245–249. *See also* Assembly group; Commitment courts; Commitment reform bill; Dilemma Report; Mental commitment

Commitment courts, 101, 102, 106–107, 108n

Commitment reform bill (AB 1220): drafting, 118, 119; sponsorship, 119, 122; organization endorsements, 124; organized support, 124–129; Assembly committee hearings, 125–129; medical opposition, 126; organized opposition, 126–131; ideological issues, 129, 131; opinions toward, table, 132; traditionalist attitudes, table, 133; in the Senate, 135–139; combined with SB 677 in Assembly, 138–139; title, 139; final revisions, 140; becomes law, 140; and legal-medical tension, 185–187; Pareto superior features, 185–188; financing formula, 187–188; evidence of support, political use, 205–206; and bargaining, 207–208. *See also* Assembly group

Communication: political, tabulated, 118–122; broadcast, 218–219; channeled, 218, 219; interpersonal, 228–229; network, in marketing development, 248

Community-based outpatient clinics, 80. *See also* Short–Doyle system

Compounding effects, 197, 205, 254

Concessions. *See* Bargaining

Conference of Local Mental Health Directors, 87; and Dilemma Report, 108–111; legislative committee and com-

mitment reform bill, 127, 128, 130 and n; and bureau transfer issue, 179

Conference on Mental Health (1949), 32

Consensus, definition, 183. *See also* Ideological consensus

"Continuity of care" principle, 40

Contra Costa County Short–Doyle program, 127, 128, 233

"County lunacy commission," 102

County mental health programs in commitment reform bill, 127–128, 127n

County supervisors, and mental health programming, 33–34

County Supervisors Association of California (CSAC), 33; and Short–Doyle system, 86; and commitment controversy, 124, 129, 130, 244; power as lobby, 224

Credibility of arguments, value of simplicity, 201

Cross-pressures, 196

Cvetic, Matt, 84

Dahl, Robert, on the political process, 7–9, 10n

Degnan, George, and commitment controversy, 127–131 *passim*, 136, 137, 204, 233

Department of Finance, 180

Department of Institutions, 79

Department of Mental Hygiene (DMH): and Mendocino Plan, 4; mapping existing policy, 16; administrative responsibility, 19–20; appropriations (1967), 20; number of employees, 20; Medical Advisory Committee (1964–1967), 34, 35; and milieu therapy, 54; function in mental health system, 77; historical development, 77–80; managerial role, 77–78; emphasis on collecting payments, 79–80; conflicting demands on, 80–81; Office of Program Review, 80; and budget process, 81; study on precommitment screening (1965), 103; and commitment issue, 105, 126; and Dilemma Report, 108–109, 115–117; positions eliminated by budget cuts, 141; threats to Bureau of Social Work, 161; Division of Hospital Services, 164; streamlining changes, 167–168; Community Services Division, 167, 167; State Services Division, 167, 168; Office of Planning, 167; Office of Program Review,